Lecture Notes in Computer Science 7257

Commenced Publication in 1973
Founding and Former Series Editors:
Gerhard Goos, Juris Hartmanis, and Jan van Leeuwen

Andy Gill   Jurriaan Hage (Eds.)

Implementation and Application of Functional Languages

23rd International Symposium, IFL 2011
Lawrence, KS, USA, October 3-5, 2011
Revised Selected Papers

 Springer

Volume Editors

Andy Gill
University of Kansas
Department of Electrical Engineering and Computer Science
2001 Eaton Hall, 1520 West 15th Street, Lawrence, KS 66045-7621, USA
E-mail: andygill@ku.edu

Jurriaan Hage
Utrecht University
Department of Information and Computing Sciences
Princetonplein 5, 3584 CC Utrecht, The Netherlands
E-mail: j.hage@uu.nl

ISSN 0302-9743   e-ISSN 1611-3349
ISBN 978-3-642-34406-0   e-ISBN 978-3-642-34407-7
DOI 10.1007/978-3-642-34407-7
Springer Heidelberg Dordrecht London New York

Library of Congress Control Number: 2012951176

CR Subject Classification (1998): F.3, D.3, D.2, F.4.1, D.1, D.2.4

LNCS Sublibrary: SL 1 – Theoretical Computer Science and General Issues

Typesetting: Camera-ready by author, data conversion by Scientific Publishing Services, Chennai, India

Printed on acid-free paper

Springer is part of Springer Science+Business Media (www.springer.com)

Preface

This volume contains the selected peer-reviewed revised articles that were presented at the 23rd International Symposium on Implementation and Application of Functional Languages (IFL 2011). IFL 2011 was held during October 3–5, 2011, at the University of Kansas, in Lawrence, USA. This was the second time the IFL symposium was held in the United States, the previous stateside IFL being in 2009. We intend to carry on this new tradition and make IFL a regular event held in the USA and in Europe by alternating the host continent every year and to foster collaborations, interactions, and friendships between researchers and practitioners on both continents and beyond.

The IFL symposia bring together researchers and practitioners that are actively engaged in the implementation and the use of functional and function-based programming languages. Every year IFL provides a venue for the presentation and discussion of new ideas and concepts, of work in progress, and of publication-ripe results. Participants are invited to submit either a draft paper or an extended abstract describing work to be presented at the symposium. These submissions are screened by the Program Committee Chair to make sure they are within the scope of IFL. The submissions accepted for presentation appear in the *draft* proceedings distributed at the symposium, which also appeared as an *Information and Telecommunication Technology Center* technical report. Submissions appearing in the draft proceedings are not peer-reviewed publications. After the symposium, authors are given the opportunity to consider the feedback received from discussions at the symposium and are invited to submit revised full articles to the formal review process. The revised submissions are reviewed by the Program Committee using prevailing academic standards and the best submissions are chosen to appear in the formal proceedings. This volume is the result of the work done by the IFL 2011 Program Committee and the contributing authors. There were 33 papers presented at IFL 2011, the Program Committee reviewed 26 revised submissions, and 11 papers were ultimately selected for this volume.

Bryan O'Sullivan, co-author of Real World Haskell and prolific open-source contributor, was the IFL 2011 guest speaker. Bryan delivered an interesting talk about his experiences as a software developer using Haskell, including a introduction to his latest package, `pronk`, an application for load-testing Web servers. Thank you Bryan for your contributions to IFL 2011.

Following the IFL tradition, IFL 2011 provided participants with an opportunity to get to know each other and to talk outside the formal setting of presentations with a social event on the second day of the symposium. This year, the participants got a walking tour of historic Lawrence, followed by a banquet in the Oread Hotel which, being one of the highest buildings in Lawrence, had panoramic views of the rolling hills of Northeast Kansas.

Carrying on a tradition started in 2003, the Program Committee selected a paper for the *Peter J. Landin Award*, given to the best article presented at the symposium. The recipients of the award for IFL 2011 were Anders Persson, Emil Axelsson, and Josef Svenningsson, from Chalmers University of Technology, for their contribution entitled "Generic Monadic Constructs for Embedded Languages."

IFL 2011 was made possible by the generous support provided by the Information and Telecommunication Technology Center and the Department of Electrical Engineering and Computer Science, both from the University of Kansas. Finally, we are also grateful to Andrew Farmer, for much of the local organization logistics, including maintaining the website, and Beth Gill for organizing the IFL banquet. We thank the authors for submitting their articles and trusting that we would do our best to positively showcase their work.

We hope that the readers will enjoy this collection of selected papers from IFL 2011. Make sure to join us at a future version of IFL!

August 2012   Andy Gill
                                                              Jurriaan Hage

Organization

Program Committee

Torben Amtoft	Kansas State University, USA
Francesco Cesarini	Erlang Solutions Ltd., UK
Olaf Chitil	University of Kent, UK
Eelco Dolstra	Delft University of Technology, The Netherlands
Martin Erwig	Oregon State University, USA
Andy Gill	University of Kansas, USA (Chair)
Alwyn Goodloe	NASA, USA
Jurriaan Hage	Universiteit Utrecht, The Netherlands (Co-chair)
Kevin Hammond	University of St. Andrews, UK
Bill Harrison	University of Missouri, USA
Ralf Hinze	Oxford University, UK
James Hook	Portland State University, USA
Garrin Kimmell	University of Iowa, USA
Andres Löh	Well-Typed LLP, Germany
Rita Loogen	Philipps University Marburg, Germany
Neil Mitchell	Standard Chartered, UK
Rex Page	Oklahoma University, USA
Rinus Plasmeijer	Radboud University Nijmegen, The Netherlands
Sven-Bodo Scholz	University of Hertfordshire, UK
Mary Sheeran	Chalmers University of Technology, Sweden
Satnam Singh	Google, USA
Walid Taha	Halmstad University, Sweden
Simon Thompson	University of Kent, UK
Geoffrey Washburn	LogicBlox, USA

Sponsoring Institutions

Information and Telecommunication Technology Center, University of Kansas
Department of Electrical Engineering and Computer Science, University of Kansas

Table of Contents

Functional Instrumentation of ActionScript Programs with Asil 1
    Arie Middelkoop, Alexander B. Elyasov, and Wishnu Prasetya

Fairness for Transactional Events 17
    Edward Amsden and Matthew Fluet

Implementing a High-Level Distributed-Memory Parallel Haskell
in Haskell 35
    Patrick Maier and Phil Trinder

Challenges for a Trace-Based Just-In-Time Compiler for Haskell 51
    Thomas Schilling

Lazy Generation of Canonical Test Programs 69
    Jason S. Reich, Matthew Naylor, and Colin Runciman

Generic Monadic Constructs for Embedded Languages 85
    Anders Persson, Emil Axelsson, and Josef Svenningsson

From Stack Traces to Lazy Rewriting Sequences 100
    Stephen Chang, Eli Barzilay, John Clements, and Matthias Felleisen

Model Based Testing with Logical Properties versus State Machines 116
    Pieter Koopman, Peter Achten, and Rinus Plasmeijer

Property-Based Testing and Verification: A Catalog of Classroom
Examples 134
    Rex Page

Describing and Optimising Reversible Logic Using a Functional
Language 148
    Michael Kirkedal Thomsen

Hardware Design with Generalized Arrows 164
    Adam Megacz

Author Index 181

Functional Instrumentation
of ActionScript Programs with Asil

Arie Middelkoop[1], Alexander B. Elyasov[2], and Wishnu Prasetya[2]

[1] LIP6-Regal, France
adriaan.middelkoop@lip6.fr
[2] Universiteit Utrecht, The Netherlands
{elyasov,wishnu}@cs.uu.nl

Abstract. Within the context of the FITTEST project, one of our tasks
was to instrument ActionScript bytecode, so that aspects of the execution
of the running application are logged. Although the decision what to log
and when requires manual intervention, the code itself can be weaved
into the system automatically by means of aspect-oriented programming
(AOP). In this paper we describe Asil, an AOP EDSL for instrumenting
ActionScript bytecode, that is firmly based on well-known functional
programming technique to provide abstraction mechanisms that other
AOP languages tend to lack.

Keywords: instrumentation, execution traces, ActionScript, aspect oriented programming, functional programming.

1 Introduction

Logs of a program's execution can provide all kinds of valuable information: usage statistics, code coverage and profiling information, and, by deeper analysis,
execution models [13], and usage patterns [15]. In some areas like internet applications, logging has become very important. In the FITTEST project [19] we
seek to develop a log-based testing approach for future internet applications. The
future internet [9] poses challenges for traditional testing approaches, because future internet applications will, more than ever, rely on dynamic compositions of
ever-changing third party components and services. In addition to conventional
unit and regression tests during development, post-deployment continuous testing will be required to make sure that such compositions still exhibit correct
behavior.

One way to accomplish this is through log-based testing. In this approach,
the execution of the system under test (SUT) is logged and later analyzed to
discover anomalies that require investigation by software testers. Logs can also
be analyzed to infer finite state models, which in turn can be used to generate
test cases.

Manually adding logging statements to the source code of the SUT is undesirable, as they easily clutter up the original code. Moreover, logging should not
interfere essentially with the execution of the program proper and this is hard

A. Gill and J. Hage (Eds.): IFL 2011, LNCS 7257, pp. 1–16, 2012.

to guarantee when manual modifications are made. Modifying the run-time environment itself may seem to be an alternative, but is generally not possible due to security restrictions on the clients that run the application, and privacy considerations.

Fortunately, other techniques exist that can help us deal with this issue more effectively. In particular, logging is a prime example of a functionality that can be injected through aspect-oriented programming (AOP) [12]. This approach is non-intrusive: the logging code can be described separately, and changed separately, without needing to change the source code of the target application. The industrial context of FITTEST specifically demands such an approach. For example, one of the FITTEST case studies is Habbo Hotel [17], which is a large Flash-based Internet application, written in ActionScript 3. For business reasons, we are restricted not to interfere with the source code, and we cannot change the Flash run-time, so that only transformation of ActionScript bytecode remains.

This paper describes the design and implementation of a tool set that facilitates the injection of logging code into client-side web applications, in ActionScript bytecode form. The implementation was made in Haskell, and the design of the AOP instrumentation language borrows heavily from functional programming techniques. Our language is called *Asil*. We decided to make it a DSL, deeply embedded inside the functional language Haskell, so that it inherits Haskell's clean syntax and higher-order feature, providing us with means of abstraction that go beyond that of traditional AOP languages. Asil also uses the well-known concepts of *monadic* [20] and *alternative* [14] interfaces to compose instrumentations.

To enable deep logging, we have to be able to log the control flow of methods. This influences the choice of our "join point model". In AOP, a *join point* represents the point where we want to inject new behavior. In our model, this point is a (static) location in the program. The behavior that we want to inject is called *advice*. The terms *instrumentation* or *aspect weaving* refer to the program transformation that carries out the injection. A join point has a static context, which can be used to determine which advice to inject. At run time it can provide additional information, which can be exploited by the advice. In our situation such a feature is useful. E.g. when we log a code block (join point x), we may want to inspect the value of some variable in a preceding block (join point y), or a parameter passed to the method (join point z) in which the block is contained. Since not all join points need to be instrumented, and different join points may require different instrumentation, there is usually also a facility for specifying groups of join points, called *point cuts*, which are to receive the same advice.

From a functional perspective, instrumentation can be viewed as a partial function that provides advice to be injected on *some* join points:

$$Instrumentation = JoinPoint \rightarrow Maybe\ Advice$$

Notice that this model implies that different join points may get different advice. In AspectJ terminology, the above function corresponds to an aspect. Asil essentially provides combinators to construct such functions.

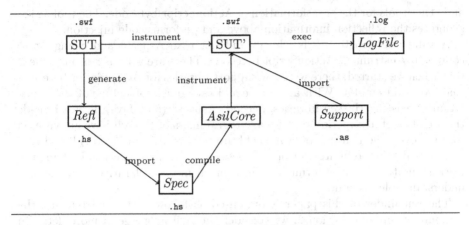

Fig. 1. Overview of the specification artifacts

In the case of logging, the advice is a state transformer that additionally yields a sequence of log events, each carrying some information to be logged. There is usually a separate logger that processes these events, possibly filtering them first based on some concept of logging level, and then takes care of the formatting and the actual I/O.

$$Advice = World \rightarrow (World \times [LogEvent])$$

Advice can be composed, and combinators can be defined to compose them in different ways. Asil performs instrumentation at compile time. In order to do so, it constructs and manipulates *representations* of advice. The actual execution of advice (the arrow in the above type) occurs of course at run time. Asil has no access to the concrete information in the *World*, which is run-time information; so it has to treat it symbolically. An alternative is to do the instrumentation dynamically [6,5], but we do not favor this due to the run-time overhead it entails (see also the discussion in Section 6).

Figure 1 shows an overview of the logging process and the artifacts involved. From the SUT (in binary form), we first generate some reflection information *Refl* (symbol information, control flow graphs), which is imported by *Spec*. The latter essentially specifies a function of type *Instrument*, describing what we want to inject and where. We convert *Spec* to an intermediate representation called *AsilCore*. This representation can be straightforwardly translated to ActionScript bytecode and injected into the SUT, together with a support library that provides log functions and the logger itself. The result is SUT'. Finally, executing SUT' generates the log.

The implementation of Asil is ongoing work within the FITTEST project[1]. The library asil[2] contains Asil as a library, including parsers, pretty printers,

---

[1] http://www.pros.upv.es/fittest/
[2] http://hackage.haskell.org/package/asil

and other tools for the transformation of ActionScript bytecode. The tool asic[3] generates the reflection information above and performs code injection.

A valid question to ask is why we did not take AspectJ and change it to compile to/instrument ActionScript bytecode. There are various reasons. One is that when we started, there were few support libraries for ActionScript bytecode that we could employ. With asic we could take quick advantage of the translation of existing Haskell libraries. Second, AspectJ (and Java) do not provide the facilities of abstraction that we as programmers of Haskell have grown used to. Moreover, the join points of AspectJ are restricted to function call and execution, which is too limited for our purposes. Finally, in a functional setting the instrumentations can be formulated in a much more declarative, and thereby, understandable fashion.

The remainder of this paper is organised as follows. After introducing the running example in Section 2, we consider the Asil language in more detail in Section 3. In Section 4 we show AsilCore and some aspects of its implementation; the aspect weaver asic is shortly discussed in Section 5. Section 6 discusses related work, and Section 7 concludes.

2   Running Example

As a simple running example, Figure 2 shows a snippet of a chess-like internet game written in ActionScript. The game proceeds in turns. In each turn, the user clicks on a square to select a piece, then clicks on an unoccupied square to move the piece there.

Just for exposition, examples of logging statements that we *plan to inject* are added as comments marked by //**. The first one is to log when the method clicked is entered, the second one to log when clicked calls move. The called Log.*method* handles the actual logging work, including serialization and formatting. These logging statements are not to be manually inserted into the program; this would be intrusive and unacceptable to our industrial partners.

The generated logs can be inspected to discover atypical execution patterns, which can be further investigated by testers or by the maintenance team.

In ActionScript an application is packaged and loaded as an swf file. At run time, it can also load another swf file to use its classes. This is a form of dynamic composition. Logs may help us detecting anomalies when such composition occurs (e.g. when it shows a move after two clicks on the same x,y).

In the next section we discuss our instrumentation language Asil.

3   The Asil Instrumentation Language

The language *Asil* is a combinator language for describing an *Instrumentation* as discussed in Section 1. It is a functional, strongly-typed, monadic Haskell EDSL for expressing *advice* that is conditionally applied at *join points*. Join

---

[3] http://hackage.haskell.org/package/asic

```
package code {
public class MyGame extends Sprite {
  private var selSquare : Square;

  public function MyGame() : void {
    addEventListener("click", clicked); }

  function clicked(event:MouseEvent) : void {
    var x : int = event.localX;
    var y : int = event.localY;

    //** Log.logEnter("clicked",x,y);
    var target : Square  = getSquare(x,y);
    var taken  : Boolean = Board.occupied(target);

    if (!this.selSquare && taken) {
      this.selSquare = target;
    } else
    if (this.selSquare && !taken) {
      //** Log.logCall("move",this.selSquare, target);
      this.move(this.selSquare, target);
      this.selSquare = null;
    }
  }
} }
```

Fig. 2. ActionScript snippet with logging code

points are predefined locations in the code where control can be transferred to. Figure 3 lists the join points in our *join point model* [4]. Our main join points are the conventional method entry and exit from the caller and callee side as in AspectJ [11], as well as blocks. A *block* is a sequence of (bytecode) instructions [10] that contains no jump instruction except for the last instruction, nor targetted by a jump instruction except for the first instruction. Each block in a method corresponds to a node in the method's control flow graph.

We refine the type *Instrumentation = JointPoint → Maybe Advice* to the monad type $I\ a$. This gives us the concept of sequentially composing instrumentations. An instrumentation $i :: I\ a$ behaves logically as an *Instrumentation*, but produces additionally a value of type a. The monadic bind $i \ggg k$ composes instrumentations sequentially over each join point: for every join point p (in the target program), it first applies i on p. The instrumentation may succeed or fail (e.g., because i does not match with p). If i succeeds, we apply $k\ a$ on the same join point, where a is the information returned by i. We also add the type $E\ a$ that (symbolically) represents bytecode fragments that at run time behave as expressions. A typed product a of these "expressions" is represented by the type $\overline{E}\ a$. Figure 4 lists Asil's combinators to construct instrumentations.

Join point	Context captured
Method entry	name, parameters, and param types
Method exit	name, return value, and return type
Method abort	nane, and exception
Method call	name, parameters, and param types
Method returned	name, return value, and return type
Method failed	name, and exception
Block entry	id, cycle root, and preceding join points
Block exit	id, cycle root, and preceding join points
Coercion call	input, input type, and intended type
Coercion returned	input, output, input type, and output type
Coercion failed	input, exception, and intended type

Fig. 3. Join points and their context

For example the operation *call m e* injects the call $m(e)$ as an advice. Both e and m are represented symbolically as types $E\ a$ and $E\ (Method\ a\ b)$. The latter indicates that at run time the expression m will return a reference to a method of type $a \to b$. Notice that the type compatibility between m and e is checked at the compile time. The instrumentation *call m e* returns the symbolic representation of m's return value.

Operations for integer arithmetic, comparisons, boolean arithmetic, field dereference, array indexing, etc are available to construct $E\ a$ expressions. We should emphasize that the actual value of an $E\ a$ will only be available at run time. Asil only has its symbolic representation, and as such it can only be manipulated (in Asil) to a limited extent. Not all Haskell expressions (lambdas in particular) can masquerade as E-expressions, nor can E-expressions be scrutinized with Haskell's case expressions. The reason is that AsilCore does not support these types and expressions, and we chose not to provide translations for them at this time. We may do so in the future, but in this first attempt we prefer to introduce only those elements that are essential and to decide later what else we might need. Only a few Haskell *values*, such as integers and strings, are also E-expressions.

The operations *matchEnter*, *matchCall*, and *matchEnter'* express matches against join points. A successful match on a join point p returns information about p, else the instrumentation fails on that join point.

For example, *matchEnter km* matches on a join point p only if p is the start of the method km. The latter is expressed as a value of type *Prop c (Method a b)* to make it type-explicit that km is supposed to be a method of type $a \to b$, belonging to an object of type c. If it succeeds, the instrumentation returns a value of type *Enter a*. The type parameter a indicates that we will get information about km's parameter(s). Notice that the type of *matchEnter* enforces that these two instances of a will bind to the same type.

The reflection information that is pre-generated and imported by an instrumentation specification (See Figure 1) contains the *Prop* representation of every

```
-- monadic combinators
(≫=)          :: I a → (a → I b) → I b
return        :: a → I a
fail          :: String → I a

-- instrumentations (I)
call          :: E (Method a b) → E̅ a → I (E b)
matchEnter    :: Prop c (Method a b) → I (Enter a)
matchCall     :: Prop c (Method a b) → I (Enter a)
matchEnter'   :: I (Enter Any)
guard         :: E Bool → I ()
onPrevious    :: I a → I a
param         :: Enter Any → Int → I (E Any)

-- alternative combinators
(⊕)           :: I a → I a → I a
(⊕)           :: I a → I a → I a
(⊗)           :: I a → I a → I a

-- expression combinators (E)
(#)           :: E c → Prop c t → E t   -- property dereference
embed         :: I a → E a
null          :: E (Object t)
static        :: E Static
param₁        :: Enter (a, r)        → E a
param₂        :: Enter (a, (b, r))   → E b

-- match context
data Enter a = ME {name :: E String, params :: E̅ a}
```

Fig. 4. Excerpt from the Asil combinators

property (field and method) of every class in the target program, in the form of a Haskell constant named:

$k\_packageName\_className\_methodName$

For example, $k\_code\_MyGame\_clicked$ represents the method *clicked* in the class *MyGame* (from Figure 2), and its type is:

$Prop\ t\_MyGame\ (Method\ t\_MouseEvent\ t\_void)$

Another example is the constant $k\_flash\_event\_MouseEvent\_localX$ which is of type $Prop\ (Field\ t\_int)$. It represents the field *localX* of the class *MouseEvent* of the package *flash.event*. If e is an Asil expression representing an instance of *MouseEvent*, we can write $e\ \#\ k\_flash\_event\_MouseEvent\_localX$ to obtain the field from e.

Figure 5 below shows an example. The operation *matchEnter* there matches against the entry of the method `clicked` of the class `MyGame`. If the match succeeds, then the variable m contains information about the join point. Different types of join points typically provide different information. In this case, we use *name* to obtain m's name and $param_1$ to obtain a (typed) reference *evt* to its first parameter. From *evt* we obtain the coordinates of the mouse click and pass these, finally, to the log method *logEnter*, along with m's name. For static properties, we use the special name *static* as object reference.

$instrLogClick =$ **do**
     $m \leftarrow matchEnter\ k\_code\_MyGame\_clicked$
     let $mname = name\ m$ -- get m's name
          $evt = param_1\ m$ -- get m's params
          $eX = evt \# k\_flash\_events\_MouseEvent\_localX$
          $eY = evt \# k\_flash\_events\_MouseEvent\_localY$
     $call\ (static \# k\_code\_Log\_logEnter)\ (mname, eX, eY)$
     $return\ ()$

Fig. 5. An example of an *Instrumentation* (so, it is also a *Spec* in Figure 1)

Alternatively, as shown below, we can do a more flexible matching. Using *matchEnter'* we can match against the entry of *any* method (including methods that have no statically fixed name nor a statically fixed signature). Then we can follow it with *guard cond* to specify a selection. The latter succeeds if *cond* evaluates (at instrumentation time) to *True*, else it fails. In the example below, we match on the entry of any method whose name contains `"clicked"` as substring, and has a first parameter of the `MouseEvent` type.

     do $m \leftarrow matchEnter'$
          $guard\ (count\ (params\ m) \equiv 1)$
          $guard\ (substr\ $`"clicked"`$\ (name\ m))$
          $p_1 \leftarrow param\ m\ 1$
          $evt \leftarrow p_1\ `cast`\ t\_flash\_events\_MouseEvent$
          ...

In this example, *params* obtains a reference to the parameters of the method from m.

We can also do contextual matching. For example, below we want to instrument calls to `move` from *inside* the method `clicked`. When tried on a join point p, the operation *onPrevious i* applies the instrumentation i to the join points that (directly) precede p in the control flow graph (ignoring back edges). The operation succeeds if i is successfully applied to such a preceding join point (at runtime).

$instrLogMove = $ **do**
  $onPrevious$ \$ $matchEnter \; k\_code\_MyGame\_clicked$
  $m \leftarrow matchCall \; k\_code\_MyGame\_move$
  let $mname = name \; m$
    $from \;\; = param_1 \; m$
    $to \;\;\;\; = param_2 \; m$
  $call \; (class \; \# \; k\_code\_Log\_logCall) \; (mname, from, to)$
  $return \; ()$

In the context of having matched against `clicked`, we match against a call to `MyGame.move`, and insert a call to `Log.logCall`, passing the name of the called method and its arguments to it.

Instrumentations can also be combined with various *alternative* operators. Given some continuation f, the meaning of $(p \otimes q) \gg= f$ is that both branches $p \gg= f$ and $q \gg= f$ are applied to the join point (and in that order). The meaning of $(p \oplus q) \gg= f$ is that p and q (in that order) are both applied, and the continuation f is parametrized with the result of the last succeeding one of the two. The strict alternative $p \oslash q$ applies q only if p fails. For example, we can now combine $instrLogMove$ and $instrLogClick$ defined before like this (*fail* is the unit of $\otimes$):

$myInstr :: I \; ()$
$myInstr = foldr \; (\otimes) \; (fail \; \texttt{"initial"})$
  $[instrLogClick, instrLogMove]$

This $myInstr$ specifies now the complete instrumentation for our running example. When evaluated on a given Flash program, this specification will inspect every joint point and applies instrumentation on it according to the semantics as specified informally in this section. However, we actually implemented an instrumentation monad such that its execution yields an AsilCore specification (Section 4) as an intermediate step. How and why we do this is the subject of the next section.

4   The AsilCore Language

The monadic bind is an obstacle in the translation of Asil to ActionScript. The right-hand side of a bind is a function, which would require a nontrivial translation of Haskell functions to ActionScript. Therefore, we partially evaluate the monadic code to AsilCore, which is sequential code. This step eliminates both functions and monads.

The AsilCore language (Figure 6) is an intermediate language that can be mapped strightforwardly to ActionScript advice (to be precise, we map directly to AVM2 bytecode). An AsilCore term has a statically fixed control flow graph, which simplifies the injection into compiled ActionScript, since it can be represented with conventional branching instructions of ActionScript.

$$
\begin{array}{llll}
i & ::= & \textbf{match } m & \text{-- match against join point } m \\
  & | & \textbf{call } o \; \overline{v} \; (x :: \tau) & \text{-- call with args } \overline{v}, \text{ binds result } x \\
  & | & \textbf{on previous } i & \text{-- lift to preceding join points} \\
  & | & \textbf{abort} & \text{-- aborts instrumentation} \\
  & | & \textbf{nop} & \text{-- no-op} \\
  & | & \textbf{coerce } v_1 \; (x_2 :: \tau) & \text{-- coerce type of } v_1 \text{ to } \tau \\
  & | & i_1 ; i_2 & \text{-- sequential composition} \\
  & | & i_1 \oplus i_2 & \text{-- parallel composition} \\
  & | & i_1 \oslash i_2 & \text{-- alternative composition} \\
  & | & \textbf{static } i & \text{-- error if } i \text{ not statically resolved} \\
  & | & \textbf{dynamic } i & \text{-- defers eval of prims in } i \\
m & ::= & \textbf{entry } (x_1 :: String) \; \overline{x_2 :: \tau} & \text{-- name } x_1, \text{ args } \overline{x_2} \\
  & | & \textbf{exit} \quad (x_1 :: String) \; (x_2 :: \tau) & \text{-- name } x_1, \text{ result } x_2 \\
  & | & \textbf{call} \quad (x_1 :: String) \; \overline{x_2 :: \tau} & \text{-- name } x_1, \text{ args } \overline{x_2} \\
  & | & ... & \text{-- etc.} \\
o & ::= & \textbf{prim } x & \text{-- primitive with the name x} \\
  & | & \textbf{static } s & \text{-- static property named s} \\
  & | & \textbf{dynamic } v_1 \; v_2 & \text{-- call closure } v_1 \text{ with } v_2 \text{ as this} \\
v & ::= & x \mid c & \text{-- identifiers and constants}
\end{array}
$$

Fig. 6. AsilCore abstract syntax

In the translation to AsilCore (Figure 7), we implement the instrumentation monad in continuation passing style [18] to deal with the $\otimes$ operator. The monadic binds are replaced with static sequencing. Even if Asil programs cannot use Haskell code to scrutinize E-values, we can parametrize a function f in the right-hand side of a bind with the (typically) symbolic value v_1 computed in the left-hand side, and continue partial evaluation. As a result, such a value v_1 will be restricted in how it can be manipulated at run-time.

We desugar Asil programs a bit further to simplify the AsilCore representation. We express all branching with the local combinators $\oplus$ and $\oslash$. Values in AsilCore are either identifiers that symbolically represent ActionScript objects, or constants that represent concrete ActionScript objects. Matches introduce identifiers for the contextual values of the match, and calls introduce identifiers for the result value. Calls take values as argument, which are either constants or identifiers. An identifier may only be introduced once, and must be introduced before being used. This property holds for AsilCore programs that are derived from well-typed Asil programs.

The fragment in Figure 8 shows the result of the translation of the running (Asil) example to AsilCore. The abstractions offered by Asil are expanded away.

The primitive *deref* takes an object and a fully qualified name as string, and returns the associated property if it exists, otherwise it fails. To invoke a property

$$\textbf{type } I\ a = Uid \rightarrow \qquad\qquad\qquad \text{-- unique id}$$
$$(Uid \rightarrow a \rightarrow Core \rightarrow (Core, Uid)) \rightarrow \qquad \text{-- continuation}$$
$$(Core, Uid)) \qquad\qquad\qquad\qquad \text{-- res. core}$$
$$run\ f = fst\ \$\ f\ 1\ (\lambda n\ \_\ i \rightarrow (i, n)) \qquad \text{-- } I\ a \rightarrow Core$$

instance *Functor I* **where**
$$fmap\ f\ g = \lambda n\ k \rightarrow g\ n\ (\lambda m\ v \rightarrow k\ m\ (f\ v))$$

instance *Monad I* **where**
$$return\ x = \lambda n\ k \rightarrow k\ n\ x\ \textbf{nop}$$
$$m_1 \ggeq f = \lambda n_1\ k \rightarrow m_1\ n_1\ \$\ \lambda n_2\ v_1\ i_1 \rightarrow$$
$$(f\ v_1)\ n_2\ \$\ \lambda n_3\ v_2\ i_2 \rightarrow k\ n_3\ v_2\ (i_1; i_2)$$
$$fail\ s \quad = \lambda n\ k \rightarrow k\ n\ (error\ s)\ \textbf{abort}$$

instance *Alternative I* **where**
$$empty \quad = \quad \lambda n_1\ k \rightarrow k\ n_1\ \bot\ \textbf{abort}$$
$$m_1 \oplus m_2 = \quad \lambda n_1\ k \rightarrow m_1\ n_1\ \$\ \lambda n_2\ v_1\ i_1 \rightarrow$$
$$m_2\ n_2\ \$\ \lambda n_3\ v_2\ i_2 \rightarrow k\ n_3\ v_2\ (i_1 \oplus i_2)$$
$$m_1 \otimes m_2 = \quad \lambda n_1\ k \rightarrow \textbf{let}\ (i_1, n_2) = m_1\ n_1\ k$$
$$(i_2, n_3) = m_2\ n_2\ k$$
$$\textbf{in}\ (i_1 \oplus i_2, n_3)$$
$$embed\ i = \lambda n\ k \rightarrow k\ n\ ()\ i \qquad\qquad \text{-- } Core \rightarrow I\ ()$$
$$fresh \quad = \lambda n\ k \rightarrow k\ (n+1)\ (ESym\ n)\ \textbf{nop} \quad \text{-- } I\ (E\ a)$$
$$matchBlockEntry = \textbf{do} \qquad\qquad \text{-- } I\ Block$$
$$vId \leftarrow fresh$$
$$embed\ (\textbf{match block guid}\ (toCoreIdent\ vId))$$
$$return\ \$\ Block\ \{\ blockGuid = vId\ \}$$

Fig. 7. Asil to Core execution

of an object, *deref* can be used to obtain a closure of type *Function*, followed by a **call dynamic**. The primitive *guard* succeeds if and only if its argument is true, and the *equals* primitive has the same semantics as the ActionScript ==.

The declarative **on previous** instruction lifts its block to all preceding join points in the static control flow graph of the method. Operationally, it also introduces an additional local boolean that keeps track whether the instrumentation was applied. If it was applied, we can access its values via the local variables that the lifted instrumentation introduced.

The obtained AsilCore instrumentation can be mapped to ActionScript code as defined in Figure 9, and can then be weaved in at join points in the program. This requires an ActionScript method for each primitive operation, and we need to construct a reflexive **thisJoinPoint** value [8] at each join point. For a typical join point, only a small part of the instrumentation is applicable (or even none at all). Therefore, our instrumentation weaver Asic (Section 5) partially evaluates the AsilCore term, and only weaves in the residual term.

```
{ match entry
     name x₁   :: String
     args  x₂   :: flash.events.MouseEvent
; call prim equals
     args  x₁, "code.MyGame:clicked"
     res   x₃   :: Boolean
; call prim guard
     args  x₃
     res   x₄   :: void
; call prim deref
     args  x₂, "flash.events.MouseEvent:localX"
     res   x₅   :: int
; call prim deref
     args  x₂, "flash.events.MouseEvent:localY"
     res   x₆   :: int
; call static "code.Log:logEnter"
     args  "code.MyGame:clicked", x₅, x₆
     res   x₇   :: void
} ⊕    -- composes the two instrumentations in parallel
{ on previous
     { match entry
         name  x₈ :: String
         inputs x₉ :: flash.events.MouseEvent
     ; call prim equals
         args   x₈, "code.MyGame:clicked"
         res    x₁₀ :: Boolean
     ; call prim guard
         args   x₁₀
         res    x₁₁ :: void }
; match call
     name  x₁₂ :: String
     inputs x₁₃ :: code.Square, x₁₄ :: code.Square
; call prim equals
     args   x₁₂, "code.MyGame:move"
     res    x₁₅ :: Boolean
; call prim guard
     args   x₁₅
     res    x₁₆ :: void
; call static "code.Log:logCall"
     args   "code.MyGame:move", x₁₃, x₁₄
     res    x₁₇ :: void
} ⊕ abort
```

Fig. 8. Translation of running example to AsilCore

$$\llbracket \textbf{abort} \rrbracket \qquad\qquad \rightsquigarrow \; thisJoinPoint.aborted = true$$

$$\llbracket \textbf{nop} \rrbracket \qquad\qquad\quad \rightsquigarrow \; ;$$

$$\llbracket \textbf{call } o \; \overline{v} \; (x :: \tau) \qquad \rightsquigarrow \; \llbracket x \rrbracket = (\tau)\,(\llbracket o \rrbracket \overline{\llbracket v \rrbracket});$$

$$\llbracket \textbf{match exit } (x_1 :: String) \; (x_2 :: \tau_2) \rrbracket \rightsquigarrow$$
$$\quad thisJoinPoint.aborted \; \vee= \; thisJoinPoint.isMethodExit;$$
$$\quad \textbf{if } (\neg \; thisJoinPoint.aborted) \; \{$$
$$\qquad \llbracket x_1 \rrbracket = thisJoinPoint.nm; \llbracket x_2 \rrbracket = thisJoinPoint.ret \, \}$$

$$\llbracket i_1; i_2 \rrbracket \qquad \rightsquigarrow \; \llbracket i_1 \rrbracket; \textbf{if } (\neg \; thisJoinPoint.aborted) \; \{ \llbracket i_2 \rrbracket \}$$

$$\llbracket i_1 \oplus i_2 \rrbracket \qquad \rightsquigarrow \; \llbracket i_1 \rrbracket; thisJoinPoint.aborted = false; \llbracket i_2 \rrbracket$$

$$\llbracket i_1 \oslash i_2 \rrbracket \qquad \rightsquigarrow \; \llbracket i_1 \rrbracket; \textbf{if } (thisJoinPoint.aborted) \; \{$$
$$\qquad\qquad\qquad thisJoinPoint.aborted = false; \llbracket i_2 \rrbracket \}$$

$$\llbracket \textbf{prim } x \rrbracket \qquad as \; \rightsquigarrow \; Primitives.\llbracket x \rrbracket (as)$$

$$\llbracket \textbf{static } C : x \rrbracket \qquad as \; \rightsquigarrow \; \llbracket C \rrbracket.\llbracket x \rrbracket (as)$$

$$\llbracket \textbf{dynamic } v_1 \; v_2 \rrbracket as \; \rightsquigarrow \; v_1.call \; (v_2, as)$$

Fig. 9. AsilCore to ActionScript translation

5   The Instrumentation Weaver Asic

The Asic tool takes an AsilCore term and applies it to all join points of the SUT. This involves yet another partial evaluation step. The success of a match is always resolved statically, and results in static bindings for identifiers related to the name of a method, unique id of a block, and possibly also the types and number of arguments. Calls to primitive methods may be performed statically, depending on what is known statically about their parameters. Reachable calls to non-primitive methods always result in a residual call in order to cater for possible side effects.

To test Asic, we have applied instrumentations to a number of examples, including the Habbo application, which is a large Flash program that consists of 3,000 classes with 25,000 methods and over 800,000 instructions.

Note that our parser combinator implementation included in Asic can be viewed as a formal specification of the ActionScript bytecode grammar in an executable, testable form. This is useful, because although the specifications of Flash and the ActionScript bytecode format are publicly available, we have discovered that these specifications are incomplete with respect to new Flash versions, and also contain errors that are hard to track down. Our implementation is consistent with recent versions of Flash, and can be viewed as an improvement of the specifications.

6   Related Work

The execution of a program can be seen as a sequence of events. Logging means to record some of these events. In AOP the term "join point model" refers to the used definition of "join point" [4]. It essentially defines where or when we can inject an advice. For logging, it makes sense to define "events" as meant above as our join points. Douence et al's join point model [6] adopts this perspective. Injection can be done at the compile time or at run time. Run-time injection is in principle more expressive, as it potentially allows the advice to change based on run-time information. However, it generates additional run-time overhead for deciding if an incoming event needs to be instrumented, and if so, which advice should be used. Compile time injection transforms the target program. It is only possible if the events we want to log can be mapped to static locations in the program. On the other hand, run-time injection is only possible if the corresponding events can be intercepted at run time. This may not be natively possible for all sorts of events. A possible solution is to inject code that facilitates interception [6] for those events. Another approach is to use a runtime system that natively facilitates run-time interception of join points. For example, Dutchyn uses continuation style interpretation [5], allowing every function call to be intercepted so that advice can be woven in.

The popular AspectJ [11] join point model only considers method calls (inside or outside) as join point. AspectJ performs compile time injection, as does Asil. The AspectJ join point model, however, is not fine grained enough to log the control flow within a method. To achieve this we would have to insert advice at the block level. Also in our case run-time injection inside methods and at blocks is not a realistic option. We cannot modify the Flash player (ActionScript's virtual machine), because it is proprietary. Besides, for security reasons altering the Flash player is unacceptable for our Habbo case study users.

AspectJ offers "after", "before", and "around" types of injection. At the moment Asil only does "after" injection, except for method/block exit, for which it does "before" injection. The "around" injection is not really sensible for logging.

Most AOP frameworks, e.g., AspectJ, AspectScheme, and AspectML [5] provide native DSLs, whereas we decided to embed Asil in Haskell, as an EDSL. The downside is that aspects are expressed in Haskell, rather than in the target program's own language (ActionScript). But in return advice are available as first class values. We can conveniently use higher order functions to compose them. On that note, we mention related work of Brady and Hammond [3] on using partial evaluation in a dependently typed setting to improve the resource usage of EDSLs. However, in our particular case we are not so much interested in efficiency of execution, but more in the declarativeness of the Asil language and the level of abstraction attainable therewith.

In FITTEST we also want to analyze logs to infer finite models, which in turn are used to generate test cases. Some previous work in this direction are [2,13]. A test-case is essentially a sequence of "top level interactions" on the SUT, interspersed with oracles [1]. To derive test-cases from logs thus requires that (a subset of) those interactions are logged. For an internet application, top level interactions are typically the user's interactions with its GUI. It is however impossible to accurately map such events to static locations in the SUT, implying that static injection is not the right approach to log them. Fortunately in ActionScript it is possible to programmatically intercept GUI events. Similar facilities exists for e.g. Java and C#. The FITTEST logging framework actually uses run-time injection to log such events [16], and uses Asil to provide the logging of lower level events.

7   Conclusion and Future Work

We presented Asil, an expressive AOP EDSL for the instrumentation of Action-Script programs. Like AspectJ, Asil allows join points and advice to be specified with constrained patterns. However, Asil's design and implementation is based on well-known functional programming techniques, such as monads. The implementation exploits Haskell's facilities for abstraction, syntactic sugar and static typing.

The possibility to write higher-order functions is an essential feature that we sorely miss in many DSLs. Fortunately, this comes for free with EDSLs in functional languages. Asil exploits higher order functions to abstract over and compose instrumentations.

Future Work. Particularly in the world of object-orientation, many metrics exist to identify code vulnerabilities, e.g., inheritance distance and coupling [7]. The ability to select join points based on the values attained for such metrics, thereby restricting the logging to parts of the code where such vulnerabilities are most likely to reside, as an interesting possibility that deserves further exploration. At the very least, it can be be used for prioritizing join points, e.g., when the target application can only afford little run-time overhead for logging.

As it is now, all join point matching is decided at compile time. We can make instrumentations more expressive if we have the option to use run-time conditions to decide upon matching. This, however, leads to a new problem. In Asil, an instrumentation may fail and this property is essential for its notion of composition (of instrumentations). However, if matching can be postponed to run time, it implies that we must be able to roll back the side effects of an instrumentation if it turns out to fail (not match) at run time. A solution is to simply insist that run time matching cannot be preceded by a side effecting instrumentation. A more generic solution is to implement a transaction-like logger.

Acknowledgement. This work has been partially funded by the European Union FP7 project FITTEST (grant agreement nr. 257574). We thank Jurriaan Hage for the feedback, discussions, and help he gave. We thank the anonymous reviewers of IFL 2011 for their constructive comments.

References

1. Baresi, L., Young, M.: Test oracles. Tech. rep., Univ. of Oregon, Dept. of Comp. and Inf. Science (2001), http://ix.cs.uoregon.edu/~michal/pubs/oracles.pdf, CIS-TR-01-02
2. Biermann, A.W., Feldman, J.A.: On the synthesis of Finite-State machines from samples of their behavior. IEEE Transactions on Computers C-21(6), 592–597 (1972)

3. Brady, E.C., Hammond, K.: Scrapping your inefficient engine: using partial evaluation to improve domain-specific language implementation. In: Procd. of 15th ACM
SIGPLAN Int. Conf. on Functional Programming, ICFP 2010, pp. 297–308. ACM
(2010)
4. Cazzola, W.: Semantic Join Point Models: Motivations, Notions and Requirements.
In: SPLAT 2006 (2006)
5. Dantas, D.S., Walker, D., Washburn, G., Weirich, S.: AspectML: A polymorphic
aspect-oriented functional programming language. ACM Transactions on Programming Languages and Systems 30(3) (May 2008)
6. Douence, R., Motelet, O., Südholt, M.: A Formal Definition of Crosscuts. In: Mat-
suoka, S. (ed.) Reflection 2001. LNCS, vol. 2192, pp. 170–186. Springer, Heidelberg
(2001)
7. Harrison, R., Counsell, S., Nithi, R.: An evaluation of the MOOD set of object oriented software metrics. IEEE Transactions on Software Engineering 24(6),
491–496 (1998)
8. Hilsdale, E., Hugunin, J.: Advice Weaving in AspectJ. In: AOSD 2004, pp. 26–35
(2004)
9. Hudson-Smith, A.: The future internet. Future Internet 1(1), 1–2 (2009)
10. Juarez-Martinez, U., Olmedo-Aguirre, J.O.: A Join-point Model for Fine-grained
Aspects. In: ECC 2008, pp. 126–131 (2008)
11. Kiczales, G., Hilsdale, E., Hugunin, J., Kersten, M., Palm, J., Griswold, W.G.:
An Overview of AspectJ. In: Lee, S.H. (ed.) ECOOP 2001. LNCS, vol. 2072,
pp. 327–353. Springer, Heidelberg (2001)
12. Kiczales, G., Lamping, J., Mendhekar, A., Maeda, C., Lopes, C.V., Loingtier, J.M.,
Irwin, J.: Aspect-Oriented Programming. In: Aksit, M., Auletta, V. (eds.) ECOOP
1997. LNCS, vol. 1241, pp. 220–242. Springer, Heidelberg (1997)
13. Lorenzoli, D., Mariani, L., Pezzè, M.: Automatic generation of software behavioral
models. In: Procd. of the 30th Int. Conf. on Software Engineering, pp. 501–510.
ACM (2008)
14. Mcbride, C., Paterson, R.: Applicative Programming with Effects. JFP 18, 1–13
(2008)
15. Pachidi, S.: Software operation data mining: techniques to analyse how software
operates in the field. Master's thesis, Dept. Inf. & Comp. Sciences, Utrecht Univ.
(2011), IKU-3317153
16. Prasetya, I.S.W.B., Middelkoop, A., Elyasov, A., Hage, J.: D6.1: FITTEST logging
approach, project no. 257574, FITTEST future internet testing (2011)
17. Sulake: Habbo Hotel (2004), http://www.habbo.com/
18. Sussman, G.J.: Scheme: An Interpreter for Extended Lambda Calculus. In: Memo
349. MIT AI Lab (1975)
19. Vos, T.E.J., Tonella, P., Wegener, J., Harman, M., Prasetya, W., Puoskari, E., Nir-
Buchbinder, Y.: Future Internet Testing with FITTEST. In: 2011 15th European
Conference on Software Maintenance and Reengineering (CSMR), pp. 355–358.
IEEE (2011)
20. Wadler, P.: Monads for Functional Programming. In: Jeuring, J., Meijer, E. (eds.)
AFP 1995. LNCS, vol. 925, pp. 24–52. Springer, Heidelberg (1995)

Fairness for Transactional Events

Edward Amsden and Matthew Fluet

Rochester Institute of Technology, Rochester NY 14623
{eca7215,mtf}@cs.rit.edu

Abstract. *Transactional events* are a recent concurrency abstraction
that combines first-class synchronous message-passing events with all-
or-nothing transactions. While prior work gave a semantics and an implementation for transactional events, it provided no guarantees about
which of the many non-deterministic executions might be exhibited by a
program.

For concurrent systems, like transactional events, it is natural to
expect certain *fairness* conditions to hold on executions. Intuitively,
fairness guarantees that any system component that could (sufficiently
often) make progress does, in fact, make progress. In this work, we investigate fairness for transactional events. We give a rigorous definition
of fair program executions in transactional events, describe a refined operational semantics that guarantees fair executions, and discuss restrictions and assumptions necessary for the correctness of an implementation
based on the refined semantics.

1 Introduction

Concurrent programming can be a difficult task. The non-deterministic nature
of a concurrent program's execution makes it difficult to reason about all of
the possible behaviors of the program. To manage the complexity of writing
and understanding concurrent programs, programmers make use of two enabling
methodologies: (1) high-level abstractions of concurrent operations and (2) assumed properties of concurrent systems.

High-level concurrency abstractions allow complex thread interactions to be abstractly packaged and exported, which increases modularity and eases reasoning.
For example, Software Transactional Memory (STM) [11,6] provides first-class,
composable operations that allow a programmer to combine shared-memory
operations into an action that can itself be treated as an atomic shared-memory
operation. Similarly, Concurrent ML (CML) [9] provides first-class, composable
operations that allow a programmer to combine synchronous message-passing operations into an action that can itself be treated as a synchronous message-passing
operation. Recently, Transactional Events [3,4] have been proposed as a concurrency abstraction that combines synchronous message-passing operations with all-
or-nothing transactions. The key to the expressive power of Transactional Events
is a sequencing combinator that allows a programmer to write an action that contains multiple communications; the action blocks until all of the constituent communications can succeed.

A. Gill and J. Hage (Eds.): IFL 2011, LNCS 7257, pp. 17–34, 2012.
© Springer-Verlag Berlin Heidelberg 2012

Safety and liveness properties assert statements that are true of all possible executions of a concurrent program. Intuitively, safety asserts that something "bad" never happens, while liveness asserts that something "good" eventually happens. Fairness [5,2,8] is a particular liveness property that is important in concurrent programming, although it is often treated informally or assumed implicitly. For example, a concurrent programmer typically assumes a "fair" thread scheduler: all threads in the program will execute, not just some threads. As another example, a concurrent programmer typically assumes that if one thread is attempting to send a message and another thread is attempting to receive the message, then the message will eventually be communicated by the system. In generally, fairness is the property that asserts that any action that is enabled often enough is eventually taken.

This paper examines fairness for transactional events. Transactional events takes synchronous message-passing on channels as the primitive concurrent operation and provides combinators for sequencing (e.g., "perform one communication *and then* perform another communication") and choosing (e.g., "perform *either* one communication *or* another communication") concurrent operations. Since synchronous message-passing requires matching a sender and a receiver and sequencing and choosing requires examining multiple communications, the enabledness of a transactional event is non-trivial, which gives rise to interesting behaviors with respect to fairness. As a simple example, consider one thread that repeatedly sends on a channel and two threads that repeatedly receive on the channel. It is intuitively unfair to repeatedly match the sending thread with exactly one of the receiving threads, never communicating with the other receiving thread. We are interested in formalizing this intuition and guaranteeing this behavior in an implementation. We make the following contributions:

- We give an intuitive, yet formal, definition of fairness for transactional events (Section 3) in terms of a high-level operational semantics (Section 2).
- We describe a lower-level operational semantics (Section 4) that refines the high-level operational semantics and demonstrate that executions in the lower-level semantics simulate fair executions (and only fair executions) of the higher-level semantics (Theorems 1 and 2).
- We discuss an implementation of the lower-level semantics and suggest a property of synchronizing events, which, if statically verified by a programmer, enables the implementation to enforce fairness (Section 5).

A companion technical report [1] provides additional background, commentary, and proof details.

2   Semantics

To begin, we review the original high-level operational semantics for transactional events. See prior work [3,4] for a longer and less formal introduction.

Syntax. Expressions naturally fall into one of four categories: standard pure functional language expressions (variables, abstractions, applications, ...), special constants (characters c, thread identifiers θ, and channel names κ), Evt combinators, and IO combinators:

> *Expressions*
> $$e ::= x \mid \lambda x.e_b \mid e_f \; e' \mid \dots \qquad \text{pure functional language expressions}$$
> $$\mid \; c \mid \theta \mid \kappa \qquad\qquad\qquad\qquad\qquad \text{special constants}$$
> $$\mid \; \texttt{alwaysEvt } e' \mid \texttt{thenEvt } e_{evt} \; e_f \qquad\quad \text{Evt combinators}$$
> $$\mid \; \texttt{neverEvt} \mid \texttt{chooseEvt } e_{evtl} \; e_{evtr}$$
> $$\mid \; \texttt{newSChan} \mid \texttt{recvEvt } e_k \mid \texttt{sendEvt } e_k \; e'$$
> $$\mid \; \texttt{unitIO } e' \mid \texttt{bindIO } e_{io} \; e_f \qquad\qquad\qquad \text{IO combinators}$$
> $$\mid \; \texttt{getChar} \mid \texttt{putChar } e_c \mid \texttt{forkIO } e_{io} \mid \texttt{sync } e_{evt}$$

Operational Semantics. The essence of the operational semantics is to interpret sequential expressions, Evt expressions, and IO expressions as separate sorts of computations. This is expressed by three levels of evaluation: sequential evaluation of pure expressions, synchronous evaluation of transactional events, and concurrent evaluation of IO threads. The bridge between the Evt and IO computations is synchronization, which moves threads from concurrent evaluation to synchronous evaluation and back to concurrent evaluation.

Sequential Evaluation ($e \hookrightarrow e'$). The "lowest" level of evaluation is the sequential evaluation of pure functional language expressions. Unsurprisingly, the sequential evaluation relation is entirely standard and thus omitted, although it is expected that sequential evaluation can express recursion and recursively defined Evt and IO computations. We note that the order of evaluation for pure expressions (whether call-by-value, call-by-name, or call-by-need) has no real impact on the behavior of transactional events or the definition of fairness.

Synchronous Evaluation ($\mathcal{E} \rightsquigarrow \mathcal{E}'$). The "middle" level of evaluation is synchronous evaluation of transactional events (see Fig. 1). A *synchronization group* is a set of *synchronizing events*, which are themselves pairs of thread identifiers and Evt expressions. Intuitively, the relation $\{\langle \theta_1, e_{evt1} \rangle, \dots\} \rightsquigarrow \{\langle \theta_1, e'_{evt1} \rangle, \dots\}$ means that the events $e_{evt1}, \dots$ make one step towards synchronization by evaluating to the events $e'_{evt1}, \dots$. All of the synchronous evaluation rules non-deterministically choose one or more events for a step of evaluation.

The EVTEVAL rule implements the sequential evaluation of an expression in the active position. The EVTTHENALWAYS rule implements sequential composition in the Evt monad. The EVTCHOOSELEFT and EVTCHOOSERIGHT rules implement a non-deterministic choice between events. The EVTNEWSCHAN rule allocates a new channel name. The EVTSENDRECV rule implements the two-way rendezvous of communication via a channel; the transition replaces the sendEvt and recvEvt events with alwaysEvt events.

Synchronizing Event	$E ::= \langle \theta, e_{evt} \rangle$	*Synchronous Evaluation Contexts*
Synchronization Group	$\mathcal{E} ::= \{E, \dots\}$	$M^{Evt} ::= [] \mid \text{thenEvt } M^{Evt} \ e_f$

EVTEVAL
$$\frac{e \hookrightarrow e'}{\mathcal{E} \uplus \{\langle \theta, M^{Evt}[e] \rangle\} \rightsquigarrow \mathcal{E} \uplus \{\langle \theta, M^{Evt}[e'] \rangle\}}$$

EVTTHENALWAYS
$$\frac{}{\mathcal{E} \uplus \{\langle \theta, M^{Evt}[\text{thenEvt } (\text{alwaysEvt } e') \ e_f] \rangle\} \rightsquigarrow \mathcal{E} \uplus \{\langle \theta, M^{Evt}[e_f \ e'] \rangle\}}$$

EVTCHOOSELEFT
$$\frac{}{\mathcal{E} \uplus \{\langle \theta, M^{Evt}[\text{chooseEvt } e_{evtl} \ e_{evtr}] \rangle\} \rightsquigarrow \mathcal{E} \uplus \{\langle \theta, M^{Evt}[e_{evtl}] \rangle\}}$$

EVTCHOOSERIGHT
$$\frac{}{\mathcal{E} \uplus \{\langle \theta, M^{Evt}[\text{chooseEvt } e_{evtl} \ e_{evtr}] \rangle\} \rightsquigarrow \mathcal{E} \uplus \{\langle \theta, M^{Evt}[e_{evtr}] \rangle\}}$$

EVTNEWSCHAN
$$\frac{\kappa' \text{ fresh}}{\mathcal{E} \uplus \{\langle \theta, M^{Evt}[\text{newSChan}] \rangle\} \rightsquigarrow \mathcal{E} \uplus \{\langle \theta, M^{Evt}[\text{alwaysEvt } \kappa'] \rangle\}}$$

EVTSENDRECV
$$\frac{}{\mathcal{E} \uplus \{\langle \theta_s, M_s^{Evt}[\text{sendEvt } \kappa \ e'] \rangle, \langle \theta_r, M_r^{Evt}[\text{recvEvt } \kappa] \rangle\} \rightsquigarrow \mathcal{E} \uplus \{\langle \theta_s, M_s^{Evt}[\text{alwaysEvt } ()] \rangle, \langle \theta_r, M_r^{Evt}[\text{alwaysEvt } e'] \rangle\}}$$

IO Thread	$T ::= \langle \theta, e_{io} \rangle$	*Program State* $\mathcal{P} ::= \mathcal{T}; \mathcal{S}$
Thread Soup	$\mathcal{T} ::= \{T, \dots\}$	*Action* $a ::= ?c \mid !c \mid \epsilon$
Synchronizing Thread	$S ::= \langle \theta, M^{IO}, e_{evt} \rangle$	*Concurrent Evaluation Contexts*
Synchronization Soup	$\mathcal{S} ::= \{S, \dots\}$	$M^{IO} ::= [] \mid \text{bindIO } M^{IO} \ e_f$

IOEVAL
$$\frac{e \hookrightarrow e'}{\mathcal{T} \uplus \{\langle \theta, M^{IO}[e] \rangle\}; \mathcal{S} \xrightarrow{\epsilon} \mathcal{T} \uplus \{\langle \theta, M^{IO}[e'] \rangle\}; \mathcal{S}}$$

IOFORK
$$\frac{\theta' \text{ fresh}}{\mathcal{T} \uplus \{\langle \theta, M^{IO}[\text{forkIO } e_{io}] \rangle\}; \mathcal{S} \xrightarrow{\epsilon} \mathcal{T} \uplus \{\langle \theta, M^{IO}[\text{unitIO } \theta'] \rangle, \langle \theta', e_{io} \rangle\}; \mathcal{S}}$$

IOUNIT
$$\frac{}{\mathcal{T} \uplus \{\langle \theta, \text{unitIO } e' \rangle\}; \mathcal{S} \xrightarrow{\epsilon} \mathcal{T}; \mathcal{S}}$$

IOBINDUNIT
$$\frac{}{\mathcal{T} \uplus \{\langle \theta, M^{IO}[\text{bindIO } (\text{unitIO } e') \ e_f] \rangle\}; \mathcal{S} \xrightarrow{\epsilon} \mathcal{T} \uplus \{\langle \theta, M^{IO}[e_f \ e'] \rangle\}; \mathcal{S}}$$

IOGETCHAR
$$\frac{}{\mathcal{T} \uplus \{\langle \theta, M^{IO}[\text{getChar}] \rangle\}; \mathcal{S} \xrightarrow{?c} \mathcal{T} \uplus \{\langle \theta, M^{IO}[\text{unitIO } c] \rangle\}; \mathcal{S}}$$

IOPUTCHAR
$$\frac{}{\mathcal{T} \uplus \{\langle \theta, M^{IO}[\text{putChar } c] \rangle\}; \mathcal{S} \xrightarrow{!c} \mathcal{T} \uplus \{\langle \theta, M^{IO}[\text{unitIO } ()] \rangle\}; \mathcal{S}}$$

IOSYNCINIT
$$\frac{}{\mathcal{T} \uplus \{\langle \theta, M^{IO}[\text{sync } e_{evt}] \rangle\}; \mathcal{S} \xrightarrow{\epsilon} \mathcal{T}; \mathcal{S} \uplus \{\langle \theta, M^{IO}, e_{evt} \rangle\}}$$

IOSYNCSYNC
$$\frac{\{\langle \theta_1, e_{evt1} \rangle, \dots\} \rightsquigarrow^* \{\langle \theta_1, \text{alwaysEvt } e_1' \rangle, \dots\}}{\mathcal{T}; \mathcal{S} \uplus \{\langle \theta_1, M_1^{IO}, e_{evt1} \rangle, \dots\} \xrightarrow{\epsilon} \mathcal{T} \uplus \{\langle \theta_1, M_1^{IO}[\text{unitIO } e_1'] \rangle, \dots\}; \mathcal{S}}$$

Fig. 1. Dynamic semantics – Synchronous (top) and Concurrent (bot) evaluation

We define SYNCABLE($\mathcal{E}$), a predicate asserting that the non-empty synchronization group $\mathcal{E}$ may successfully synchronize by evaluating to a configuration in which all events are alwaysEvts.

$$\text{SYNCABLE}(\{\langle\theta_1, e_{evt1}\rangle, \ldots\}) \overset{\text{def}}{=}$$
$$\exists e'_1, \ldots. \{\langle\theta_1, e_{evt1}\rangle, \ldots\} \rightsquigarrow^* \{\langle\theta_1, \texttt{alwaysEvt } e'_1\rangle, \ldots\}$$

Concurrent Evaluation ($\mathcal{P} \overset{a}{\rightarrow} \mathcal{P}'$). The "highest" level of evaluation is concurrent evaluation of threads (see Fig. 1). A *thread soup* is a set of *IO threads*, which are themselves pairs of thread identifiers and IO expressions. A *synchronization soup* is a set of *synchronizing threads*, which correspond to IO threads that are actively synchronizing and are themselves triples of a thread identifier, an IO evaluation context, and an Evt expression. Finally, a *program state* pairs a thread soup and a synchronization soup. *Actions* represent the input/output behavior of the program. The observable actions correspond to reading a character c from standard input ($?c$) or writing a character c to standard output ($!c$). The silent action ϵ indicates no observable input/output behavior. All of the concurrent evaluation rules non-deterministically choose one or more threads for a step of evaluation and are labeled with an action.

The IOEVAL rule implements the sequential evaluation of an expression in the active position. The IOFORK rule implements thread creation by adding a new IO thread to the thread soup. The IOUNIT rule implements thread termination when a thread has evaluated to a unitIO action. The IOBINDUNIT rule implements sequential composition in the IO monad. The IOGETCHAR and IOPUTCHAR rules perform the appropriate labeled transition, yielding observable actions.

The IOSYNCINIT and IOSYNCSYNC rules implement event synchronization. The IOSYNCINIT rule initiates event synchronization by changing an IO thread into a synchronizing thread. The IOSYNCSYNC rule completes event synchronization by selecting some non-empty collection of synchronizing threads, passing the event expressions to the synchronous evaluation relation, which takes *multiple transitions* to a configuration in which all events are alwaysEvts, and resuming all of the synchronizing threads as IO threads with their synchronization results.

Note that the IOSYNCINIT and IOSYNCSYNC rules have silent actions. Synchronization is not observable, though it may unblock a thread so that subsequent I/O actions are observed. Also note that the IOSYNCSYNC rule takes multiple synchronous evaluation steps in a single concurrent evaluation step; this guarantees that synchronization executes "atomically," although the synchronization of a single event is not "isolated" from the synchronizations of other events. (Indeed, it is imperative that multiple events synchronize simultaneously in order to enable synchronous communication along channels.)

3 Fairness

Intuitively, fairness is a property that asserts that every thread that could make progress does, in fact, make progress. Alternatively, unfairness is a property that asserts that some thread that could make progress does not make progress. Hence, fairness and unfairness are a properties of a program's execution, rather than a property of a program's state. We start by formalizing a representation of a program's execution and then introduce two distinct notions of fairness.

Traces. A *program trace* is a representation of a program's execution. Since many interesting concurrent programs do not terminate, a program trace must represent both terminating and non-terminating executions. Furthermore, a program trace must represent a maximal execution, where a terminating execution is witnessed by a terminal program state that cannot evolve. A program trace $\mathcal{P} \Uparrow$ is defined using a coinductive relation, in order to represent both terminating and non-terminating executions.

$$
\text{Term} \quad \frac{\neg \exists a, \mathcal{P}'.\ \mathcal{P} \xrightarrow{a} \mathcal{P}'}{\mathcal{P} \Uparrow}\ \text{co}
\qquad\qquad
\text{Step} \quad \frac{\mathcal{P} \xrightarrow{a} \mathcal{P}' \qquad \mathcal{P}' \Uparrow}{\mathcal{P} \Uparrow}\ \text{co}
$$

The Term rule indicates that $\mathcal{P}$ is a terminal program state, while the Step rule indicates that $\mathcal{P}$ may evolve to a new program state.

Since a program trace may be seen to define a finite or infinite sequence of program steps and program states, it is convenient to index a program trace in order to extract the ith program step or program state. These recursive, partial, indexing operations $I^{\rightarrow}(\mathcal{P} \Uparrow, i)$ for steps and $I^{\mathcal{P}}(\mathcal{P} \Uparrow, i)$ for states, are defined as follows:

$$
I^{\rightarrow} \left(\frac{\text{Step}}{\dfrac{\mathcal{P} \xrightarrow{a} \mathcal{P}' \quad \mathcal{P}' \Uparrow}{\mathcal{P} \Uparrow}\ \text{co}}, 0 \right) = \mathcal{P} \xrightarrow{a} \mathcal{P}'
$$

$$
I^{\rightarrow} \left(\frac{\text{Step}}{\dfrac{\mathcal{P} \xrightarrow{a} \mathcal{P}' \quad \mathcal{P}' \Uparrow}{\mathcal{P} \Uparrow}\ \text{co}}, i+1 \right) = I^{\rightarrow}(\mathcal{P}' \Uparrow, i)
$$

$$
I^{\mathcal{P}}(\mathcal{P} \Uparrow, 0) = \mathcal{P}
$$

$$
I^{\mathcal{P}} \left(\frac{\text{Step}}{\dfrac{\mathcal{P} \xrightarrow{a} \mathcal{P}' \quad \mathcal{P}' \Uparrow}{\mathcal{P} \Uparrow}\ \text{co}}, i+1 \right) = I^{\mathcal{P}}(\mathcal{P}' \Uparrow, i)
$$

As a convenience, we define $I^{\mathcal{T}}(\mathcal{P} \Uparrow, i)$ and $I^{\mathcal{S}}(\mathcal{P} \Uparrow, i)$ to extract the ith thread soup and the ith synchronization soup, respectively, from a program trace:

$$
\begin{aligned}
I^{\mathcal{T}}(\mathcal{P} \Uparrow, i) &= \mathcal{T} & \text{where } \mathcal{T}; \mathcal{S} = I^{\mathcal{P}}(\mathcal{P} \Uparrow, i) \\
I^{\mathcal{S}}(\mathcal{P} \Uparrow, i) &= \mathcal{S} & \text{where } \mathcal{T}; \mathcal{S} = I^{\mathcal{P}}(\mathcal{P} \Uparrow, i)
\end{aligned}
$$

While a program trace is a representation of a program's complete execution, an *action trace* is a representation of a program's observable input/output behavior. An action trace is a finite or infinite sequence of actions, defined using a coinductive interpretation.

$$Action\ Trace \qquad \mathcal{A} \overset{co}{::=} \bullet \mid a : \mathcal{A}$$

We define $Acts(\mathcal{P} \Uparrow)$ as a corecursive, total operation that constructs an action trace from a program trace:

$$Acts \left(\dfrac{\text{TERM} \quad \dfrac{\neg \exists a, \mathcal{P}'. \ \mathcal{P} \overset{a}{\rightarrow} \mathcal{P}'}{\mathcal{P} \Uparrow}}{} \ co \right) = \bullet$$

$$Acts \left(\dfrac{\text{STEP} \quad \dfrac{\mathcal{P} \overset{a}{\rightarrow} \mathcal{P}' \quad \mathcal{P}' \Uparrow}{\mathcal{P} \Uparrow}}{} \ co \right) = a : Acts(\mathcal{P}' \Uparrow)$$

Two programs that have the same action trace have the same observable input/output behavior. However, we would like to consider two programs that have action traces that differ only in the insertion and deletion of silent actions to have the same observable input/output behavior. Nonetheless, we do not wish to consider a terminating program with only silent actions to have the same observable behavior as a non-terminating program with only silent actions. This motivates defining *action trace bisimilarity* $\mathcal{A}_1 \cong \mathcal{A}_2$ as follows:

$$\dfrac{}{\mathcal{A} \succeq \mathcal{A}} \qquad \dfrac{\mathcal{A} \succeq \mathcal{A}'}{\epsilon : \mathcal{A} \succeq \mathcal{A}'}$$

$$\dfrac{}{\bullet \simeq \bullet}\ co \qquad \dfrac{\mathcal{A}_1 \cong \mathcal{A}_2}{a : \mathcal{A}_1 \simeq a : \mathcal{A}_2}\ co$$

$$\dfrac{\mathcal{A}_1 \succeq \mathcal{A}_1' \quad \mathcal{A}_2 \succeq \mathcal{A}_2' \quad \mathcal{A}_1' \simeq \mathcal{A}_2'}{\mathcal{A}_1 \cong \mathcal{A}_2}\ co$$

$\mathcal{A} \succeq \mathcal{A}'$ is an inductively defined relation that holds when $\mathcal{A}'$ may be obtained from $\mathcal{A}$ by dropping an arbitrary, but finite, prefix of ϵ actions. $\mathcal{A}_1 \simeq \mathcal{A}_2$ and $\mathcal{A}_1 \cong \mathcal{A}_2$ are mutually, coinductively defined relations; the former holds when $\mathcal{A}_1$ and $\mathcal{A}_2$ are either both $\bullet$ or have equal heads and bisimilar tails, while the latter holds when $\mathcal{A}_1$ and $\mathcal{A}_2$ match after dropping ϵ-prefixes.

IO Fairness. Our first notion of fairness, dubbed *IO fairness*, captures the behavior of a fair scheduler for the program's IO threads. Intuitively, a fair IO-thread scheduler ensures that every IO thread in the program makes progress. We formalize this intuitive notion as $\mathsf{IO\_FAIR}(\mathcal{P} \Uparrow)$:

$$\mathsf{IO\_FAIR}(\mathcal{P} \Uparrow) \overset{def}{=} \forall i \in \mathbb{N}. \ \forall \langle \theta, e_{io} \rangle \in I^{\mathcal{T}}(\mathcal{P} \Uparrow, i). \ \exists j > i. \ \langle \theta, e_{io} \rangle \notin I^{\mathcal{T}}(\mathcal{P} \Uparrow, j)$$

This predicate asserts that every IO thread in every thread soup in the program trace eventually "leaves" the thread soup; a thread $\langle \theta, e \rangle$ "leaves" the thread soup by either terminating (IOUNIT), synchronizing and moving to the synchronization soup (IOSYNCINIT), or transitioning to a new IO expression (IOEVAL,

IOFORK, IOBINDUNIT, IOGETCHAR, and IOPUTCHAR).[1] Note that in order to satisfy $\langle \theta, e_{io} \rangle \notin I^{\mathcal{T}}(\mathcal{P} \Uparrow, j)$, $I^{\mathcal{T}}(\mathcal{P} \Uparrow, j)$ must be defined.

Sync Fairness. Our second notion of fairness, dubbed *sync fairness*, captures the behavior of a fair "synchronizer" for the program's synchronizing threads. A "synchronizer" is the mechanism by which the collection of synchronizing threads in the IOSYNCSYNC rule are chosen. Intuitively, a fair "synchronizer" ensures that every synchronizing thread that could synchronize often enough does, in fact, synchronize. To capture the idea that a synchronizing thread could synchronize, we define $\mathsf{ENABLED}(\theta, \mathcal{S})$, a predicate asserting that θ is a sychronizing thread in the synchronization soup $\mathcal{S}$ that may synchronize with (zero or more) other synchronizing threads.

$$\mathsf{ENABLED}(\theta, \mathcal{S}) \overset{\mathrm{def}}{=}$$
$$\exists \{\langle \theta, M^{IO}, e_{evt} \rangle, \langle \theta_1, M_1^{IO}, e_{evt1} \rangle, \ldots\} \subseteq \mathcal{S}.$$
$$\mathsf{SYNCABLE}(\{\langle \theta, e_{evt} \rangle, \langle \theta_1, e_{evt1} \rangle, \ldots\})$$

Using enabledness, we formalize sync fairness as $\mathsf{SYNC\_FAIR}(\mathcal{P} \Uparrow)$:

$$\mathsf{SYNC\_FAIR}(\mathcal{P} \Uparrow) \overset{\mathrm{def}}{=}$$
$$\forall i \in \mathbb{N}. \ \forall \langle \theta, M^{IO}, e_{evt} \rangle \in I^{\mathcal{S}}(\mathcal{P} \Uparrow, i).$$
$$\exists j > i. \ \langle \theta, M^{IO}, e_{evt} \rangle \notin I^{\mathcal{S}}(\mathcal{P} \Uparrow, j) \vee$$
$$\forall k \geq j. \ \neg \mathsf{ENABLED}(\theta, I^{\mathcal{S}}(\mathcal{P} \Uparrow, k))$$

This predicate asserts that every synchronizing thread in every synchronization soup in the program trace eventually either "leaves" the synchronization soup (and moves to the thread soup (IOSYNCSYNC)) *or* is never again enabled. Since we described the behavior of a fair "synchronizer" as one that ensures that every synchronizing thread that is enabled often enough does synchronize, one may be confused by the appearance of the negation of the enabledness predicate in this definition. Consider sync unfairness, the negation of sync fairness:

$$\mathsf{SYNC\_UNFAIR}(\mathcal{P} \Uparrow) \overset{\mathrm{def}}{=} \neg \mathsf{SYNC\_FAIR}(\mathcal{P} \Uparrow) \equiv$$
$$\exists i \in \mathbb{N}. \ \exists \langle \theta, M^{IO}, e_{evt} \rangle \in I^{\mathcal{S}}(\mathcal{P} \Uparrow, i).$$
$$\forall j > i. \ \langle \theta, M^{IO}, e_{evt} \rangle \in I^{\mathcal{S}}(\mathcal{P} \Uparrow, j) \wedge \exists k \geq j. \ \mathsf{ENABLED}(\theta, I^{\mathcal{S}}(\mathcal{P} \Uparrow, k))$$

This predicate asserts that some synchronizing thread in some synchronization soup in the program trace always remains in the synchronization soup and eventually becomes enabled. Given an unfairly treated thread, we can witness an infinite number of indices in which the thread could synchronize in the corresponding program states by repeatedly instantiating $\forall j > i. \exists k \geq j. \mathsf{ENABLED}(\theta, I^{\mathcal{S}}(\mathcal{P} \Uparrow, k))$.

---

[1] We assume that sequential evaluation does not admit any expression e such that $e \hookrightarrow e$. This assumption implies that there is no program state $\mathcal{P}$ such that $\mathcal{P} \overset{a}{\rightarrow} \mathcal{P}$. This does not preclude expressions or program states that evaluate to themselves, but simply that such evaluations take more than one step.

Thus, a trace is sync unfair when it does not synchronize a synchronizing thread that is enabled infinitely often.[2]

Examples. It is instructive to consider some examples that demonstrate what executions are admitted and required by IO and sync fairness.[3]

A classic example is a program with two threads that repeatedly send on a channel and a third thread that repeatedly receives on the channel:

$\langle \theta_A,$ `forever (sync (sendEvt k 'a'))`$\rangle$ $\langle \theta_B,$ `forever (sync (sendEvt k 'b'))`$\rangle$
$\langle \theta_C,$ `forever (sync (recvEvt k))`$\rangle$

IO and sync fairness demand that θ_C receive both `'a'`s and `'b'`s; that is, it would be unfair if, for example, θ_C only communicated with θ_A.

Another classic example is a program with two threads that repeatedly send on different channels and a third thread that repeatedly chooses between receiving on the two channels:

$\langle \theta_A,$ `forever (sync (sendEvt ka 'a'))`$\rangle$ $\langle \theta_B,$ `forever (sync (sendEvt kb 'b'))`$\rangle$
$\langle \theta_C,$ `forever (sync ((recvEvt ka) ˙chooseEvt˙ (recvEvt kb)))`$\rangle$

Again, IO and sync fairness demand that θ_C receive both `'a'`s and `'b'`s.

Note that in the previous example, the fact that a fair execution exercises both sub-events of the `chooseEvt` is due to the fact that the different sub-events are independently enabled by different threads. Consider this example, where one thread chooses between sending `'a'` and sending `'b'` to another thread:

$\langle \theta_A,$ `forever (sync ((sendEvt k 'a') ˙chooseEvt˙ (sendEvt k 'b')))`$\rangle$
$\langle \theta_B,$ `forever (sync (recvEvt k))`$\rangle$

IO and sync fairness admit executions of this program where θ_B receives only `'a'`s or only `'b'`s.

In this example, θ_A sends to θ_B, either directly or indirectly via θ_C:

$\langle \theta_A,$ `forever (sync (sendEvt k 'a'))`$\rangle$ $\langle \theta_B,$ `forever (sync (recvEvt k))`$\rangle$
$\langle \theta_C,$ `forever (sync ((recvEvt k) ˙thenEvt˙ (sendEvt k)))`$\rangle$

---

[2] Our notion of sync fairness is, therefore, an instance of *strong fairness* [5,2,8]. We could define *weak sync fairness* as follows:

WEAK_SYNC_FAIR$(\mathcal{P} \Uparrow) \overset{\text{def}}{=}$
$\quad \forall i \in \mathbb{N}. \; \forall \langle \theta, M^{IO}, e_{evt} \rangle \in I^S(\mathcal{P} \Uparrow, i).$
$\quad\quad \exists j > i. \; \langle \theta, M^{IO}, e_{evt} \rangle \notin I^S(\mathcal{P} \Uparrow, j) \vee \exists k \geq j. \; \neg \text{ENABLED}(\theta, I^S(\mathcal{P} \Uparrow, k))$

A trace is weakly sync unfair when it does not synchronize a synchronizing thread that is enabled continuously. Note that weak sync fairness admits an execution of the threads $\{\langle \theta_A,$ `forever (sync (recvEvt k))`$\rangle, \langle \theta_B,$ `forever (sync (recvEvt k))`$\rangle,$ $\langle \theta_3,$ `forever (sync (sendEvt k ()))`$\rangle\}$ in which θ_C never synchronizes, since θ_A is not enabled whenever θ_C is not synchronizing. Weak sync fairness, therefore, seems to be of limited utility for reasoning about transactional events.

[3] For convenience, we use Haskell syntax.

IO and sync fairness demand that thread θ_C repeatedly synchronizes, because, once thread θ_C is synchronizing, neither thread θ_A nor thread θ_B can synchronize until all three threads are synchronizing, in which case θ_C is enabled.

This final example is a program with five threads:

$\langle\theta_A,$ `forever (sync (sendEvt k1 'a'))`$\rangle$ $\langle\theta_B,$ `forever (sync (recvEvt k1))`$\rangle$
$\langle\theta_C,$ `forever (sync (sendEvt k2 'c'))`$\rangle$ $\langle\theta_D,$ `forever (sync (recvEvt k2))`$\rangle$
$\langle\theta_E,$ `forever (sync ((sendEvt k1 'e') `thenEvt` (\ _ -> sendEvt k2 'e')))`$\rangle$

Perhaps counterintuitively, IO and sync fairness admit program executions of this program where thread θ_E synchronizes only a finite (including zero) number of times. Consider the program execution where (1) θ_E executes until it is synchronizing, then (2) θ_A and θ_B execute until they are synchronizing and synchronize θ_A and θ_B, then (3) θ_C and θ_D execute until they are synchronizing and synchronize θ_C and θ_D, then repeat (2) and (3) infinitely. At no time is θ_E enabled, since θ_B and θ_D are never synchronizing at the same time.

4   Instrumented Semantics

The operational semantics of Section 2 and the fairness predicates of Section 3 provide a specification for fair transactional events, but do not immediately suggest an implementation. In this section, we instrument the original operational semantics and demonstrate that the instrumented operational semantics refines the original operational semantics in the sense that every IO-fair program trace in the instrumented semantics corresponds to an IO- and sync-fair program trace in the original semantics with the same observable input/output behavior.

Concurrent Evaluation ($\mathcal{P} \xrightarrow{a}_{\text{inst}} \mathcal{P}'$). To motivate the instrumented operational semantics, we observe that if there is a program state where the IOSYNCSYNC rule does not apply and a later program state where the IOSYNCSYNC rule does apply, then there must be an occurrence of the IOSYNCINIT rule in the program trace that takes the former program state to the later. Hence, it is only necessary to check for the applicability of the IOSYNCSYNC rule immediately after applications of the IOSYNCINIT rule. In fact, the instrumented operational semantics checks for the existence of a synchronizable group when evaluating an IO thread of the form $\langle\theta, M^{IO}[\text{sync } e_{evt}]\rangle$. If a synchronizable group exists, then the IO thread commits (with zero or more synchronizing threads) and continues as an IO thread (with its synchronization result); if no synchronizable group exists, then the IO thread blocks and transitions to a synchronizing thread. Thus, an IO thread has "one shot" to initiate its own synchronization.

The instrumented semantics also adds a *weight* to each synchronizing thread:

$$\begin{array}{lll} \textit{Weight} & w \in \mathbb{N} \\ \textit{Synchronizing Thread} & S ::= \langle\theta, M^{IO}, e_{evt}, w\rangle \end{array}$$

Intuitively, the weight measures how long a synchronizing thread has been waiting to synchronize. When choosing a synchronization group to synchronize, the semantics selects a group with a synchronizing thread that has been waiting the longest (among all synchronizing threads that could synchronize).

We formalize the instrumented semantics by replacing the IOSyncInit and IOSyncSync rules of Fig. 1 with these IOSyncCommit and IOSyncBlock rules:

IOSyncCommit

$$\frac{\begin{array}{c} \{\langle\theta, e_{evt}\rangle, \langle\theta_1, e_{evt1}\rangle, \ldots\} \leadsto^* \{\langle\theta, \text{alwaysEvt } e'\rangle, \langle\theta_1, \text{alwaysEvt } e'_1\rangle, \ldots\} \\ W = \max\{0, w_1, \ldots\} \\ \forall\{\langle\theta_a, M_a^{IO}, e_{evtz}, w_a\rangle, \ldots\} \subseteq \mathcal{S} \uplus \{\langle\theta_1, M_1^{IO}, e_1, w_1\rangle, \ldots\}. \\ \text{SYNCABLE}(\{\langle\theta, e_{evt}\rangle, \langle\theta_a, e_{evtz}\rangle, \ldots\}) \Rightarrow W \geq \max\{0, w_a, \ldots\} \end{array}}{\mathcal{T} \uplus \{\langle\theta, M^{IO}[\text{sync } e_{evt}]\rangle\}; \mathcal{S} \uplus \{\langle\theta_1, M_1^{IO}, e_{evt1}, w_1\rangle, \ldots\} \\ \xrightarrow{\epsilon}_{\text{inst}} \mathcal{T} \uplus \{\langle\theta, M^{IO}[\text{unitIO } e']\rangle, \langle\theta_1, M_1^{IO}[\text{unitIO } e'_1]\rangle, \ldots\}; incw(\mathcal{S})}$$

IOSyncBlock

$$\frac{\begin{array}{c} \neg\exists\{\langle\theta_1, M_1^{IO}, e_{evt1}, w_1\rangle, \ldots\} \subseteq \mathcal{S}. \\ \text{SYNCABLE}(\{\langle\theta, e_{evt}\rangle, \langle\theta_1, e_{evt1}\rangle, \ldots\}) \end{array}}{\mathcal{T} \uplus \{\langle\theta, M^{IO}[\text{sync } e_{evt}]\rangle\}; \mathcal{S} \xrightarrow{\epsilon}_{\text{inst}} \mathcal{T}; \mathcal{S} \uplus \{\langle\theta, M^{IO}, e_{evt}, 0\rangle\}}$$

The IOSyncCommit rule synchronizes one IO thread ($\langle\theta, M^{IO}[\text{sync } e_{evt}]\rangle$) along with a (possibly empty) set of synchronizing threads ($\{\langle\theta_1, M_1^{IO}, e_{evt1}, w_1\rangle, \ldots\}$). The weight of this group is $\max\{0, w_1, \ldots\}$; the 0 represents the weight of the IO thread and ensures that the group weight is defined if the set of synchronizing threads is empty. This group weight is required to be greater than or equal to the group weight of every other synchronizable group. All synchronizing threads that do not synchronize ($\mathcal{S}$) have their weights incremented ($incw(\mathcal{S})$), whether or not they could have synchronized along with the synchronizing IO thread. The IOSyncBlock rule transitions an IO thread that cannot synchronize with any existing synchronizing threads to a synchronizing thread with zero weight.

Traces, IO Fairness, and Sync Fairness. We easily adapt the definitions of program traces and IO fairness from Section 3 as $\mathcal{P} \Uparrow_{\text{inst}}$ and $\text{IO\_FAIR}_{\text{inst}}(\mathcal{P} \Uparrow_{\text{inst}})$.[4]

Adapting the definition of sync fairness requires a more substantial change. Since the instrumented semantics only adds a synchronizing thread to the synchronization soup if doing so does not create a synchronizable group, no synchronizing thread is ever ENABLED in any synchronization soup in a instrumented program trace. Instead, a synchronizing thread is enabled by a particular IOSyncCommit step in a program trace:

$$\begin{array}{l} \text{ENABLED}_{\text{inst}}(\theta, \mathcal{T}; \mathcal{S} \xrightarrow{a}_{\text{inst}} \mathcal{P}') \overset{\text{def}}{=} \\ \quad \exists\langle\theta_s, M_s^{IO}[\text{sync } e_{evts}]\rangle \in \mathcal{T}. \\ \qquad \mathcal{T}; \mathcal{S} \xrightarrow{a}_{\text{inst}} \mathcal{P}' \equiv \text{IOSyncCommit}(\langle\theta_s, M_s^{IO}[\text{sync } e_{evts}]\rangle) \wedge \\ \qquad \exists\{\langle\theta, M^{IO}, e_{evt}, w\rangle, \langle\theta_1, M_1^{IO}, e_{evt1}, w_1\rangle, \ldots\} \subseteq \mathcal{S}. \\ \qquad \text{SYNCABLE}(\{\langle\theta_s, e_{evts}\rangle, \langle\theta, e_{evt}\rangle, \langle\theta_1, e_{evt1}\rangle, \ldots\}) \end{array}$$

---

[4] In order to avoid excessive notation, we overload the $I^{\rightarrow}$, $I^{\mathcal{P}}$, $I^{\mathcal{T}}$, $I^{\mathcal{S}}$, and $Acts$ operations on instrumented program traces.

This predicate asserts that the program step $\mathcal{T}; \mathcal{S} \xrightarrow{a}_{\text{inst}} \mathcal{P}'$ is an instance of IOSYNCCOMMIT that commits the IO thread $\langle \theta_s, M_s^{IO}[\texttt{sync } e_{evts}] \rangle$ and that θ is a synchronizing thread in the synchronization soup $\mathcal{S}$ that may synchronize with the committing thread and with (zero or more) other synchronizing threads. Sync fairness for instrumented program traces is defined similarly to sync fairness for original program traces, but uses the ENABLED$_{\text{inst}}$ predicate rather than the ENABLED predicate and does not allow a synchronizing thread to "leave" the synchronization soup by simply changing its weight:

$$\text{SYNC\_FAIR}_{\text{inst}}(\mathcal{P} \Uparrow_{\text{inst}}) \overset{\text{def}}{=}$$
$$\forall i \in \mathbb{N}. \ \forall \langle \theta, M^{IO}, e_{evt}, w \rangle \in I^{\mathcal{S}}(\mathcal{P} \Uparrow_{\text{inst}}, i).$$
$$\exists j > i. \ \forall v. \ \langle \theta, M^{IO}, e_{evt}, v \rangle \notin I^{\mathcal{S}}(\mathcal{P} \Uparrow_{\text{inst}}, j) \vee$$
$$\forall k > j. \ \neg \text{ENABLED}_{\text{inst}}(\theta, \mathcal{I}^{\rightarrow}(\mathcal{P} \Uparrow_{\text{inst}}, k))$$

Refines Original Semantics. We show that the instrumented semantics refines the original semantics by demonstrating a translation from instrumented program traces to original program traces that preserves the properties of interest: observable input/output behavior, IO fairness, and sync fairness.

Fig. 2 gives the corecursively defined translation, using a simple erasure of weights from synchronizing threads. A IOSYNCBLOCK step is translated to a IOSYNCINIT step; a IOSYNCCOMMIT step is translated to a IOSYNCINIT step followed by a IOSYNCSYNC step; all other steps in the instrumented semantics are translated to the corresponding step in the original semantics. A terminal program state in the instrumented semantics is translated to a terminal program state in the original semantics. There is a subtlety that makes the translation partial: a program state such as $\{\}; \{\langle \theta, M^{IO}, \texttt{alwaysEvt } e', w \rangle\}$ is terminal in the instrumented semantics (all rules in the instrumented semantics require an IO thread), but is non-terminal in the original semantics (the IOSYNCSYNC rule may step to the program state $\{\langle \theta, M^{IO}[\texttt{unitIO } e'] \rangle\}; \{\}$). However, if the initial program state in the instrumented program trace does not contain a syncable set of synchronizing threads, then terminal program states coincide (since the absence of syncable sets is preserved by the instrumented semantics).

The following theorem establishes that every instrumented program trace that is IO and sync fair corresponds to an original program trace with the same observable input/output behavior that is IO and sync fair.

Theorem 1 (Instrumented semantics refines original semantics)

If $\mathcal{P} \Uparrow_{\text{inst}}$ is a program trace in the instrumented semantics such that

- $\forall \{\langle \theta_1, M_1^{IO}, e_{evt1}, w_1 \rangle, \ldots\} \subseteq I^{\mathcal{S}}(\mathcal{P} \Uparrow_{\text{inst}}, 0). \ \neg \text{SYNCABLE}(\{\langle \theta_1, e_{evt1} \rangle, \ldots\})$,
- $\text{IO\_FAIR}_{\text{inst}}(\mathcal{P} \Uparrow_{\text{inst}})$, *and*
- $\text{SYNC\_FAIR}_{\text{inst}}(\mathcal{P} \Uparrow_{\text{inst}})$,

then

- $[\![\mathcal{P} \Uparrow_{\text{inst}}]\!]$ *is defined,*
- $Acts(\mathcal{P} \Uparrow_{\text{inst}}) \cong Acts([\![\mathcal{P} \Uparrow_{\text{inst}}]\!])$,
- $\text{IO\_FAIR}([\![\mathcal{P} \Uparrow_{\text{inst}}]\!])$, *and*
- $\text{SYNC\_FAIR}([\![\mathcal{P} \Uparrow_{\text{inst}}]\!])$.

$$[\![\{\langle \theta, M^{IO}, e_{evt}, w\rangle, \ldots\}]\!] = \{\langle \theta, M^{IO}, e_{evt}\rangle, \ldots\}$$

$$[\![\mathcal{T}; \mathcal{S}]\!] = \mathcal{T}; [\![\mathcal{S}]\!]$$

$$\left[\!\left[\begin{array}{c} \text{TERM} \\ \dfrac{\neg \exists a, \mathcal{P}'.\mathcal{P} \xrightarrow{a}_{\text{inst}} \mathcal{P}'}{\mathcal{P} \Uparrow_{\text{inst}}} \ \text{CO} \end{array} \right]\!\right] = \begin{array}{c} \text{TERM} \\ \dfrac{\left[\!\left[\neg \exists a, \mathcal{P}'.\mathcal{P} \xrightarrow{a}_{\text{inst}} \mathcal{P}'\right]\!\right]}{[\![\mathcal{P}]\!] \Uparrow} \ \text{CO} \end{array}$$

$$\left[\!\left[\begin{array}{c} \text{STEP} \\ \dfrac{\mathcal{P} \xrightarrow{a}_{\text{inst}} \mathcal{P}' \quad \mathcal{P}' \Uparrow_{\text{inst}}}{\mathcal{P} \Uparrow_{\text{inst}}} \ \text{CO} \end{array} \right]\!\right] =$$

$$\begin{cases} \begin{array}{c} \text{STEP} \\ \dfrac{[\![\mathcal{P}]\!] \xrightarrow{a} [\![\mathcal{P}']\!] \quad [\![\mathcal{P}' \Uparrow_{\text{inst}}]\!]}{[\![\mathcal{P}]\!] \Uparrow} \ \text{CO} \quad \text{if } \mathcal{P} \xrightarrow{a}_{\text{inst}} \mathcal{P}' \notin \{\text{IOSYNCCOMMIT, IOSYNCBLOCK}\} \end{array} \\[2em] \hline \end{cases}$$

STEP

$$\dfrac{[\![\mathcal{P}]\!] \xrightarrow{a} \mathcal{P}'' \qquad \begin{array}{c} \text{STEP} \\ \dfrac{\mathcal{P}'' \xrightarrow{a''} [\![\mathcal{P}']\!] \quad [\![\mathcal{P}' \Uparrow_{\text{inst}}]\!]}{\mathcal{P}'' \Uparrow} \ \text{CO} \end{array}}{[\![\mathcal{P}]\!] \Uparrow} \ \text{CO}$$

IOSYNCCOMMIT

$$\text{if } \mathcal{P} \xrightarrow{a}_{\text{inst}} \mathcal{P}' \equiv \dfrac{\begin{array}{c} \{\langle \theta, e_{evt}\rangle, \langle \theta_1, e_{evt1}\rangle, \ldots\} \rightsquigarrow^* \{\langle \theta, \text{alwaysEvt } e'\rangle, \langle \theta_1, \text{alwaysEvt } e'_1\rangle, \ldots\} \\ W = \max\{0, w_1, \ldots\} \\ \forall \{\langle \theta_a, M_a^{IO}, e_{evtz}, w_a\rangle, \ldots\} \subseteq \mathcal{S} \uplus \{\langle \theta_1, M_1^{IO}, e_1, w_1\rangle, \ldots\}. \\ \text{SYNCABLE}(\{\langle \theta, e_{evt}\rangle, \langle \theta_a, e_{evtz}\rangle, \ldots\}) \Rightarrow W \geq \max\{0, w_a, \ldots\} \end{array}}{\begin{array}{c} \mathcal{T} \uplus \{\langle \theta, M^{IO}[\text{sync } e_{evt}]\rangle\}; \mathcal{S} \uplus \{\langle \theta_1, M_1^{IO}, e_{evt1}, w_1\rangle, \ldots\} \\ \xrightarrow{\epsilon}_{\text{inst}} \mathcal{T} \uplus \{\langle \theta, M^{IO}[\text{unitIO } e']\rangle, \langle \theta_1, M_1^{IO}[\text{unitIO } e'_1]\rangle, \ldots\}; incw(\mathcal{S}) \end{array}}$$

IOSYNCINIT

$$\text{where } [\![\mathcal{P}]\!] \xrightarrow{a} \mathcal{P}'' = \dfrac{}{\begin{array}{c} \mathcal{T} \uplus \{\langle \theta, M^{IO}[\text{sync } e_{evt}]\rangle\}; [\![\mathcal{S}]\!] \uplus \{\langle \theta_1, M_1^{IO}, e_1\rangle, \ldots\} \\ \xrightarrow{\epsilon}_{\text{inst}} \mathcal{T}; [\![\mathcal{S}]\!] \uplus \{\langle \theta, M^{IO}, e_{evt}\rangle, \langle \theta_1, M_1^{IO}, e_1\rangle, \ldots\} \end{array}}$$

IOSYNCSYNC

$$\text{and } \mathcal{P}'' \xrightarrow{a''} [\![\mathcal{P}']\!] = \dfrac{\{\langle \theta, e\rangle, \langle \theta_1, e_1\rangle, \ldots\} \rightsquigarrow^* \{\langle \theta, \text{alwaysEvt } e'\rangle, \langle \theta_1, \text{alwaysEvt } e'_1\rangle, \ldots\}}{\begin{array}{c} \mathcal{T}; [\![\mathcal{S}]\!] \uplus \{\langle \theta, M^{IO}, e_{evt}\rangle, \langle \theta_1, M_1^{IO}, e_{evt1}\rangle, \ldots\} \\ \xrightarrow{\epsilon} \mathcal{T} \uplus \{\langle \theta, M^{IO}[\text{unitIO } e']\rangle, \langle \theta_1, M_1^{IO}[\text{unitIO } e'_1]\rangle, \ldots\}; [\![\mathcal{S}]\!] \end{array}}$$

$$\hline$$

STEP

$$\dfrac{[\![\mathcal{P}]\!] \xrightarrow{a} [\![\mathcal{P}']\!] \quad [\![\mathcal{P}' \Uparrow_{\text{inst}}]\!]}{[\![\mathcal{P}]\!] \Uparrow} \ \text{CO}$$

IOSYNCBLOCK

$$\text{if } \mathcal{P} \xrightarrow{a}_{\text{inst}} \mathcal{P}' \equiv \dfrac{\begin{array}{c} \neg \exists \{\langle \theta_1, M_1^{IO}, e_{evt1}, w_1\rangle, \ldots\} \subseteq \mathcal{S}. \\ \text{SYNCABLE}(\{\langle \theta, e_{evt}\rangle, \langle \theta_1, e_{evt1}\rangle, \ldots\}) \end{array}}{\mathcal{T} \uplus \{\langle \theta, M^{IO}[\text{sync } e_{evt}]\rangle\}; \mathcal{S} \xrightarrow{\epsilon}_{\text{inst}} \mathcal{T}; \mathcal{S} \uplus \{\langle \theta, M^{IO}, e_{evt}, 0\rangle\}}$$

IOSYNCINIT

$$\text{where } [\![\mathcal{P}]\!] \xrightarrow{a} [\![\mathcal{P}']\!] = \dfrac{}{\mathcal{T} \uplus \{\langle \theta, M^{IO}[\text{sync } e_{evt}]\rangle\}; [\![\mathcal{S}]\!] \xrightarrow{\epsilon} \mathcal{T}; [\![\mathcal{S}]\!] \uplus \{\langle \theta, M^{IO}, e_{evt}\rangle\}}$$

Fig. 2. Translation of instrumented program traces to original program traces

The proof defines and uses a strictly monotonic function to map the index of a program state in $\mathcal{P} \Uparrow_{\text{inst}}$ to the index of the equal program state in $[\![\mathcal{P} \Uparrow_{\text{inst}}]\!]$. Note that the proof does not make use of the weights of synchronizing threads.

Guarantees Sync Fairness. We defined sync fairness for instrumented program traces in order to simplify the proof of Theorem 1. Of course, the instrumentation of the instrumented semantics is meant to guide program executions towards sync fairness. The following theorem establishes that every instrumented program trace is sync fair, without additional assumptions.

Theorem 2 (Instrumented semantics is sync fair)
If $\mathcal{P} \Uparrow_{\text{inst}}$ is a program trace in the instrumented semantics,
then $\mathsf{SYNC\_FAIR}_{\text{inst}}(\mathcal{P} \Uparrow_{\text{inst}})$.

The proof is by contradiction and, intuitively, proceeds as follows. Suppose there is a sync-unfair instrumented program trace. Then there is a synchronizing thread that never "leaves" the synchronization soup, but is enabled at an infinite number of future program steps; call this the *unfair thread*. After the first of IOSYNCCOMMIT step at which the unfair thread is enabled but does not synchronize, the thread will necessarily have a weight greater than zero. Now consider the set of synchronizing threads that have weight greater than or equal to the unfair thread. This set can only decrease, since new synchronizing threads enter the synchronization soup with weight zero and existing synchronizing threads that remain in the synchronization soup have their weights incremented together. Furthermore, this set must decrease at each IOSYNCCOMMIT step at which the unfair thread is enabled, since the IOSYNCCOMMIT rule must commit an enabled synchronizing thread with weight greater than or equal to that of the unfair thread. Since there are an infinite number of future program steps at which the unfair thread is enabled, the set of synchronizing threads that have weight greater than or equal to the unfair thread must eventually be exhausted. At this point, the unfair thread must have weight greater than that of any other enabled synchronizing threads and must commit. But, this contradicts the assumption that the thread never "leaves" the synchronization soup. Thus, there cannot be a sync-unfair instrumented program trace.

5   Implementation

The obvious difficulty with implementing the instrumented semantics of Section 4 is knowing when to apply the IOSYNCCOMMIT and IOSYNCBLOCK rules and which of the two rules to apply. While the two rules are mutually exclusive, they effectively require enumerating all of the enabled synchronization groups. Unfortunately, for the general case of transactional events, the enabledness of a set of event synchronizations is undecidable. To see this, we simply recall that sequential evaluation can express recursively defined Evt and IO computations. Thus, an $\mathcal{E} \rightsquigarrow^*$ evaluation may diverge by being either infinitely deep (recursing through thenEvt) or infinitely wide (recursing through chooseEvt).

We therefore introduce *decidable synchronization groups*. A synchronization group $\mathcal{E}$ is a decidable synchronization group if all evaluations of $\mathcal{E} \rightsquigarrow^*$ terminate. That is, for all events in the synchronization group, all "paths" through the event are finite. Note that this is a property of a synchronization group, not an event, since an event synchronization may have control-flow that is based on values received from other events synchronizing in the group.

An implementation of fair transactional events, under the assumption of decidable synchronization groups, works as follows. When the fair IO thread scheduler selects a thread performing a synchronization, its event expression is evaluated with the blocked event expressions in the synchronization soup. If enabled synchronization groups emerge, then the IOSYNCCOMMIT rule is taken, choosing the synchronization group with maximum weight. If no enabled synchronization groups emerge, then the IOSYNCBLOCK rule is taken. Note that the implementation may utilize many of the techniques described in the previous (non-fair) implementation of transactional events [4]. In particular, search threads and channel stores may be used to represent the synchronization soup in a manner that keeps all potential synchronizations evaluated "as much as possible" so that all work performed upon selecting a thread for synchronization is "new" work.

To represent thread weights, it suffices to use a global counter that records the number of IOSYNCCOMMIT steps taken. When a IOSYNCBLOCK step is taken, the newly synchronizing thread records the current value of the global counter. Thus, the thread with maximum weight is simply the thread with the minimum recorded value.

Note that this suggested implementation will fail in the presence of non-terminating synchronization computations. In particular, if it is not possible to decide which of IOSYNCCOMMIT or IOSYNCBLOCK applies to a particular thread synchronization, then no subsequent thread synchronizations can be initiated.

We conjecture that it is impossible to construct an implementation which enforces fairness in the presence of undecidable synchronization computations, since sync fairness depends upon knowing the enabledness of these computations. Verifying that all synchronization groups that arise during any execution of a program are decidable synchronization groups can be challenging, but appears to be reasonable in practice. In fact, all of the examples from prior work (e.g., guarded receive, Concurrent ML encoding, three-way rendezvous, boolean satisfiability encoding) [3,4] give rise to only decidable synchronization groups. A notion similar to decidable synchronization groups, that of "obstruction freedom", is often employed in the context of Software Transactional Memory (STM). Obstruction-freedom asserts that a transaction executed in isolation commits in a finite number of steps. Again, this condition can be challenging to reason about in the presence of first-class transactions, and so the criticism applies equally well to STM systems such as STM Haskell [6].

The "global lock" approach, where there is exactly one thread attempting a synchronization at any time, might be relaxed by permitting multiple threads to begin searching for a synchronization, but tracking the order in which they began and requiring that they commit or block in that order. Alternatively, an implementation might track weights but permit unrestricted synchronization until a blocked thread's weight grows too large, after which point the global lock is enforced until no threads have weights above the threshold.

6 Related Work

Concurrent ML. Reppy discusses fairness for Concurrent ML (CML) [9, Appendix B], but does not completely formalize the definition and there is no proof that the implementation of CML is fair. One notable difference is that CML discusses enabledness of synchronization objects (channels and conditions) in addition to enabledness of threads. Consider the following program:

$$\langle\theta_A, \texttt{forever (sync ((sendEvt k1 'a') `chooseEvt` (sendEvt k2 'b')))}\rangle$$
$$\langle\theta_B, \texttt{forever (sync ((recvEvt k1) `chooseEvt` (recvEvt k2)))}\rangle$$

CML's notion of fairness demands that thread θ_B receive both 'a's and 'b's (since channels k1 and k2 are both enabled infinitely often), while our notion of fairness allows thread θ_B to receive only 'a's or 'b's. As another example, consider the following program:

$$\left\langle\theta_A, \begin{array}{l}\texttt{let evt = (alwaysEvt 'a') `chooseEvt` (alwaysEvt 'b') in}\\ \texttt{forever (sync evt)}\end{array}\right\rangle$$

CML adopts a call-by-value evaluation strategy and the evaluation of an alwaysEvt allocates a fresh condition; hence, in the program above, the thread repeatedly synchronizes on the same conditions and the synchronization must yield both 'a's and 'b's. Our semantics for transactional events treats alwaysEvt as a pure expression and allows the synchronization to yield only 'a's or 'b's.

The implementation of CML enforces fairness through a combination of channel priorities and an ordered queue of threads blocked on a channel. The choice of synchronization among a collection of enabled events with equal priority is resolved by a pseudo-random number generator; hence, the implementation of CML provides only a probabilistic guarantee of fairness.

Software Transactional Memory. While it seems reasonable to propose a notion of fairness for Software Transactional Memory (STM) [11] similar in spirit to those proposed for CML and transactional events, the discussion is often informal or absent. For instance, STM Haskell [6] offers no discussion of fairness and the semantics allows a transaction that could commit to remain blocked indefinitely. Most work on STM has focused on the use of *contention managers* [7,10,12] that use heuristics to increase the throughput of an STM implementation (and behave "fair enough"), but without providing a guarantee of (complete) fairness. Various STM implementations are shown to be non-blocking (wait-free, lock-free, obstruction-free), although it is not always clear whether the property applies to the low-level implementation (threads attempting transactions make progress, but progress includes observing a conflict and aborting) or the high-level semantics (threads attempting transactions make progress and commit). Furthermore, properties such as obstruction freedom, which assert that a transaction completes so long as no other transactions are being attempted, are not directly applicable to transactional events. Any thread performing a synchronization that involves a send or receive necessarily requires another thread to be performing a synchronization with the matching communication, so such isolation properties are not appropriate.

7   Conclusion

We have formally characterized a notion of fairness in Transactional Events, a combination of first-class synchronous message-passing and all-or-nothing transactions. Our fairness notion permits programmers to reason with the guarantee that a synchronizing thread will not be blocked indefinitely from synchronizing by the mechanism which chooses synchronizations. We have given an instrumented operational semantics for transactional events along with theorems establishing that all program executions in this semantics are fair. Finally, we have described a condition on event synchronizations that permits an implementation of this semantics to successfully complete enabled synchronizations

Acknowledgments. This work was supported in part by an RIT Center for Student Innovation Undergraduate Summer Research and Innovation Fellowship.

References

1. Amsden, E., Fluet, M.: Fainess for transactional events. Tech. rep., Rochester Institute of Technology (March 2012), https://ritdml.rit.edu/handle/1850/14852
2. Costa, G., Stirling, C.: Weak and strong fairness in CCS. Information and Computation 73(3), 207–244 (1987)
3. Donnelly, K., Fluet, M.: Transactional events. In: Proceedings of the Eleventh ACM SIGPLAN International Conference on Functional Programming (ICFP 2006), pp. 124–135. ACM Press (2006)
4. Donnelly, K., Fluet, M.: Transactional events. The Journal of Functional Programming 18(5-6), 649–706 (2008)
5. Francez, N.: Fairness. Texts and Monographs in Computer Science. Springer, New York (1986)
6. Harris, T., Marlow, S., Peyton Jones, S., Herlihy, M.: Composable memory transactions. In: Proceedings of the Tenth ACM SIGPLAN Symposium on Principles and Practice of Parallel Programming (PPoPP 2005), pp. 48–60. ACM Press (2005)
7. Herlihy, M., Luchangco, V., Moir, M., Scherer III, W.N.: Software transactional memory for dynamic-sized data structures. In: Proceedings of the 22nd Annual Symposium on Principles of Distributed Computing (PODC 2003), pp. 92–101. ACM Press (2003)
8. Kwiatkowska, M.: Survey of fairness notions. Information and Software Technology 31(7), 371–386 (1989)
9. Reppy, J.: Concurrent Programming in ML. Cambridge University Press, Cambridge (1999)

10. Scherer III, W.N., Scott, M.L.: Advanced contention management for dynamic software transactional memory. In: Proceedings of the 24th Annual Symposium on Principles of Distributed Computing (PODC 2005), pp. 240–248. ACM Press (2005)
11. Shavit, N., Touitou, D.: Software transactional memory. Distributed Computing 10(2), 99–116 (1997)
12. Spear, M.F., Dalessandro, L., Marathe, V.J., Scott, M.L.: A comprehensive strategy for contention management in software transactional memory. In: Proceedings of the 14th ACM SIGPLAN Symposium on Principles and Practice of Parallel Programming (PPoPP 2005), pp. 141–150. ACM Press (2009)

Implementing a High-Level Distributed-Memory Parallel Haskell in Haskell

Patrick Maier and Phil Trinder

School of Mathematical and Computer Sciences, Heriot-Watt University, Edinburgh, UK
{P.Maier,P.W.Trinder}@hw.ac.uk

Abstract. We present the initial design, implementation and preliminary evaluation of a new distributed-memory parallel Haskell, HdpH. The language is a shallowly embedded parallel extension of Haskell that supports high-level semi-explicit parallelism, is scalable, and has the potential for fault tolerance. The HdpH implementation is designed for maintainability without compromising performance too severely. To provide maintainability the implementation is modular and layered and, crucially, coded in vanilla Concurrent Haskell. Initial performance results are promising for three simple data parallel or divide-and-conquer programs, e. g., an absolute speedup of 135 on 168 cores of a Beowulf cluster.

1 Introduction

The multicore revolution is driving renewed interest in parallel functional languages. Early parallel Haskell variants like GpH [20] and Eden [13] use elaborate runtime systems (RTS) to support their high-level coordination constructs - evaluation strategies and algorithmic skeletons respectively. More recently the multicore Glasgow Haskell Compiler (GHC) implementation also extends the RTS [17]. However these bespoke runtime systems have development and maintainability issues: they are complex stateful systems engineered in low-level C and use message passing for distributed architectures. Worse still, they must be continuously re-engineered to keep up with the ever evolving GHC research compiler.

To preserve maintainability and ease development several recent parallel Haskells use Concurrent Haskell [18] as a systems language on a vanilla GHC rather than changing the GHC RTS; examples include CloudHaskell [6], and the Par Monad [16]. Our new language, *Haskell distributed parallel Haskell (HdpH)*, also follows this approach.

Table 1 compares the key features of general purpose parallel Haskells, and each of these languages is discussed in detail in Sect. 2. Most of the entries in the table are self-explanatory. Fault Tolerance means that the language implementation isolates the heaps of each distributed node, and hence has the *potential* to tolerate individual node failures - few Haskells have implemented fault tolerance. Determinism identifies whether the language model guarantees that a function will be a function even if its body is evaluated in parallel.

The crucial differences between HdpH and other parallel Haskells can be summarised as follows. Both GHC and the Par Monad provide parallelism only on a single multicore, where HdpH scales onto distributed-memory architectures with many multicore

A. Gill and J. Hage (Eds.): IFL 2011, LNCS 7257, pp. 35–50, 2012.

Table 1. Parallel Haskell comparison

Property \ Language	Low-level RTS			Haskell-level RTS		
	GpH-GUM	Eden	GHC	Par Monad	CloudHaskell	HdpH
Scalable (distributed memory)	+	+	−	−	+	+
Fault Tolerance (isolated heaps)	−	(+)			+	+
Polymorphic Closures	+	+	+	+	−	+
Pure, i.e. non-monadic, API	+	+	+	−	−	−
Determinism	(+)	−	(+)	+	−	−
Implicit Task Placement	+	+	+	+	−	+
Automatic Load Balancing	+	+	+	+	−	+

nodes. CloudHaskell replicates Erlang style [1] explicit distribution. It is most closely related to HdpH, but provides lower level coordination with explicit task placement and no load management. As CloudHaskell distributes only monomorphic closures it is not possible to construct general coordination abstractions like evaluation strategies or algorithmic skeletons.

Section 3 describes the key features of HdpH as follows.

– HdpH is *scalable* with a distributed memory model that manages computations on more than one multicore node.
– HdpH provides *high-level semi-explicit parallelism* with

  • Implicit task placement: the programmer is not required to explicitly place tasks on specific nodes. Idle nodes seek work automatically.
  • Automated and dynamic load management: the programmer is not required to ensure that all nodes are utilised effectively. The implementation continuously manages load.
  • Polymorphism: polymorphic closures can be transferred between nodes.
  • Powerful coordination abstractions: specifically both evaluation strategies and algorithmic skeletons can be defined using a small set of polymorphic coordination primitives, see examples in Sect. 3.3.

– HdpH is designed with *fault tolerance* in mind.

  • The separation of heaps provides *fault isolation*, making it possible to recover from remote node failure.
  • Fault tolerance necessitates non-determinism, as we will argue in Sect. 3.1.

HdpH is a distributed-memory *parallel* language, but not (yet) a *distributed* programming language as it lacks crucial features such as support for distributed data and exceptions. We leave the implementation of such features and of fault tolerant skeletons to future work as discussed in Sect. 6.

Section 4 outlines the HdpH implementation design which aims to deliver acceptable performance while being maintainable. Implementing the system in vanilla (GHC) Concurrent Haskell is crucial to preserving maintainability, and enables the language design space to be explored more readily than modifying an RTS written in C. Moreover the implementation is layered and modular with coordination aspects such as communication, thread management, global address management, scheduling etc. realised in independent modules. This design represents a middle ground between monolithic runtime systems like GUM [21] and Eden/EDI [11,2], and kernel-based proposals [12,3].

Section 5 reports initial performance results for three simple data parallel or divide-and-conquer programs on up to 168 cores of a Beowulf cluster. The HdpH system is available for download [9], and an extended version of this paper is available [14].

2 Related Work

This section outlines parallel functional languages and implementations that have influenced the design and implementation of HdpH. As HdpH is primarily control-oriented, we do not consider data oriented parallel languages like DPH [4] or SAC [7] here. A comprehensive survey of parallel functional languages is available in [22].

2.1 Shared-Memory Languages

There have been a number of parallel Haskell extensions [22], and several have extended the GHC compiler. A crucial feature of GHC is its concurrency support: lightweight threads with extremely low thread management overheads.

The Par Monad [16] provides monadic control of concurrency, realising deterministic pure parallelism. Moreover, the Par Monad allows the lifting of system-level functionality (in the form of a work-stealing scheduler) to the Concurrent Haskell level. Performance results demonstrate that the overhead associated with the Par Monad remains low.

The GpH extension of Haskell focuses on pure parallelism and keeps many details of the parallel execution hidden from the programmer. Both shared- and distributed-memory implementations [17,21] are available. The specification of parallelism in GpH is non-monadic and less intrusive than in the Par Monad. Effective parallel programming requires specifying both evaluation order and evaluation degree. To do so elegantly evaluation strategies, i. e., high-level coordination abstractions have been developed [20,15].

2.2 Distributed-Memory Languages

Eden extends Haskell with distributed-memory parallelism [13]. It supports process abstractions, analogous to lambda abstractions, and uses process application to instantiate parallelism. Placement of the generated threads and synchronisation between them is implicit, and managed by the RTS. A higher level of abstraction is provided through skeletons, capturing specific patterns of parallel execution, implemented using these parallelism primitives.

Erlang is a distributed functional language originally developed by Ericsson for constructing server-side telecommunications [1], and has experienced rapid uptake in a range of industrial sectors. Erlang broadly follows the Actor model and is widely recognised as a beacon language for distributed computing, influencing the design of many languages and frameworks, for example Scala and F#. The key aspects of Erlang style concurrency are first class processes that may fail without damaging others, fast process creation and destruction, scalability, fast asynchronous message passing, copying message-passing semantics (share-nothing concurrency), and selective message reception [23].

A recent development that heavily influenced our work, was the design and implementation of CloudHaskell [6] It emulates Erlang's distributed programming model, explicitly targeting distributed-memory systems, and implementing all parallelism extensions (processes with explicit message passing and closure serialisation) entirely on the Haskell level. Initial performance results indicate that the overhead from using Haskell as a system language is acceptable.

2.3   Parallel Functional Language Implementations

Many parallel functional language implementations use a sophisticated and low-level RTS to coordinate parallelism. That is, the RTS schedules and distributes work, synchronises and communicates with threads, and so forth. Implementations taking this approach include Dream/EDI [13] for Eden, GUM [21] for distributed-memory GpH, and the threaded GHC RTS [17] for shared-memory GpH.

The use of a low-level systems language may be necessary when the performance impact of layers of abstraction cannot be tolerated. However, low-level implementations of parallel coordination tend to suffer from high maintenance cost, as seemingly unrelated internal changes to the RTS, e. g., to the memory layout of closures, may break parallel coordination. In contrast, the implementations of CloudHaskell [6] and the Par Monad [16] leave the GHC RTS unchanged, and implement all coordination functionality on the Haskell level. Using Haskell's advanced abstraction mechanisms ensures ease of maintainability and more readable implementations. Moreover GHC's light-weight threads deliver good performance.

3   Language Design

This section presents the initial design of HdpH. The design is strongly influenced by GpH, by Eden's EDI layer, and by two recent developments that lift functionality normally provided by a low-level RTS to the Haskell level.

The Par Monad [16], a shallowly embedded domain specific language (DSL) for deterministic shared-memory parallelism. Section 3.1 adapts this DSL to distributed-memory parallelism, including semantic provisions for fault tolerance.

Closure serialisation in CloudHaskell [6]. Section 3.2 extends CloudHaskell's closure representation to support polymorphic closure transformations, which Section 3.3 exploits to implement high-level coordination abstractions.

3.1   Primitives

Figure 1 shows the basic primitives that HdpH exposes to the programmer, with shared-memory primitives inherited from the Par Monad [16] to the left, and distributed-memory primitives to the right.

The Par type constructor is a monad[1] for encapsulating a parallel computation. The basic primitive for generating shared-memory parallelism is fork, which forks a new

---

[1] Par is a continuation monad like Claessen's Poor Man's Concurrency monad [5]; alternatively Par could be based on Harrison's resumption monad [8].

```
data Par a  -- Par monad          data NodeId     -- explicit locations
eval :: a -> Par a                allNodes :: Par [NodeId]

                                  data Closure a  -- explicit, serialisable closures
fork :: Par () -> Par ()          spark  :: Closure(Par ()) -> Par ()
                                  pushTo :: Closure(Par ()) -> NodeId -> Par ()

data IVar a -- buffers            data GIVar a    -- global handles to IVars
new :: Par (IVar a)               glob :: IVar (Closure a) -> Par (GIVar (Closure a))
put :: IVar a -> a -> Par ()      rput :: GIVar (Closure a) -> Closure a -> Par ()
get :: IVar a -> Par a            at   :: GIVar (Closure a) -> NodeId
```

Fig. 1. HdpH primitives. To the left types and primitives for shared memory inherited from the `Par` Monad [16]; to the right types and primitives for distributed memory.

thread and returns nothing. To communicate the results of computations (and to block waiting for their availability), threads employ IVars, which are essentially mutable variables that are writable exactly once. The programmer has access to these via three operations: IVar creation (new), blocking read (get), and write (put). Note that put does not normalise its argument, unlike the put in [16]. Instead the programmer can force expressions to weak-head normal form explicitly using eval; full normalisation can be defined by combining eval with deepseq.

To extend the DSL towards distributed memory HdpH exposes abstract data types for explicit locations, explicit closures (discussed in detail in Sect. 3.2), and global IVars. An explicit location identifies a *node*, i. e., an operating system process running HdpH, within the GHC RTS, possibly on multiple cores. HdpH is *location-aware*: The programmer can test locations for equality, query the set of all locations (allNodes) and query the current location (by myNode = fmap at (new >>= glob)).

The basic primitives for generating distributed-memory parallelism are spark and pushTo. The former operates much like fork, generating a computation (henceforth referred to as a *spark*) that *may* be executed on a different node. However, it can't just take a Par computation as an argument because such a computation can't be serialised. Instead, the argument to be sparked must be converted to an explicit closure first. The pushTo primitive is similar except that it eagerly pushes a closure containing a Par computation to a target node, where it is eagerly unwrapped and executed. In contrast, spark just stores its argument in a local *spark pool*, where it sits waiting to be distributed or scheduled by an on-demand work-stealing scheduler (Sect. 4.2).

To retrieve the results of remote closures or synchronise distributed computations, HdpH introduces *global IVars*. These are simply global references to IVars, with three operations: Creation (glob) by globalising a local IVar, remote write (rput), and information (at) about the location of the underlying IVar. To ensure that the values written by rput are serialisable, these operations restrict the base type of their underlying IVars to closures. Hence all values transported between nodes, be it computations or results, are closures — so results may again be computations. Note that there is no remote read on global IVars — in this respect they are much like channels in Eden and CloudHaskell, supporting remote write but only local read.

For comparison and demonstration we present three parallel Fibonacci functions in Fig. 2. All three functions take two arguments: the second is the argument to the Fibonacci function, and the first a granularity threshold below which to generate no parallelism.

```
fib :: Int -> Int                    pfib :: Int -> Int -> Int
fib n                                pfib t n
  | n <= 1    = 1                      | n <= t    = fib n
  | otherwise = x + y                  | otherwise = x `par` y `pseq` x + y
    where x = fib (n-1)                  where x = pfib t (n-1)
          y = fib (n-2)                        y = pfib t (n-2)

spfib :: Int -> Int -> Par Int       dpfib :: Int -> Int -> Par Int
spfib t n                            dpfib t n
  | n <= t    = return $ fib n         | n <= t    = return $ fib n
  | otherwise = do                     | otherwise = do
      v <- new                             v <- new
                                           gv <- glob v
      fork $ spfib t (n-1) >>=             spark $(mkClosure [|dpfib t (n-1) >>=
             eval >>=                                         eval >>=
             put v                                            rput gv . toClosure|])
      y <- spfib t (n-2)                   y <- dpfib t (n-2)
      x <- get v                           clo_x <- get v
      return (x + y)                       return (unClosure clo_x + y)
```

Fig. 2. Fibonacci numbers. To the left sequential code and shared-memory parallel code in HdpH; to the right GpH code and distributed-memory parallel code in HdpH.

The first variant, pfib, uses the GpH par and pseq primitives. It can be executed either on a shared-memory multicore using the GHC RTS or on distributed-memory architectures using the GUM RTS. The second variant, spfib, uses the shared-memory primitives of the Par Monad, and is thus confined to the shared-memory GHC RTS. The third variant, dpfib, employs the HdpH primitives and can be executed on shared or distributed-memory architectures using the HdpH implementation.

There are many similarities between spfib and dpfib; the difference is that spfib can simply fork the first recursive call, whereas dpfib must globalise the IVar v, yielding global IVar gv, and wrap the first recursive call in an explicit closure generated by the Template Haskell splice $(mkClosure [|...|]), before sparking. Moreover, dpfib must convert the result of the sparked computation to an explicit closure with toClosure before writing to gv, and that closure must be eliminated again with unClosure before adding the results of both recursive calls.

The HdpH primitives constitute a deliberately low-level language, much like the GpH primitives. Section 3.3 will show how to build common abstractions on top.

Non-determinism, fault tolerance and the semantics of IVars. There is a subtle difference in the semantics of put in HdpH versus the Par Monad [16]. The latter forbids racing put; any attempt to do so, i. e., any attempt to put into an already filled IVar, will abort the program in the name of determinism. HdpH opts for a different and non-deterministic semantics: putting into a full IVar has no effect. That is, only the first put succeeds but subsequent puts aren't fatal. The price we pay for the more flexible semantics is that Par computations remain confined to the monadic world. HdpH only offers the monadic function runParIO :: Par a -> IO a to extract Par computations, in contrast to the pure runPar :: Par a -> a of [16].

There are good reasons for accepting non-determinism in the distributed-memory setting. Firstly, for a distributed computation to survive node failures, it must be able to speculatively restart supposedly failed tasks. Such a speculative restart must share the global IVar expecting its result with the original task, opening up a race if the original task happens to be alive (e. g., because the executing node didn't fail but was temporarily unreachable or unresponsive). Secondly, many distributed algorithms are non-deterministic by nature — insisting on determinism would severely limit expressiveness.

3.2 Explicit Closures

CloudHaskell [6] introduced the idea of making a thunk thk serialisable[2] by constructing an *explicit closure* consisting of an environment env storing the variables captured by thk, and a function fun such that fun env = thk. Because all variables captured by thk have been abstracted out to env, fun does not itself capture any variables, that is all its free variables are top-level, which implies that fun itself could be defined at top-level. CloudHaskell pulls two tricks to make explicit closures serialisable, i. e., an instance of class Binary. It assumes (1) that env is already serialised and represented as a byte string that will be deserialised by fun, and (2) that fun is serialisable as its code address. The latter trick requires a Haskell extension: a primitive type constructor Static for reflecting code addresses of terms, plus term formers static :: a -> Static a for obtaining the address of a term which could be top-level, and unstatic :: Static a -> a for resolving such an address. Though not (yet) implemented in GHC 7, we proceed with our language design in this section as if Static were fully supported.[3] Details about Static can be found in [6] and are not relevant for the rest of this paper, save for the fact that Static is an instance of the classes Binary and NFData.

CloudHaskell represents explicit closures as a pair of a serialised environment of type Env, a synonym for byte strings, and a static deserialiser, i. e., the address of a deserialiser.

```
data Closure a = MkClosure (Static (Env -> a)) Env

unClosure :: Closure a -> a
unClosure (MkClosure fun env) = (unstatic fun) env
```

Other than serialisation the only operations on closures that CloudHaskell exposes are introduction by the constructor, and elimination by unClosure. As introduction is lazy it delays serialising the environment until demanded, either by the closure being serialised or eliminated. Oddly, closure introduction and elimination are asymmetric: unClosure. MkClosure is not an identity, because unClosure eliminates not only the constructor but also the closure representation. This does not matter as long as closures are just used to ferry computations from one node to another, to be unpacked and executed at the target node.

We consider the CloudHaskell Closure constructor too limited. Firstly, the constructor should be generalised to support both computation with closures as well as their transportation. Ideally, Closure should be a *functor*, so closures can be transformed without eliminating them. In addition there should be a special closure transformation

---

[2] In keeping with the programming languages community, we take *serialisation* to mean the process of encoding in-memory data structures into byte strings to be sent over the network. This is not to be confused with the notion of *serialisability* in concurrency theory.

[3] Like CloudHaskell, we emulate Static support by requiring the programmer to register all Static functions in a lookup table.

```
data Closure a = UnsafeMkClosure
                 a                      -- actual thunk
                 (Static (Env -> a))    -- static deserialiser
                 Env                    -- serialised environment

instance Binary (Closure a) where
  put (UnsafeMkClosure _ fun env) = put fun >> put env
  get = do fun <- get
           env <- get
           let thk = (unstatic fun) env
           return $ UnsafeMkClosure thk fun env

instance NFData (Closure a) where
  rnf (UnsafeMkClosure _ fun env) = rnf fun `seq` rnf env

unClosure :: Closure a -> a
unClosure (UnsafeMkClosure thk _ _) = thk

toClosure :: (Binary a) => a -> Closure a
toClosure thk = UnsafeMkClosure thk (static decode) (encode thk)

mapClosure :: Closure (a -> b) -> Closure a -> Closure b
mapClosure clo_f clo_x = $(mkClosure [|unClosure clo_f $ unClosure clo_x|])
```

Fig. 3. HdpH closure representation and operations on closures

that *forces*, i. e., evaluates to normalform, its content. Finally, we'd like to avoid unnecessary serialisation, e. g., when eliminating a closure immediately after introduction.[4] We use strategies to force the evaluation of a closure (Sect. 3.3), and will address the other issues while introducing the enhanced HdpH closure representation in Fig. 3.

Dual closure representation. To avoid unnecessary serialisation HdpH maintains a dual representation of closures, extending CloudHaskell's closure representation with the actual thunk being represented, see the first argument of UnsafeMkClosure in Fig. 3. This representation avoids unnecessary serialisation as Closure elimination is just a projection on the first argument, involving no serialisation. Dual representation implies the obligation to maintain the invariant that the two representations, the actual thunk thk and its serialisable representation fun and env, are semantically and computationally equivalent. When constructing closures explicitly this obligation rests on the programmer, which is why the constructor is termed UnsafeMkClosure.

The Binary instance maintains the invariant by serialising only the serialisable representation fun and env, reconstructing the actual thunk thk upon deserialisation by applying the static deserialiser fun to the serialised environment env in the same way as CloudHaskell eliminates its explicit closures. Note that the reconstruction of thk is lazy, and hence delayed until the explicit Closure is eliminated.

The NFData instance normalises only the serialisable representation fun and env, not the actual thunk thk. Normalising thk, too, would break the dual representation invariant because the actual closure would be in normal form but the serialisable representation would not. Specifically, unClosure $ decode $ encode $ clo and unClosure clo would not have the same strictness properties if the actual thunk thk were normalised.

---

[4] This is not a concern if all closures are guaranteed to be serialised because they are to be shipped across the network. However, computing with closures tends to create lots of intermediate closures, so treating them efficiently becomes important.

Safe closure construction. As using `UnsafeMkClosure` is cumbersome and error-prone, there are *safe* `Closure` constructions that guarantee the dual representation invariant. The simplest such construction is `toClosure`, albeit only for serialisable types, i.e., instances of class `Binary`. The function `toClosure` simply pairs a serialised value with the appropriate static deserialiser which exists thanks to the `Binary` context. Note that `toClosure` lazily delays serialising its argument until the resulting `Closure` is serialised or normalised. In particular, `unClosure . toClosure` is an identity that does not involve serialisation.

A more general safe `Closure` construction generates the arguments to the constructor `UnsafeMkClosure` automatically by macro expansion, using Template Haskell. This is done by function `mkClosure :: Q Exp -> Q Exp`, which safely converts a *quoted* thunk, i.e., an expression in Template Haskell's quotation brackets `[| ... |]`, into a quoted `Closure`, to be spliced into the code using Template Haskell's splicing parentheses `$( ... )`. To explain what `mkClosure` does, we show what the call in Fig. 2 expands to.

```
mkClosure [|dpfib t (n-1) >>= eval >>= rput gv . toClosure|]
==> [|let thk = dpfib t (n-1) >>= eval >>= rput gv . toClosure
          env = encode (gv, t, n)
          fun = static (\env -> let (gv, t, n) = decode env in
                        dpfib t (n-1) >>= eval >>= rput gv . toClosure)
      in UnsafeMkClosure thk fun env|]
```

To start, `mkClosure` finds the variables captured by the given thunk and packs them into a tuple, here `(gv, t, n)`. Then, it constructs the explicit `Closure` expression `(UnsafeMkClosure thk fun env)`, where `thk` is the given thunk, `env` is the serialised environment, i.e., the serialised tuple of captured variables, and `fun` is a static deserialiser. The latter is actually the code address of a wrapper around the given thunk, abstracting over its serialised environment. That is, the wrapper is a λ-abstraction whose body is the given thunk yet the captured variables (here `gv`, `t` and `n`) are now let-bound as a result of deserialising the parameter `env`. The wrapper itself does not capture any variables hence `static` is applicable.

Note how `mkClosure` eliminates two pitfalls that `UnsafeMkClosure` exposed programmers to: (1) It guarantees the dual representation invariant, and (2) it ensures that the tuple of captured variables is serialised and deserialised in exactly the same shape and order.

Transforming closures. One might think that `Closure` should be an instance of the `Functor` class. It would appear that `fmap` can be implemented by generating an explicit `Closure` which applies a function another closure, like so:

```
fmap :: (a -> b) -> Closure a -> Closure b
fmap f clo_x = $(mkClosure [|f $ unClosure clo_x|])
```

This implementation of `fmap`, however, does not compile because the argument to `mkClosure` captures the function `f`, requiring `f` to be serialisable. Yet arbitrary functions are not serialisable — that is the very reason for introducing the `Closure` type.

Nonetheless, the idea of an `fmap`-like `Closure` transformation can be salvaged if we insist on the function argument being a `Closure` itself. Figure 3 shows the resulting

```
type Strategy a = a -> Par a

using :: a -> Strategy a -> Par a
x 'using' strat = strat x

forceClosure :: (Binary a, NFData a) => Strategy (Closure a)
forceClosure clo = unClosure clo' 'deepseq' return clo'
  where clo' = toClosure $ unClosure clo

parList :: Closure (Strategy (Closure a)) -> Strategy [Closure a]
parList clo_strat = mapM spawn >=> mapM get
  where spawn :: Closure a -> Par (IVar (Closure a))
        spawn clo = do
          v <- new
          gv <- glob v
          spark $ $(mkClosure [|(clo 'using' unClosure clo_strat) >>= rput gv|])
          return v

parListNF :: (Binary a, NFData a) => Strategy [Closure a]
parListNF = parList $(mkClosure [|forceClosure|])

parMap :: (Binary a, Binary b, NFData b) => Closure (a -> b) -> [a] -> Par [b]
parMap clo_f xs = do clo_ys <- map f clo_xs 'using' parListNF
                     return $ map unClosure clo_ys
                       where f = mapClosure clo_f
                             clo_xs = map toClosure xs
```

Fig. 4. Task-farm skeleton implemented via closure strategies

functor-like transformation mapClosure, promoting a function Closure to a function on Closures. Note how mapClosure is implemented in terms of Closure elimination and introduction; that is why our efforts in curbing unnecessary serialisation overhead are relevant.

In fact, mapClosure is not just a functor-like transformation; it actually *is* (the morphism part of) a functor, just not the type of functor that would fit into the Functor class. Instead, it is a functor mapping function Closures to functions on Closures, see the technical report [14] for details.

3.3 Strategies and Skeletons

Directly using coordination primitives, like those in Sect. 3.1, does introduce parallelism but obscures code by intertwining computation and coordination aspects. To disentangle coordination and computation we aim to develop higher-level abstractions over the primitives, and Fig. 4 shows some simple examples.

Strategies are compositional building blocks for coordination developed for GpH in [20,15]. Following [15], strategies in HdpH are identity functions in the Par monad, i.e. functions of type a -> Par a whose denotational semantics is the identity. A strategy may cause sequential or parallel evaluation of their argument as a side effect. Being based on the Par monad rather than the Eval monad of [15] has implications because the Par monad can't be escaped as easily as the Eval monad. For example, strategy application with using must stay in Par. Moreover, the strategy composition dot that was used extensively in the strategies library of [15] cannot be expressed without leaving the monad, nor can strategies for infinite data structures like rolling buffers for lazy streams. Nevertheless, many useful strategy combinators can.

Since all distributed-memory parallelism in HdpH involves explicit `Closure`s, we focus on `Closure` strategies. The most basic of these is `forceClosure` (see Fig. 4), which fully normalises the thunk inside a `Closure`. It does so by eliminating the `Closure` with `unClosure`, then converting the resulting thunk into a new `Closure` with `toClosure`, before normalising the thunk with `deepseq` and returning the new closure. Note how this is different from just `deepseq`ing the thunk and returning the original `Closure`, which would result in an evaluated `Closure` that would revert to its unevaluated state upon serialisation.

The `parList` strategy combinator applies a strategy to a all elements of a list in parallel. The list elements are of type `Closure a`, so we expect an argument of type `Strategy (Closure a)`; however, the strategy argument needs to be serialised itself, see the definition of `spawn`, so it must be wrapped in another `Closure`. The implementation of `parList` is straightforward: Spawn all strategy applications with `mapM spawn` producing a list of IVars, then read the results back with `mapM get`; the structure of the code for `spawn` itself is similar to that of `dpfib` in Fig. 2. The strategy `parListNF`, which fully normalises a list of closures in parallel, is derived by applying `parList` to `forceClosure` after wrapping the latter in another `Closure`.

Skeletons are polymorphic higher order functions that abstract common parallel programming patterns, e. g., task farms. Thanks to polymorphic closure transformations like `mapClosure` and polymorphic strategies like `parListNF`, we can build simple skeletons like GpH does. For example, Fig. 4 shows the task farm skeleton `parMap`, which applies a function closure to all elements of a list in parallel using the strategy `parListNF`. A sample use of `parMap` to implement a data-parallel computation can be found in the technical report [14].

In the implementation of `parMap`, we can still observe the separation of computation (the `clo_ys <- map f clo_xs` part of the first line) and coordination (the `'using' parListNF`) though it is muddied in the rest of the function that deals with the necessary closure conversions and eliminations.

4   Implementation Design

For maintainability HdpH is implemented in a layered fashion with coordination aspects such as communication, global reference management, spark management, scheduling, etc. realised in independent modules. Figure 5 depicts the HdpH architecture in terms of state, i. e., mutable data structures in Haskell, and agents, i. e., Haskell IO threads. Each node runs several thread schedulers, typically one per core. Each scheduler owns a dedicated thread pool (a concurrent deque) that may be accessed by other schedulers for stealing work. Each node runs a message handler, which shares access to the spark pool (another concurrent deque) with the schedulers. Each node also has a registry (a concurrent map) of global IVars that is shared between message handler and schedulers.

Inter-node communication is abstracted into a *communication layer*, that provides startup and shutdown functionality, node IDs, and seamless peer-to-peer send/receive of arbitrarily sized byte strings. Currently this layer is based on MPI; we plan ports to other network protocols with better support for fault tolerance.

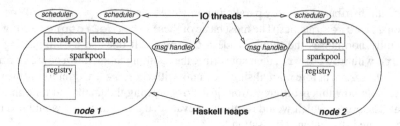

Fig. 5. HdpH system architecture; coupling a dual core and a uni-core node

Thread scheduling is based on the work-stealing scheme of the Par Monad [16], except that HdpH implements a two-tier work pool. Idle schedulers first try to steal threads from other thread pools; if that fails they try to pick sparks from the spark pool.

4.1   Global References and Global IVars

Global references provide a type-safe way of accessing remotely hosted objects (Fig. 6). A global reference records the type of the referred-to object as a phantom type, i.e., ref :: GRef t refers to an object of type t. A global reference is represented by a pair of a node ID identifying the host of the referred-to object and a name that is unique on that host (and stays unique over the life span of the host). This yields globally unique identifiers with cheap projection, at, to the node component, and straightforward seri-alisation and normalisation.

The link between a global reference (whose host is the current node) and its referred-to object is established by the *registry*, a concurrently mutable lookup table, much like the GALA table in the GUM RTS, except that the registry is implemented in Haskell (currently as mutable reference to an immutable finite map). There are two basic operations on global references: (1) Introducing a fresh one (by globaliseing a local object) and (2) eliminating an existing one (by dereferencing it). However, to avoid having to implement a global garbage collection, we add a third operation for freeing a global reference. Thus, we are faced with the problem that a global reference may be

```
data GRef a                                at :: GRef a -> NodeId
instance Eq (GRef a) where { ... }         globalise :: a -> IO (GRef a)
instance Binary (GRef a) where { ... }     deref :: GRef a -> IO (Maybe a)
instance NFData (GRef a) where { ... }     free :: GRef a -> IO ()

type GIVar a = GRef (IVar a)

glob :: IVar (Closure a) -> Par (GIVar (Closure a))
glob = lift . globalise

rput :: GIVar (Closure a) -> Closure a -> Par ()
rput gv clo = pushTo clo' (at gv)
                 where clo' = $(mkClosure [|lift (deref gv) >>=
                                 maybe
                                 (return ())
                                 (\v -> put v clo >> lift (free gv))|])
```

Fig. 6. API of global references and implementation of global IVars

dead (because it has been `freed` earlier) when we attempt to `dereference` it, which explains why `deref` returns a `Maybe` type.

In many ways, global references are like stable names: they provide stable, global and type-safe identifiers for the objects they refer to. There is one essential difference: The life time of a stable name is tied to the life time of its referred-to object — stable names whose objects have vanished may be garbage collected and re-used. In contrast, the life time of a global reference is decoupled from the life time of its object (since the object may live in a different heap). Hence global references must never be re-used.

Global references aren't exposed in HdpH. Instead they serve to implement *global IVars*: a `GIVar` is simply a global reference to an IVar (Fig. 6) and inherits the properties of global references, including serialisability. Moreover, `glob` simply lifts the respective operation on global references to the `Par` monad.

The semantics of `rput` is more complex: it pushes a computation to the node hosting the IVar referred to by `gv`. That computation dereferences the global reference and, depending on the outcome, either returns immediately (in case the global reference was dead) or else writes `clo` to the referred-to IVar and `frees` the global reference `gv`. Note that the action on dead references is consistent with the semantics for IVars. If `rput` encounters a dead global IVar `gv` then `gv` must have been filled by an earlier, successful `rput`, and in that case `put` would fail silently, just as `rput` does.

4.2 Spark Management

HdpH re-implements the spark management of GUM [21] at the Haskell level. Each node stores *sparks*, i. e., values of type `Closure (Par ())`, in a pool. Sparks enter the pool either on being `sparked` or on being received in a SCHEDULE message. Sparks leave the pool either to be turned into local threads (by eliminating the `Closure`), or to be SCHEDULEd on another node, which entails serialising the `Closure`. Currently the spark selection strategy is purely age-based: the youngest ones are turned into threads, the oldest ones are SCHEDULEd away.

When the spark pool is running low, a FISH message is sent to a random node (or to a node known to have had excess sparks recently). If a node receives a FISH, it either replies with a SCHEDULE (in case it has excess sparks to give away) or forwards the FISH to a random node. To avoid FISH messages circulating forever, each FISH counts the number of times it is forwarded. If the counter reaches a threshold, the FISH expires and a NOWORK message is returned to its originating node, which will wait for some time before sending the next FISH.

Executing `pushTo clo node` sends a PUSH message containing `clo` to `node`. Upon receiving a PUSH the message handler eliminates the `Closure` and executes the resulting computation without waiting for a scheduler to become available. Thus `pushTo` is suitable for very short and urgent actions like writing to an IVar or forking a thread.

4.3 Current Limitations of the HdpH Implementation

At the time of writing, two issues handicap the usability of HdpH. Firstly, the lack of `Static` support in GHC necessitates work-arounds that bloat the number of top-level

nodes	cores	Fibonacci			SumEuler (prim)			SumEuler (parMap)		
		runtime	error	speedup	runtime	error	speedup	runtime	error	speedup
sequential		424.58s	6%		355.69s	8%		*see columns to the left*		
1	6	75.64s	1%	5.6	62.31s	< 0.5%	5.7	62.65s	< 0.5%	5.7
2	12	42.29s	< 0.5%	10.0	32.72s	< 0.5%	10.9	32.71s	< 0.5%	10.9
3	18	28.32s	1%	15.0	22.07s	< 0.5%	16.1	22.14s	1%	16.1
4	24	20.25s	< 0.5%	21.0	16.42s	1%	21.7	16.47s	< 0.5%	21.6
6	36	14.09s	1%	30.1	11.13s	1%	31.9	11.12s	1%	32.0
8	48	10.37s	1%	41.0	8.48s	1%	42.0	8.47s	< 0.5%	42.0
12	72	6.81s	1%	62.3	5.91s	2%	60.2	5.91s	1%	60.2
16	96	5.26s	2%	80.7	4.47s	3%	79.5	4.53s	1%	78.5
20	120	4.21s	2%	100.9	3.79s	5%	93.8	3.83s	9%	92.9
24	144	3.55s	2%	119.7	3.99s	13%	89.1	3.29s	16%	108.0
28	168	3.14s	7%	135.4	3.72s	7%	95.6	3.25s	7%	109.5

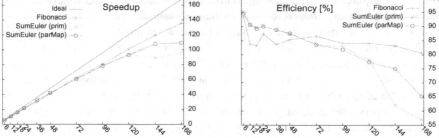

Fig. 7. Results of three benchmarks: runtime, absolute speedup and efficiency

declarations and burden the programmer with explicit `Static` registration. Secondly, the MPI-based communication layer is performing poorly on large messages, which severely affects data-intensive applications.

5 Preliminary Performance Results

To investigate the scalability and efficiency of HdpH we have benchmarked three simple parallel programs on a Beowulf cluster. Each Beowulf node comprises two Intel quad-core CPUs (Xeon E5504) at 2GHz, sharing 12GB of RAM. Nodes are connected via Gigabit Ethernet and run Linux (CentOS 5.7 x86_64). HdpH (version 0.3.0) and the benchmarks were built with GHC 7.2.1 and linked against the MPICH2 library (version 1.2.1p1). Benchmarks were run on up to 28 cluster nodes; to limit variability we used only 6 cores per node. Reported runtime is median wall clock time over 7 executions. Reported error is standard deviation relative to median runtime; percentages in the low single digits indicate high quality measurements.

Figure 7 summarises our results in terms of runtime, absolute speedup and efficiency. The *Fibonacci* benchmark is a regular divide-and-conquer algorithm computing `dpfib 30 50` from Fig. 2. The program generates 17710 sparks with an average granularity of 25 milliseconds. With efficiency declining very slowly, Fibonacci scales very well, yielding a maximum speedup of 135 on 168 cores. The reason is that a regular divide-and-conquer algorithm tends to generate work on many nodes, so work stealing via random fishing tends to be very effective.

The two *SumEuler* benchmarks map Euler's totient function over [1..65536] and reduce the result to a sum. Both are regular, flat data-parallel algorithms, where the main thread deals the input list in a round-robin fashion to 1024 sparks (with a granularity of about 350 milliseconds each), and sums up the results. The two SumEuler benchmarks differ in that one is implemented solely in terms of the HdpH primitives whereas the other relies on the parMap skeleton (and hence on polymorphic closure operations). Code for both versions can be found in the technical report [14].

Both SumEuler benchmarks scale worse than Fibonacci, with efficiency declining faster and maximum speedup limited to about 110 on 168 cores, because the main node is bound to become a bottleneck. Remarkably though, both SumEuler benchmarks perform virtually the same,[5] suggesting that the overhead of parMap is negligible.

Finally, we observe that all benchmarks achieve their peak efficiency, about 95%, on a single node. Efficiency drops steeply (to 80–90%) when adding a second node and then declines more slowly and steadily. The reason for this single-node efficiency boost is that HdpH completely avoids serialisation overheads when running on a single node.

6   Conclusion and Future Work

We have presented the initial design, implementation and preliminary evaluation of a new distributed-memory parallel Haskell, HdpH. The language supports high-level semi-explicit parallelism, is scalable, and has the potential for fault tolerance (Sect. 3). The HdpH implementation is designed for maintainability. It does not rely on a bespoke low-level RTS but is implemented in Concurrent Haskell as supported by the GHC (Sect. 4). Initial performance results for simple benchmarks are promising with good efficiency and absolute speedups (Sect. 5).

HdpH is still a young project, and development continues in several directions. We are experimenting with fault tolerant skeletons, e. g., task farms that guarantee evaluation of all tasks despite repeated node failures. We are exploring how to extend HdpH towards fully-fledged distributed programming, specifically how to handle distributed data and exceptions in the style of GdH [19]. We are also developing a profiler to analyse HdpH programs as well as the HdpH implementation. Finally, we plan to benchmark HdpH on realistic problems and compare its performance to other parallel Haskells.

In the medium term we plan to use HdpH as the implementation language for the SymGridPar2 middleware providing parallel execution of large GAP computational algebra problems [10]. Key requirements for SymGridPar2 are the scalability and reliability supported by the HdpH distributed-memory programming model.

Acknowledgements. Thanks to Andrew Black, Jeff Epstein, Hans-Wolfgang Loidl, and Rob Stewart for stimulating discussions. This research is supported by the projects HPC-GAP (EPSRC EP/G05553X), SCIEnce (EU FP6 RII3-CT-2005-026133), and RELEASE (EU FP7-ICT 287510).

---

[5] The speedup and efficiency graphs suggest that the parMap-based SumEuler outperforms the other beyond 120 cores, but the measurement errors are too high to support such a conclusion.

References

1. Armstrong, J.L., Virding, S.R., Williams, M.C., Wikstrom, C.: Concurrent Programming in Erlang, 2nd edn. Prentice-Hall (1996)
2. Berthold, J.: Explicit and implicit parallel functional programming: concepts and implementation. Ph.D. thesis, Philipps-Universität Marburg, Germany (2008)
3. Berthold, J., Al Zain, A., Loidl, H.-W.: Scheduling Light-Weight Parallelism in ARTCOP. In: Hudak, P., Warren, D.S. (eds.) PADL 2008. LNCS, vol. 4902, pp. 214–229. Springer, Heidelberg (2008)
4. Chakravarty, M.M.T., Leshchinskiy, R., Peyton-Jones, S.L., Keller, G., Marlow, S.: Data Parallel Haskell: a status report. In: DAMP 2007, Nice, France, pp. 10–18. ACM Press (2007)
5. Claessen, K.: A poor man's concurrency monad. J. Funct. Program. 9(3), 313–323 (1999)
6. Epstein, J., Black, A.P., Peyton-Jones, S.L.: Towards Haskell in the cloud. In: Haskell 2011, Tokyo, Japan. pp. 118–129. ACM Press (2011)
7. Grelck, C., Scholz, S.B.: SAC - a functional array language for efficient multi-threaded execution. International Journal of Parallel Programming 34(4), 383–427 (2006)
8. Harrison, W.L.: The Essence of Multitasking. In: Johnson, M., Vene, V. (eds.) AMAST 2006. LNCS, vol. 4019, pp. 158–172. Springer, Heidelberg (2006)
9. Haskell distributed parallel Haskell, https://github.com/PatrickMaier/HdpH
10. HPC-GAP: High Performance Computational Algebra and Discrete Mathematics, http://www-circa.mcs.st-andrews.ac.uk/hpcgap.php
11. Klusik, U., Ortega, Y., Peña, R.: Implementing Eden - or: Dreams Become Reality. In: Hammond, K., Davie, T., Clack, C. (eds.) IFL 1998. LNCS, vol. 1595, pp. 103–119. Springer, Heidelberg (1999)
12. Li, P., Marlow, S., Peyton-Jones, S.L., Tolmach, A.P.: Lightweight concurrency primitives for GHC. In: Haskell 2007, Freiburg, Germany, pp. 107–118. ACM Press (2007)
13. Loogen, R., Ortega-Mallén, Y., Peña-Marí, R.: Parallel functional programming in Eden. J. Funct. Program. 15(3), 431–475 (2005)
14. Maier, P., Trinder, P.W.: Implementing a high-level distributed-memory parallel Haskell in Haskell. Tech. Rep. HW-MACS-TR-0091, Heriot-Watt University (2011), http://www.macs.hw.ac.uk/~pm175/papers/Maier_Trinder_IFL2011_XT.pdf
15. Marlow, S., Maier, P., Loidl, H.W., Aswad, M.K., Trinder, P.W.: Seq no more: Better strategies for parallel Haskell. In: Haskell 2010, Baltimore, USA, pp. 91–102. ACM Press (2010)
16. Marlow, S., Newton, R., Peyton-Jones, S.L.: A monad for deterministic parallelism. In: Haskell 2011, Tokyo, Japan, pp. 71–82. ACM Press (2011)
17. Marlow, S., Peyton-Jones, S.L., Singh, S.: Runtime support for multicore Haskell. In: ICFP 2009, Edinburgh, Scotland, pp. 65–78. ACM Press (2009)
18. Peyton-Jones, S.L., Gordon, A., Finne, S.: Concurrent Haskell. In: POPL 1996, St. Petersburg Beach, USA, pp. 295–308 (1996)
19. Pointon, R.F., Trinder, P.W., Loidl, H.-W.: The Design and Implementation of Glasgow Distributed Haskell. In: Mohnen, M., Koopman, P. (eds.) IFL 2000. LNCS, vol. 2011, pp. 53–70. Springer, Heidelberg (2001)
20. Trinder, P.W., Hammond, K., Loidl, H.W., Peyton-Jones, S.L.: Algorithms + strategy = parallelism. J. Funct. Program. 8(1), 23–60 (1998)
21. Trinder, P.W., Hammond, K., Mattson Jr., J.S., Partridge, A.S., Peyton-Jones, S.L.: GUM: A portable parallel implementation of Haskell. In: PLDI 1996, Philadelphia, USA, pp. 79–88. ACM Press (1996)
22. Trinder, P.W., Loidl, H.W., Pointon, R.F.: Parallel and distributed Haskells. J. Funct. Program. 12(4&5), 469–510 (2002)
23. Wiger, U.: What is Erlang-style concurrency?, http://ulf.wiger.net/weblog/2008/02/06/what-is-erlang-style-concurrency/

Challenges for a Trace-Based Just-In-Time Compiler for Haskell

Thomas Schilling

School of Computing
University of Kent, UK
ts319@kent.ac.uk

Abstract. Haskell's use of lazy evaluation and type classes has endowed it with enhanced expressiveness, but also poses difficult challenges for compiler writers if high performance is a requirement. Most research so far has used static compilation techniques to solve these issues.

In this work, we argue that an implementation based on a virtual machine with a dynamic optimizer based on trace-compilation may be able to remove Haskell's execution overheads with similar efficacy. This could improve on static techniques in the following ways: (1) more predictable optimization in hot spots, (2) cross-module optimization while retaining binary compatibility, and (3) no need to compile multiple module variants for profiling or debugging.

We present a work-in-progress prototype that implements a trace-based just-in-time compiler for Haskell and identify the missing pieces of the puzzle required to achieve an implementation that can be competitive with state of the art ahead-of-time Haskell compilers.

1 Introduction

To the implementer of a runtime system, Haskell's most interesting characteristics are:

- *Lazy evaluation.* Function arguments in Haskell are only evaluated when required by the computation (and no sooner). In the function call (f x (g y)) the expression g y is not evaluated before passing control to f. Instead a heap object called a *thunk* is allocated and a reference to that heap object is passed as the second argument to f. If f requires the value of its second argument it *evaluates* the thunk to weak head normal form (WHNF) and then *updates* the thunk with that value.
- *Curried function definitions.* Functions are first class values and can be passed as arguments and return values. Functions may also be applied to fewer or more arguments than the function arity, known as *partial application* and *overapplication* respectively. The runtime system must handle both cases if they cannot be ruled out statically [23].
- *Mostly immutable data structures.* Haskell encourages the use of immutable (or *persistent*) data structures. For example, to add an element to a set

A. Gill and J. Hage (Eds.): IFL 2011, LNCS 7257, pp. 51–68, 2012.

data structure, a new set data structure is constructed which contains the new element. To make this efficient many data structures are implemented in terms of tree structures to allow sharing of common parts between the original and the updated data structure. While immutable data structures are often less efficient than mutable structures, immutability makes it easier to introduce concurrency [24] or improve garbage collection on multicore.

- *Type classes.* Haskell uses type classes [36] to support overloaded functions. They are typically implemented using indirect function calls. A source expression (plus x y) where plus is an overloaded function of type class C is internally rewritten to (plus dict x y). The dict argument is a record of functions definitions for all overloaded functions of the C class. The plus function merely looks up its implementation in this record and calls it with the two arguments x and y. Many common operations such as equality and addition are implemented using type classes.

Haskell has traditionally been a stronghold of static optimization. The Glasgow Haskell Compiler (GHC)[1] has a sophisticated inliner [30] to eliminate function call overhead and expose further optimisations. Library authors can specify rewrite rules to be applied during compilation [31]. This is used in particular to implement *deforestation*, the removal of intermediate data structures [10,16,22].

There are certain downsides to static optimization. Optimizations can be fragile and sensitive to small changes in the input program (in particular if rewrite rules are involved). Inliner behavior must be carefully fine-tuned to avoid too much code size increase while not missing optimizations in hot spots. Rewrite rules must usually be re-implemented from scratch for each data structure. Finally, programs (and all dependencies) must be recompiled to enable certain forms of profiling or debugging.

Trace-based Just-in-time (TJIT) compilation [2,1] has been used successfully to optimize statically typed languages such as Java [13] and C#/CIL [3] as well as dynamically typed languages such as JavaScript [14], Lua [27] and Python [32,7].

In the following we argue that trace-based compilation is indeed a good fit for optimizing lazy functional languages at runtime. We also note that an approach based on a virtual machine (VM) is necessary in order to enable deforestation and cannot be achieved by trace-compiling a lower-level representation such as LLVM bitcode. We have implemented a prototype TJIT compiler and believe that it has the potential to remove many or even most drawbacks of static compilation. Our prototype uses GHC as a front-end, which allows it to take advantage of *both* static and dynamic optimization if desired.

2   Trace-Based Just-In-Time Compilation

Traditional JIT compilers use basic blocks or single functions as a unit of compilation. Using a form of runtime profiling, hot functions are identified and then compiled and optimized using standard compilation techniques on the control

---

[1] http://haskell.org/ghc/

flow graph of the full function (and possibly inlined functions). The compiler typically has to traverse the program until a fixed-point is reached slowing down compilation speed. If a function is inlined, its whole body is inlined increasing the problem size further. In practice, however, only a few parts of a function are actually hot and the compiler may spend a lot of time optimizing code that is executed rarely or never.

Trace-based compilation, on the other hand, compiles only straight-line code—a trace—with no control flow join points except that the last instruction might loop back to the beginning. Iterative fixed-point analyses are no longer necessary and compilation can be implemented as a single forward pass and a single backwards pass (combined with, or followed by, machine code generation). A trace follows the execution of the program and is not limited to a single function. Traces usually correspond to loops in the source program which tends to result in greater scope for optimisations and removal of redundancies. E. g., if an object is allocated in one iteration of the loop only to be destructed and discarded in the next iteration, then the allocation can often be removed altogether.

A trace only corresponds to a single path through the loop. If the original code contains a conditional branch, the recorded trace will contain a *guard*. A guard verifies that execution is allowed to continue on the trace; if the guard fails execution leaves the current trace and continues in the interpreter or another trace. If a guard fails frequently it usually becomes the start of another trace.

Figure 1 gives an overview of the main phases of a trace-based JIT.

1. Execution starts in the interpreter. Only special instructions can cause the start of a new trace (e.g., function calls). Whenever the interpreter executes any of these instructions a hot counter is incremented. If the hot counter reaches a predefined threshold, the instruction is considered hot and the next execution phase begins.
2. Execution continues in trace recording mode. The interpreter still executes bytecode instructions but additionally emits intermediate code to the trace recorder. Recording continues until either of the following conditions occurs:

   – A loop is found, i.e., execution reaches the point where recording started.
   – The start of an existing trace is found.
   – An abort condition is triggered, e.g., an exception is thrown or the recorded trace has become too long.

3. If recording finished successfully, the recorded intermediate code is now optimized and translated into machine code. The machine code is then placed into the *fragment cache* and execution continues in machine code.
4. Eventually, a guard fails and execution leaves the fragment cache and falls back to the interpreter. Execution continues in the interpreter until an existing trace is encountered or another instruction becomes hot.

Traces may be linked together so that most of the executed code comes from the fragment cache. A trace covers only a single execution path through a loop. If there are multiple hot paths through a single loop, a side trace will be attached

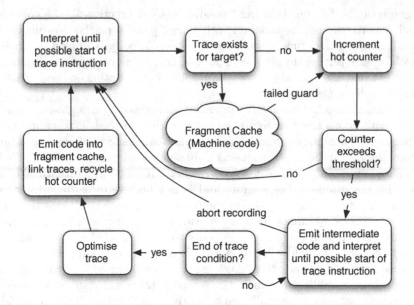

Fig. 1. Overview of trace-based just-in-time compilation

at an exit point of the trace which was generated first, the root trace. The side trace eventually loops back to the beginning of the root trace. The control flow *graph* of the original program gets turned into a trace *tree* [13].

Trace-based JIT compilers have become popular for implementing dynamically typed languages [27,32,7,14]. Dynamically typed languages are difficult to optimize because the static control flow graph is much larger as each instruction often has related but different semantics for each possible type. Indeed, in the next section we will show that Haskell's execution behavior is also "dynamic" despite being a statically-typed language.

3   Lazy Evaluation and Trace Compilation

This section explains how trace-based compilation could help reduce the overheads of lazy evaluation. There are a number of open issues that we are addressing in ongoing work. We identify them here as Challenges 1 through 3.

3.1   Thunks and Evaluation

Despite being a statically-typed language, compiled Haskell code exhibits fairly complex control flow behavior. The reason for this is lazy evaluation. For example, the data type `Int` (a heap allocated fixed precision integer) has only a single constructor `CInt`. Nevertheless, a runtime value of type `Int` can either be an object constructed with `CInt`, or it can be a *thunk*, that is, an unevaluated (or delayed) expression. In this paper we will use the term *shape* to refer to which code would execute when an object is evaluated. Thus a heap object of type Int has only one constructor but may have many different shapes at runtime.

If the value of an object is needed and the object may be a thunk, then the object needs to be evaluated first. The code that needs to be executed depends on where the thunk was created. Due to the large number of different possible code paths, GHC implements the evaluation operation using an indirect function call (with no arguments). For the case where the object was not a thunk the called code will return immediately.

Evaluation is very frequent in Haskell code and indirect function calls are typically very expensive. When GHC introduced a pointer-tagging scheme to reduce the number of these calls, it improved performance by 12%-14% on average [25]. In this scheme the lower two to three bits of a pointer (which would normally all be zero due to heap data alignment restrictions) are used to encode the tag of the pointed-to heap object (unless it is a thunk).

Pointer-tagging removes branch mispredictions and memory accesses. It does not, however, enable higher-level optimizations. For example, the fact that, say, an object is a cons rather than nil may be used to optimize later parts of the code. Trace compilation would allow us to do just that. A trace is automatically specialized for the particular constructor or thunk code that has been encountered when the trace was recorded. A guard is inserted that checks the object shape (by looking at the object header).

This only works, though, if the number of different dynamically encountered object shapes is small; otherwise, trace trees may grow very large. We expect this to be true in many cases, but there are likely to be cases where an argument may contain many possible shapes.

Challenge 1. *Can we use specialization to remove the overhead of evaluation and indirect function calls due to type class dictionaries? If the number of possible shapes per evaluation site is small, then the size of trace trees will remain small and thus remain efficient. It is, however, likely that there a few functions which are* megamorphic, *i.e., exhibit a large amount of different argument shapes.*

For example given two expressions e_1 and e_2, the calls (length e_1) and (length e_2) will result in different traces because the evaluation of length and e_1 (or e_2, respectively) will be interleaved (due to non-strictness). Thus, if length becomes the root of a trace, then it will contain a guard for the shape of its argument (i.e., its info table). The problem is that in these cases the shape checks degenerate to linear search which becomes inefficient past a certain length (say, ten). Other candidates for this issue are frequently used utility functions and functions that pattern match on arguments with many possible constructors. We plan to investigate several strategies to handle such cases: (1) if the function is non-recursive inline it into the parent, i.e., disallow the function as a root trace, (2) re-balance the search code to obtain logarithmic complexity, or (3) create multiple traces for such functions and index them by argument shape. Strategy (3) would be similar to polymorphic inline caches [20] which are often used in object-oriented languages.

3.2   Deforestation

Lazy evaluation can increase software modularity because it allows decomposing programs into a consumer and a (lazy) producer [21]. As a simple example consider these two functions:

```
upto :: Int -> Int -> [Int]
upto lo hi =
  if lo > hi then [] else lo : upto (lo + 1) hi

sum :: [Int] -> Int
sum xs = loop 0 xs
  where loop !acc [] = acc
        loop !acc (x:xs) = loop (acc + x) xs
```

The upto function generates a list of integers from lo to hi (inclusive). Note, though, that upto does not call itself recursively. Instead a thunk is constructed (upto (lo + 1) hi) which when evaluated will call upto again. In other words, upto produces a lazy stream of increasing integers.

The sum function consumes a (finite) list of integers and returns their sum. It uses a local function loop which takes an extra accumulator argument which contains the sum of the values consumed so far.[2]

We can use both functions to concisely (yet naïvely) compute the sum of the numbers between 1 and 100: sum (upto 1 100). Unfortunately, this high level of abstraction comes with a performance cost. The loop function causes upto to run and return a value, namely a heap allocated cons object (the ":" operator). This heap object is then immediately examined, its contents extracted, and finally discarded. The recursive call to loop will then do the same thing all over again until upto eventually returns the empty list. In short, communication between consumer and producer occurs through very short-lived heap objects. GHC also uses boxed (heap-allocated) integers which causes further allocation.

A modern copying garbage collector makes short-lived objects very cheap, but there are still unnecessary overheads such as: writing data to memory rather than keeping it in registers, repeated heap-overflow checks, and more frequent garbage collections. The process of removing such intermediate data structures only used for communicating between two functions is called *deforestation* [35] and has been the topic of much research in the functional programming community [16,15,10]. Existing techniques are performed at compile time and rely on sufficient inlining to be applicable. They also require that both consumer and producer are written in a certain way, hence the above definitions would not be optimized automatically.[3]

---

[2] The exclamation mark (pronounced "bang") is a *strictness annotation* which intentionally forbids its argument to be in thunk form. This ensures that the sum is produced immediately instead of constructing a long chain of thunks; a stumbling block to look out for when writing tail-recursive functions in Haskell.

[3] A more general technique called *supercompilation* [26,5] would be able to deforest this example, but it currently has other drawbacks.

Deforestation in a Trace-Based JIT Compiler. A trace-based JIT can automatically remove short-lived allocations if they are allocated on the trace and do not escape [6]. In the case of lazy functional languages, however, it is not so straightforward due to thunk updates.

Consider again the expression (sum (upto 1 100)). At some point the loop function is identified as hot and becomes the entry point to a trace. The traced code will then read a pointer to an upto thunk, e.g., the thunk t_i representing the expression (upto 42 100).

$$t_i = \langle \text{pointer to thunk not created on trace} \rangle$$

Eventually t_i will be evaluated to a list l with a new thunk in the tail position.

$t_{i+1} = $ new $Thunk$(upto 43 100)
$l = $ new $Cons$(42, t_{i+1})
update(t_i, l)   ; Overwrite t_i with indirection to l

Because the thunk t_i came from outside the trace it might be shared, so we have to update it. In a few more instructions the list object l will see its last use on the trace. However, we cannot eliminate its allocation because a reference to it escapes from the trace due to the update of thunk t_i. The same will happen to the thunk t_{i+1} in the next iteration of the loop. (If we do not do this then we degrade to call-by-name which can result in unbounded duplication of work.)

Updating a *shared* thunk is necessary to avoid duplicated work and the allocation cannot be eliminated in this case. If, however, a thunk is not shared, then omitting the update allows us to also omit the allocation. If we have a way to find out whether a thunk is non-shared and omit the update for such thunks, then TJIT compilation would be able to perform automatic deforestation.

Much research has gone into eliminating unnecessary updates, mainly using static analysis [8,34,17,37,18], but it is not clear whether any of these systems would be applicable (and beneficial) for dynamic compilation. Even the simpler of these systems are either tricky to implement, or require a whole-program analysis which is likely to be too expensive for a dynamic optimization system. We plan to investigate the costs and benefits of a one-bit pointer tagging scheme that only requires a very simple static phase.

Challenge 2. *Sharing information at runtime is important to enable deforestation with a dynamic compiler. Both static and dynamic approaches are possible and likely have different trade-offs in terms of accuracy, implementation cost, and runtime overhead. It is not clear which trade-offs will work best for dynamic optimization systems.*

3.3 Trace Selection

Functional programming languages usually have no built-in looping constructs and instead use (tail) recursion to express repetition. Loops can span multiple recursive functions and often use non-constant stack space. The trace selection mechanism must support these cases. Our prototype currently treats every function entry point as a possible trace head. This most likely needs refinement such as false loop filtering [19].

Challenge 3. *Evaluate different trace selection schemes by their coverage and code size. Functional programming benchmarks may exhibit different execution behavior from standard benchmarks for imperative/object-oriented languages.*

4   Implementation

In order to evaluate the applicability of TJIT compilation for Haskell we implemented a prototype VM.[4] We use GHC as our compiler front-end to compile Haskell programs down to GHC's Core intermediate language. Our bytecode compiler then compiles Core into our custom bytecode format.

Our prototype adopts many ideas and techniques from LuaJIT 2 [27] but adapts them to accommodate Haskell-specific needs (such as the different calling convention, lazy evaluation support) and makes use of static type information. We use an interpreter instead of dynamically generating machine code for each execution mode [4]. Like LuaJIT, we also implement trace linking using snapshots (Sect. 4.4) rather than trace trees [13]. The bytecode instruction set is shown in Fig. 2 and the JIT compiler intermediate language is shown in Fig. 3.

4.1   Bytecode and Interpreter

Our bytecode is register-based. Many bytecodes are designed to pop their operands off an operand stack and push their results back onto it. This allows compact bytecode at the cost of more instructions overall due to additional stack management instructions. In an interpreter, instruction decoding and dispatch tend to dominate the execution time. In a register-based bytecode each instruction reads its inputs from and writes back its result to arbitrary locations in the stack. These arbitrary stack locations are called *virtual registers* and need to be encoded in the instruction. This increases bytecode size, but leads to fewer instructions executed overall. It has been shown that register-based interpreters tend to be faster despite the increase in bytecode size [12,33].

Instruction sizes are multiples of four bytes. Some instructions such as call may be longer than four bytes because they take a variable number of arguments. The implementation of call and callt (tail call) are indeed the most complex because Haskell allows both partial application and over-application. We currently use the eval/apply model to support this [23].

The other non-standard instruction is eval which takes one argument and evaluates it to weak head normal form (WHNF). The interpreter implements eval r the same way as the STG machine [29]: Each heap-allocated object has a header word which is a pointer to an *info table*. The info table is a static structure that mainly describes the object to the garbage collector but also

---

[4] https://github.com/nominolo/lambdachine

add d, s_1, s_2, etc.	ALU instructions, two arguments (e.g., $d \leftarrow s_1 + s_2$).
mov d, s	Copy register.
loadk d, n	Load constant n from constant table into register d.
alloc $d, C, s_1, \ldots, s_n$	Allocation ($d \leftarrow$ new $C(s_1, \ldots, s_n)$).
loadf d, p, n	Load field n of p into d.
loadfv d, n	Load free variable of current closure.
loadslf d	Load pointer to current closure into d.
loadbh d	Load reference to blackhole (error thunk) into d.
storef p, n, v	Store v into field n of p. For mutually recursive data only.
islt s_1, s_2, n, etc.	Conditional branch to offset n if $s_1 < s_2$.
jmp n	Goto program counter + n.
case s	Case dispatch on constructor tag.
eval p	Evaluate closure p.
update s_1, s_2	Overwrite object s_1 with indirection to s_2.
call $f, a_1, \ldots, a_n$	Call f with arguments $a_1, \ldots, a_n$.
callt $f, a_1 \ldots, a_n$	Tail-call f with arguments $a_1, \ldots, a_n$.
movrslt $d_1, \ldots, d_n$	Move results of last function call into registers $d_1, \ldots, d_n$.
ret $s_1, \ldots, s_n$	Return results $s_1, \ldots, s_n$.

Fig. 2. The bytecode instruction set. Some instructions take an arbitrary number of arguments, but all instructions are multiples of 4 bytes in size. callt expects its n arguments in registers $r0$ through $r(n-1)$ to avoid copying in the case where f has arity n. loadbh and storef are only used to initialize mutually recursive data structures. There are additional specialized versions of some instructions.

contains the bytecode for evaluating a thunk. The implementation of eval first checks if the object is a thunk and if so calls the evaluation code. Before returning, the evaluation code will execute the special update instruction which overwrites the thunk with the computed value. The computed value is returned from the evaluation code and written into r. If the object has already been evaluated, r will point to the value that it has been updated with. In short, after eval r, the register r will never contain a thunk.

The update instruction is currently the only instruction in our prototype which can modify an initialized object. Haskell also supports mutable arrays, but our prototype does not yet support these. Mutable references (IORef, STRef) in Haskell can be implemented as pointers to a one-element mutable array where the only element is a pointer to the current (immutable) value. The storef instruction is only used to initialize freshly-allocated, mutually-recursive structures. The remaining bytecode instructions are standard.

4.2   Intermediate Representation

When the VM is in trace recording mode, execution continues in the interpreter, but as a side effect emits trace intermediate representation (IR) code into a buffer. All optimizations are performed on the trace IR which is eventually translated into machine code.

Our IR is a fairly standard low-level compiler intermediate representation. IR instructions take up to two operands and return zero or one result. In memory instructions are represented as a graph: to refer to the output of one instruction we use a pointer to the IR instruction that produced the output. In this paper we explicitly name the result of an instruction for better readability. Figure 3 summarizes the trace IR instruction set.

$x = op\ x_1, x_2$; $op \in \{\text{add}, \text{sub}, ...\}$	ALU operation.
guard $(x_1\ op\ x_2)$; $op \in \{<, >, \leq, ..\}$	Guard (leave trace if predicate not true).
heapcheck n	Allocate n words or leave trace if allocation fails.
$x = $ sload n	Load value from stack slot n.
$p = $ iload p	Load pointer to info table of heap object p.
$x = $ fload p, n	Load field n of heap object p.
fstore p, n, x	Store x into field n of object p.
update p_1, p_2	Update p_1 with indirection to p_2.
new p, h	Allocate closure (see text).
frame n_1, n_2	Stack increases by n_1, frame size n_2.
ret	Pop stack frame.
loop	Special marker.
phi x_1, x_2	ϕ instruction (see text).

Fig. 3. Intermediate representation (IR) of the trace compiler. Meta variables names describes the types required: p is a pointer, n is a constant integer, x is any type (for which the operation makes sense).

The sload instruction loads an operand from the stack ("load slot"), iload loads a pointer to the info table from the header of the given object (used only for guards). The new instruction initializes a new heap object whose memory has previously been allocated with heapcheck. The first argument is the info table, and the second is a reference into the abstract heap which describes the contents of the object. The abstract heap is explained in Sect. 4.5 below. The frame, ret and loop instructions are operational no-ops; frame and ret are used during loop unrolling to keep track of the stack level, and the loop marker marks the start of an unrolled loop. The phi instruction correspond to ϕ-instructions from SSA [11]. It can be read as a move instruction copying x_2 into x_1 (multiple phi instructions are executed in parallel). However, phi instructions are treated specially during loop optimization and the register allocator tries to allocate both arguments to the same register to avoid emitting the move instruction.

4.3   Optimizations

We perform only standard optimizations with a good cost/benefit ratio. All forward optimizations are performed immediately when the instruction is recorded by sending it through a simple optimization pipeline. Optimizations that need to traverse the IR recording buffer backwards (e.g., dead code elimination) are performed at the end before machine code generation. Our prototype performs the following optimizations:

- Common sub-expression elimination.
- Constant folding, algebraic optimizations and reassociation.
- Redundant load removal.
- Store-to-load forwarding. Because heap objects are immutable this optimization is not hindered by aliasing issues.
- Redundant guard removal.
- Dead code elimination.
- Loop unrolling. Wherever possible, we unroll loops to remove redundancies across loop boundaries.
- Allocation removal. See Sect. 4.5.

4.4   Snapshots

When execution exits a trace due to a failing guard, we need to reconstruct the VM state, in particular, the stack. Instead of writing back all intermediate results to the stack before each guard, we use *snapshots* to describe how to reconstruct the stack state from machine register contents in case a guard fails.

During translation of bytecode into trace IR we maintain an *abstract stack* which maps stack slots to IR references. The abstract stack is updated whenever a slot is read or written. If the abstract stack contains an entry for a slot that is about to be read, the reference from the abstract stack is used instead of emitting a slot load instruction. Similarly, instead of emitting a write instruction of y to slot i, the entry for slot i in the abstract stack is updated to map to y.

Whenever a guard is added to the IR buffer, a snapshot is generated from the current contents of the abstract stack. In addition to the values from the abstract stack, the snapshot contains the program counter at the given guard, the (relative) location of the stack frame pointer, a heap snapshot (see Sect. 4.5), and a hot counter. During trace compilation snapshots contain IR references, but the register allocator will turn these into appropriate register or stack references.

Snapshots can be used in two ways to reconstruct the VM state. They can either be used to generate machine code (known as *exit stubs* [2,9]) or they can be interpreted at runtime when a trace is exited [28].

Note that snapshots may extend the live ranges of trace variables and thereby increase register pressure. This can be ameliorated by taking snapshots into account during register allocation. If a variable needs to be spilled to the stack, it can be spilled into the stack slot it would take in the nearest snapshot.

Some snapshots can be omitted. If a guard is (a) very unlikely to fail, (b) not suitable as the start of a side trace, and (c) no globally visible side effect has been performed since the last snapshot (e.g, an update), then the snapshot can be omitted. If the corresponding guard fails, the trace will be exited at the previous guard. The virtual machine state is essentially rewound to an earlier state. The interpreter then re-executes the (small amount of) code between the two guards, then reaches the point where the guard failed again and then continues execution as appropriate. Examples of guards where it is worthwhile to omit snapshots are rarely failing guards such as the zero-check before a division or stack and heap overflow checks.

When a particular guard fails frequently and a new side trace is being recorded, the snapshot of the guard is used to initialize the abstract stack for the side trace. The compiled side trace will then read values from the registers or stack slots used by the parent trace.

4.5   Allocation Sinking and Abstract Heaps

Allocation is one of the most important performance aspects of a modern garbage-collected language. While allocation is relatively cheap on modern garbage collectors in terms of instructions (a pointer increment and overflow check followed by initialization code), allocating many objects causes many garbage collection cycles which increases to the total program execution time. Haskell programs perform particularly many allocations due to the design of the calling convention (allocation of thunks, boxed representation basic types). Therefore it is important to try to remove allocations on traces.

Traces ideally correspond to loops and (hopefully) execute for several iterations before a guard fails. If an object is both allocated and consumed on the same trace (or on a side trace), then the allocation can be eliminated and any field load from the allocated object can be replaced by the value used to initialize the object. Only if a guard fails is it actually necessary to allocate the object.

Based on these ideas, we try to *sink* as many allocations as possible into snapshots, that is, we try to push allocations down into side exits. A sunken allocation is only performed when leaving the trace. Not all instructions can be sunken, e.g., if an object reference is written (via update) into a shared object outside the heap then it cannot be sunken. The same holds for all objects reachable from an unsinkable object.

To implement allocation sinking we use a structure analogous to the abstract stack, the *abstract heap*. The abstract heap tracks the contents of freshly allocated heap objects. It contains an entry for each allocation instruction. Each entry maps each field of the allocated object to the IR instruction that produced the value to initialize that field.

If an allocation *cannot* be sunken, then the code generator will emit the necessary code to perform the allocation on the trace. If an allocation *can* be sunken, then no code will be generated on the trace. Instead the relevant parts of the abstract heap are added to all snapshots that contain a reference to the omitted allocation instruction. If a trace exits at a guard with such a snapshot, the abstract heap is used to perform the allocation before execution continues in the interpreter.

Short-lived objects often are allocated in one loop iteration and become unreachable in the next. To eliminate such objects, we need to perform optimizations across loop boundaries. Moving loop-invariant code outside the loop body and into the loop header is also helpful.

4.6   Loop Optimizations

A simple but effective way of turning a recorded loop into a loop header and a loop body is to simply unroll the loop (also known as *loop peeling*) and perform optimizations while unrolling [28]. The initially recorded loop becomes the loop header and the unrolled loop becomes the loop body. The last instruction of the unrolled loop jumps back to the beginning of the unrolled loop, not to the head of the trace.

This is implemented as follows. First, we emit the special instruction loop which marks the beginning of the unrolled loop. We maintain a renaming, a mapping from original instruction to its unrolled counterpart. The renaming is initialized with the identity map. Now, for each instruction in the trace buffer, apply the renaming to each of its references and emit the renamed instruction into the IR buffer, going through the same optimisation pipeline as when recording an instruction. If an instruction I_1 is emitted, the result will be a reference to an instruction I_2. This I_2 may be a newly-emitted instruction (i.e., it refers to an instruction after the loop marker) or it may refer to an existing instruction, in which case the original instruction is loop-invariant. The renaming is updated with $(I_1 \mapsto I_2)$. This continues until the loop marker is reached.

At the end of the unrolled loop, the necessary ϕ instructions are constructed from the renaming. A ϕ node is needed for each renaming entry $(I_1 \mapsto I_2)$ where $I_1 \neq I_2$. Additional ϕ nodes are needed for all fields of allocated objects involved in a ϕ node. That is, if there is a ϕ node $x = \phi(x_1, x_2)$ and $x_1 = $ new T $a_1, \cdots, a_n$ and $x_2 = $ new T $b_1, \cdots, b_n$, then there must be nodes $a_i = \phi(a_i, b_i)$ for $i \in \{1, ..., n\}$. This may introduce unnecessary ϕ nodes, but these can be eliminated by a subsequent dead code elimination pass.

4.7   Results

Our prototype currently can generate machine code for basic Haskell programs that use only a small subset of built-in types, Char, Bool and Int. All user defined types are supported, but the IO monad or arrays are not supported. All our benchmarks and tests produce a single number or boolean as result. Traces can have increasing or decreasing stacks, but only traces with constant stack usage are unrolled and profit from loop unrolling (i.e., traces resulting from tail-recursive functions). Side traces are not yet implemented.

Fig. 5 and Fig. 6 show the counts of different kinds of operations for two very small benchmarks. Benchmark sumFromTo is simply

```
sumFromTo n = sum (upto 1 n)
```

with sum and upto defined as in Sect. 3.2. Benchmark sumSquare is a slightly more complicated version of that benchmark:

```
sumSquare n = sum [ a * b | a <- upto 1 n, b <- upto a n ]
```

While sumFromTo only contains one loop, sumSquare consists of two nested loops. Our prototype currently only produces a trace for the inner loop. The outer loop is currently executed by the interpreter. The operation counts shown in Fig. 5 and Fig. 6 are as follows:

- Alloc(Words): The number of machine words allocated.
- Load: The number of machine words loaded from heap objects.
- Eval(WHNF): The number of calls to eval where the object turned has been evaluated before (was in weak head normal form).
- Eval(Thunk): The number of calls to eval where the evaluated object was a thunk.
- Calls: The total number of function calls (of any arity).
- ALU: Basic arithmetic operations (addition, comparison, multiplication, etc.).

The Load operation does not include any loads due to the interpreter (like reading virtual registers). We ignore interpreter overheads in order to approximate the number of operations the program would execute if compiled.

Each benchmark is run in four configurations, every combination of static and dynamic optimization:

- O0/O2: The GHC front end was invoked with optimization level -O0 (no optimizations) and -O2 (full optimizations) respectively. List fusion [16] was disabled in both benchmarks because the consumer (sum) is not written in terms of foldr.
- Interp/JIT: Our JIT was run in interpreter-only mode or with JIT compiler enabled. Note again that the operation counts do not include interpreter overhead thus simulating GHC performance. The JIT-compiled code also omits thunk updates (which is safe for both benchmarks) to enable full deforestation. That is, the optimized code uses call-by-name rather than call-by-need. This is indeed a valid implementation of the Haskell 2010 specification, but can lead to severe performance degeneration for some programs. As explained in Sect. 3.2, this optimization can be proved safe for our benchmarks using a suitable sharing analysis.

Both Fig. 5 and Fig. 6 show that the static compiler is quite good at removing calls to eval on values that are already in WHNF and did remove some allocations. However, without code specially tailored to enable list fusion it is not able to remove the intermediate lists.

Our tracing JIT was able to remove all allocations on the trace. The remaining allocations stem from the interpreter before a loop was detected as hot. For sumFromTo the loop was reduced to only ALU instructions (the optimized code is shown in Fig. 4). For sumSquare the outer loop is still executed in the interpreter because our prototype currently does not fully support side traces. This causes some extra allocations and loads. The increased number of ALU operations are guards executed when re-entering the trace for the inner loop.

We are in the process of expanding our work to handle larger programs with more complicated control flow behavior. Some standard benchmarks seem to rely on thunk updates and are hard to optimize. Many recursive Haskell functions are also not tail-recursive, hence it is important to handle loops with increasing or decreasing stack levels.

$t_{01} = $ sload 0	guard $(t_{10} \leq t_{19})$
$t_{02} = $ iload t_{01}	$t_{21} = $ new thunk_B_info(t_{10}, t_{13})
guard $(t_{02} = $ Int_info$)$	$t_{22} = $ new :_info(t_{11}, t_{21})
$t_{04} = $ sload 1	$t_{28} = $ fload $t_1, 1$
$t_{05} = $ iload t_{04}	$t_{29} = $ add t_{28}, t_{10}
guard $(t_{05} = $ thunk_B_info$)$	$t_{30} = $ new Int_info(t_{29})
$t_{09} = $ fload $t_{04}, 1$	loop:
$t_{10} = $ add $t_{09}, 1$	$t_{36} = $ addt$_{10}, 1$
$t_{11} = $ new Int_info(t_{10})	guard $(t_{36} \leq t_{19})$
$t_{13} = $ fload $t_{04}, 2$	$t_{49} = $ add t_{29}, t_{36}
$t_{15} = $ iload t_{13}	phi t_{10}, t_{36}
guard $(t_{15} = $ Int_info$)$	phi t_{29}, t_{49}
$t_{19} = $ fload $t_{13}, 1$	goto loop

Fig. 4. Example of loop unrolling applied to the example from Sect. 3.2. Snapshots information is not shown. Variables which appear to be dead are used in snapshots. Names ending with _info are the static addresses of info tables which form the header word of each heap object.

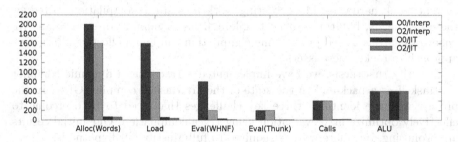

Fig. 5. Operation execution counts for sumFromTo. Hotness threshold is 7, $n = 200$. JIT compiler overhead not included.

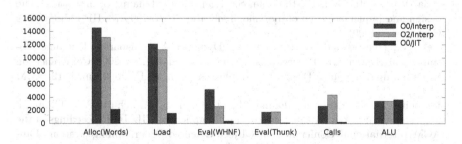

Fig. 6. Operation execution counts for sumSquare. Hotness threshold is 7, $n = 40$. JIT compiler overhead not included. Configuration O2/JIT omitted due to an unsupported feature in our prototype JIT compiler.

5 Related Work

We are not aware of published previous efforts to apply trace-based compilation to a lazy functional language. Trace-based compilation has been applied to languages with higher-order functions such as Lua [27] and JavaScript [14], but, as we showed in this paper, these techniques are not necessarily sufficient to optimize a lazy functional language.

Some of the problems we hope to address, such as automatic deforestation can also be addressed statically by a powerful technique called *supercompilation* [26,5]. However, being a static compilation technique it shares the drawbacks of other static techniques such as the need to recompile code for profiling or debugging. Supercompilation also currently does not scale to large programs.

6 Conclusion

Haskell's execution model poses interesting challenges for compiler and runtime implementors. Haskell's lazy evaluation strategy provides quite some expressive power to the programmer, but it can be difficult to implement efficiently on current stock hardware. Most existing work uses static compilation to reduce these overheads, but this can be fragile and has a number of drawbacks. We believe that trace-based just-in-time compilation can be an effective alternative approach to tackle these issues.

To verify this thesis, we have implemented a trace-based dynamic compiler for Haskell as a back-end to the state-of-the-art Haskell compiler GHC. In the process we have identified three key challenges that need to be overcome to effectively optimize lazy evaluation using trace-compilation. Our initial results are promising, but more work is required to fully justify our hypothesis.

References

1. Bala, V., Duesterwald, E., Banerjia, S.: Transparent dynamic optimization: The design and implementation of dynamo. Tech. Rep. HPL-1999-78, HP Laboratories Cambridge (1999)
2. Bala, V., Duesterwald, E., Banerjia, S.: Dynamo: A Transparent Dynamic Optimization System. In: Proceedings of the ACM SIGPLAN 2000 Conference on Programming Language Design and Implementation, PLDI 2000, pp. 1–12. ACM (2000)
3. Bebenita, M., Brandner, F., Fahndrich, M., Logozzo, F., Schulte, W., Tillmann, N., Venter, H.: SPUR: A Trace-based JIT Compiler for CIL. In: Proceedings of the ACM International Conference on Object Oriented Programming Systems Languages and Applications, OOPSLA 2010, pp. 708–725. ACM, New York (2010)
4. Bebenita, M., Chang, M., Wagner, G., Gal, A., Wimmer, C., Franz, M.: Trace-based compilation in execution environments without interpreters. In: PPPJ 2010, pp. 59–68. ACM, New York (2010)
5. Bolingbroke, M., Peyton Jones, S.: Supercompilation by Evaluation. In: Proceedings of the Third ACM Haskell Symposium on Haskell, Haskell 2010, pp. 135–146. ACM (2010)

6. Bolz, C.F., Cuni, A., Fijałkowski, M., Leuschel, M., Pedroni, S., Rigo, A.: Allocation Removal by Partial Evaluation in a Tracing JIT. In: Proceedings of the 20th ACM SIGPLAN Workshop on Partial Evaluation and Program Manipulation, PEPM 2011, pp. 43–52. ACM (2011)
7. Bolz, C.F., Cuni, A., Fijalkowski, M., Rigo, A.: Tracing the Meta-Level: PyPy's Tracing JIT compiler. In: ICOOOLPS 2009: Proceedings of the 4th Workshop on the Implementation, Compilation, Optimization of Object-Oriented Languages and Programming Systems, pp. 18–25 (2009)
8. Boquist, U., Johnsson, T.: The GRIN Project: A Highly Optimising Back End for Lazy Functional Languages. In: Implementation of Functional Languages, pp. 58–84 (1996)
9. Bruening, D.L.: Effient, Transparent, and Comprehensive Runtime Code Manipulation. Ph.D. thesis, Massachusetts Institute of Technology (September 2004)
10. Coutts, D., Leshchinskiy, R., Stewart, D.: Stream fusion: From lists to streams to nothing at all. In: Proceedings of the 12th ACM SIGPLAN International Conference on Functional Programming, ICFP 2007, pp. 315–326. ACM (2007)
11. Cytron, R., Ferrante, J., Rosen, B.K., Wegman, M.N., Zadeck, F.K.: Efficiently computing static single assignment form and the control dependence graph. ACM Trans. Program. Lang. Syst. 13(4), 451–490 (1991)
12. Davis, B., Beatty, A., Casey, K., Gregg, D., Waldron, J.: The Case for Virtual Register Machines. In: Proceedings of the 2003 Workshop on Interpreters, Virtual Machines and Emulators, IVME 2003, pp. 41–49. ACM Press (2003)
13. Gal, A., Franz, M.: Incremental Dynamic Code Generation with Trace Trees. Tech. Rep. ICS-TR-06-16, University of California, Irvine (2006)
14. Gal, A., Orendorff, J., Ruderman, J., Smith, E., Reitmaier, R., Bebenita, M., Chang, M., Franz, M., Eich, B., Shaver, M., Anderson, D., Mandelin, D., Haghighat, M.R., Kaplan, B., Hoare, G., Zbarsky, B.: Trace-based Just-in-time type Specialization for Dynamic Languages. In: PLDI 2009, pp. 465–478. ACM (2009)
15. Gill, A.: Cheap deforestation for non-strict functional languages. Ph.D. thesis, The University of Glasgow (January 1996)
16. Gill, A., Launchbury, J., Peyton Jones, S.: A short cut to deforestation. In: Proceedings of the Conference on Functional Programming Languages and Computer Architecture, FPCA 1993, pp. 223–232. ACM (1993)
17. Gustavsson, J.: A type based sharing analysis for update avoidance and optimisation. In: Proceedings of the Third ACM SIGPLAN International Conference on Functional Programming, ICFP 1998, pp. 39–50. ACM (1998)
18. Hage, J., Holdermans, S., Middelkoop, A.: A generic usage analysis with subeffect qualifiers. In: Proceedings of the 12th ACM SIGPLAN International Conference on Functional Programming, ICFP 2007, pp. 235–246. ACM (2007)
19. Hayashizaki, H., Wu, P., Inoue, H., Serrano, M.J., Nakatani, T.: Improving the Performance of Trace-based Systems by False Loop Filtering. In: ASPLOS 2011, pp. 405–418. ACM (2011)
20. Hölzle, U., Chambers, C., Ungar, D.: Optimizing Dynamically-typed Object-oriented Languages with Polymorphic Inline Caches. In: America, P. (ed.) ECOOP 1991. LNCS, vol. 512, pp. 21–38. Springer, Heidelberg (1991)
21. Hughes, J.: Why Functional Programming Matters. The Computer Journal 32(2), 98–107 (1989)
22. Leshchinskiy, R.: Recycle Your Arrays! In: Gill, A., Swift, T. (eds.) PADL 2009. LNCS, vol. 5418, pp. 209–223. Springer, Heidelberg (2008)

23. Marlow, S., Peyton Jones, S.: Making a Fast Curry: Push/Enter vs. Eval/Apply for Higher-order Languages. In: Proceedings of the Ninth ACM SIGPLAN International Conference on Functional Programming, ICFP 2004, pp. 4–15. ACM (2004)
24. Marlow, S., Peyton Jones, S., Singh, S.: Runtime Support for Multicore Haskell. In: Proceedings of the 14th ACM SIGPLAN International Conference on Functional Programming, ICFP 2009, pp. 65–78. ACM (2009)
25. Marlow, S., Yakushev, A.R., Peyton Jones, S.: Faster laziness using dynamic pointer tagging. In: Proceedings of the 12th ACM SIGPLAN International Conference on Functional Programming, ICFP 2007, pp. 277–288. ACM (2007)
26. Mitchell, N.: Rethinking Supercompilation. In: Proceedings of the 15th ACM SIGPLAN International Conference on Functional Programming, ICFP 2010, pp. 309–320. ACM (2010)
27. Pall, M.: LuaJIT 2, http://luajit.org/
28. Pall, M.: LuaJIT 2.0 intellectual property disclosure and research opportunities. Lua-l mailing list message (2009), http://lua-users.org/lists/lua-l/2009-11/msg00089.html
29. Peyton Jones, S.: Implementing lazy functional languages on stock hardware: the Spineless Tagless G-machine. Journal of Functional Programming 2, 127–202 (1992)
30. Peyton Jones, S., Marlow, S.: Secrets of the glasgow haskell compiler inliner. Journal of Functional Programming 12(5), 393–434 (2002)
31. Peyton Jones, S., Tolmach, A., Hoare, T.: Playing by the rules: rewriting as a practical optimisation technique in GHC. In: Haskell 2001, pp. 203–233 (2001)
32. Rigo, A., Pedroni, S.: PyPy's Approach to Virtual Machine Construction. In: OOPSLA 2006: Companion to the 21st ACM SIGPLAN Symposium on Object-Oriented Programming Systems, Languages, and Applications (2006)
33. Shi, Y., Gregg, D., Beatty, A., Ertl, M.A.: Virtual machine showdown: Stack versus registers. In: Proceedings of the 1st ACM/USENIX International Conference on Virtual Execution Environments, VEE 2005, pp. 153–163. ACM (2005)
34. Mogensen, T.Æ.: Types for 0, 1 or Many Uses. In: Clack, C., Hammond, K., Davie, T. (eds.) IFL 1997. LNCS, vol. 1467, pp. 112–122. Springer, Heidelberg (1998)
35. Wadler, P.: Deforestation: Transforming programs to eliminate trees. Theoretical Computer Science 73, 231–248 (1990)
36. Wadler, P., Blott, S.: How to make ad-hoc polymorphism less ad hoc. In: Proceedings of the 16th ACM SIGPLAN-SIGACT Symposium on Principles of Programming Languages, POPL 1989, pp. 60–76. ACM (1989)
37. Wansbrough, K., Peyton Jones, S.: Simple Usage Polymorphism. In: The Third ACM SIGPLAN Workshop on Types in Compilation (2000)

Lazy Generation of Canonical Test Programs

Jason S. Reich, Matthew Naylor, and Colin Runciman

Department of Computer Science, University of York
{jason,mfn,colin}@cs.york.ac.uk

Abstract. Property-based testing can be a highly effective form of lightweight verification, but it relies critically on the method used to generate test cases. If we wish to test properties of compilers and related tools we need a generator for source programs as test cases.

We describe experiments[1] generating functional programs in a core first-order language with algebraic data types. Candidate programs are generated freely over a syntactic representation with positional names. Static conditions for program validity and canonical representatives of large equivalence classes are defined separately. The technique is used to investigate the correctness properties of a program optimisation and two language implementations.

Keywords: automated testing, SmallCheck, lightweight verification, compiler correctness, search-based software engineering.

1 Introduction

Testing, when used effectively, can reveal a wide variety of programming errors. For the time invested in the implementation of testing, it can return a large improvement in confidence of software correctness. For example, a suite of programs is often used [11, 5] for verifying a compiler's correct behaviour.

In property-based testing, program properties are defined in the host language as functions returning a Boolean. A property-based testing library then instantiates the arguments of these functions, searching for negative results. The QuickCheck [4] property-based testing library for Haskell uses generators that randomly select test values of the appropriate types. This approach relies on failure cases occurring frequently enough to appear in a random sample of a few hundred or a few thousand tests. SmallCheck and Lazy SmallCheck [12] instead fully explore a bounded enumeration of all possible test values up to some size. This approach appeals to the *Small Scope hypothesis* [6, page 15] that programming errors will appear for small data values.

In this paper, we use Lazy SmallCheck to enumerate all small test programs that are *valid* (well-formed, well-scoped and well-typed, §2), *canonical* (of a regular form detailed in §3) and *terminating* (also §3).

---

[1] Source code available at https://github.com/jasonreich/ProgGen

A. Gill and J. Hage (Eds.): IFL 2011, LNCS 7257, pp. 69–84, 2012.

```
data Pro    = Pro (Seq1 Nat) Exp (Seq RedDef)
data RedDef = Lam Nat   Bod
data Bod    = Solo Exp
            | Case Exp   (Seq1 Alt)
data Exp    = Var  Varld
            | App Decld (Seq Exp)
data Varld  = Arg  Nat
            | Pat  Nat
data Decld  = Con  Nat
            | Red  Nat
data Alt    = Nat :→: Exp
```

Fig. 1. Initial definition of our core language

Rather than directly constructing programs that satisfy these conditions, we freely generate abstract syntax trees and filter out those for which some required condition does not hold. With careful representation choices for the freely generated abstract syntax, a lazy and condition-driven approach to test generation can efficiently and effectively prune large classes of unwanted test programs.

2   Generating Valid Programs of a Core Language

Our Core Language. We choose to work with a first-order core functional language with algebraic data types. In order to generate programs in this language, we first define a datatype for its abstract syntax, as in Figure 1.

A program *Pro cds e rds* consists of a single datatype definition represented as a sequence *cds* of one or more constructor arities, a main expression *e* to be evaluated and zero or more top-level value definitions *rds* whose applications are reducible. A top-level value definition *Lam ar b* is a lambda abstraction of arity *ar*. The body may be just a single applicative expression *Solo e* or it may be a case expression *Case e as* with alternatives for different constructions of the subject *e*.

Expressions are, as usual, recursively composed applications with either variables or zero-arity applications as leaves. Variable references are explicitly tagged: *Arg* for argument variables and *Pat* for pattern variables in alternatives. Applied references are also tagged: *Con* for constructors and *Red* for top-level names whose applications are reducible. These are all referenced by the natural-number positions of their definitions.

Free Generation. Using SmallCheck [12] we can now define functions to enumerate all values of these AST datatypes bounded by a given depth of construction. The *Serial* instances are defined in Figure 2.

The type *Seq a* is synonymous with the list type [a] but the depth-bound is the same for all elements of the list — a *Seq a* list bounded by depth *d* has at most *d* items, each of which has depth at most $d - 1$. The *Seq1* variant is for lists with at least one element.

It is often convenient not to count simple tags or tupling structures when determining the depth of a construction. The compositions with *depth* 0 are for that purpose.

Let's run the *Pro* series generator with increasing depth bounds, and count the number of programs generated.

> [*length* (*series* i :: [*Pro*]) | i ← [0..]]
[0, 4, 3504, 27700575980220, ...

What do the four *Pro* values at depth one look like? These can be rendered as follows,[2] with the convention that arguments are renamed x,y,..., pattern variables p,q,..., constructors A,B,... and top-level functions f,g,....

```
data D = A        data D = A        data D = A        data D = A
> x               > p               > A               > f
```

As these programs are freely generated from the abstract syntax type, they are as yet unconstrained by any static semantics. Only one of them is valid — the third one. At depth two there are already thousands of similar-looking *Pro* values, hardly any of which are valid. Beyond depth two our machines are overwhelmed by the task of enumeration.

Validity Test. Only one of the programs generated at depth one was valid. The other three referred to *undefined* variables or functions. At greater depths another form of invalidity can occur: there may be *arity disagreement* between uses and definitions. We must avoid, or cut short, the work of generating such invalid programs.

We can define a predicate *valid*, as in Figure 3. The auxiliary functions *validr*, *valide* and *valida* test the validity of reducibles, expressions and applications respectively. The first two arguments to *valide* are the enclosing scopes for argument and pattern variables.

If we test the property λp → *valid* p ⟹ *True*, of the 3,504 syntactically generated programs at depth two, just 160 are found to be valid. So even this simple validity check greatly reduces the number of programs to be tested. But as things stand, we still have to generate a large number of invalid programs, only to reject them as test cases.

Lazy Free Generation. The problem of generating test cases that satisfy conditions was a large part of the motivation for *Lazy* SmallCheck [12]. This tool applies conditions to *partially defined* values. If a test value is sufficiently defined to allow a condition to be evaluated to True (or to False), then it is

---

[2] Text in sans-serif indicates Haskell (host language) code. Code in the typewriter typeface represents the target *core* language.

```
instance Serial Pro where
    series = cons3 Pro ∘ depth 0
instance Serial RedDef where
    series = cons2 Lam ∘ depth 0
instance Serial Bod where
    series = (cons1 Solo ∪ cons2 Case) ∘ depth 0
instance Serial Exp where
    series = cons1 Var ∪ cons2 App
instance Serial VarId where
    series = (cons1 Arg ∪ cons1 Pat) ∘ depth 0
instance Serial DecId where
    series = (cons1 Con ∪ cons1 Red) ∘ depth 0
instance Serial Alt where
    series = cons2 (:→:) ∘ depth 0
```

Fig. 2. The series generators for our initial syntactic representation

```
-- Test a program is well-scoped and arity consistent.
valid :: Pro → Bool
valid (Pro (Seq1 cons) m (Seq eqns)) = valide 0 0 m ∧ all validr eqns
  where
      -- Test a reducable is well-scoped and arity consistent.
    validr (Lam a (Solo e))              = valide a 0 e
    validr (Lam a (Case s (Seq1 alts))) = valide a 0 s ∧
        and [indexThen c cons (λp → valide a p e) | (c :→: e) ← alts]
      -- Test an expression is well-scoped and arity consistent, in context.
    valide a _ (Var (Arg v))    = a ≢ 0 ∧ v < a
    valide _ p (Var (Pat v))    = p ≢ 0 ∧ v < p
    valide a p (App d (Seq es)) = valida d (N $ length es) ∧ all (valide a p) es
      -- Test an application is well-scoped and arity correct.
    valida (Con c) n = indexThen c cons (λn'           → n ≡ n')
    valida (Red f) n = indexThen f eqns (λ(Lam n' _) → n ≡ n')
-- Index an element from a list and apply predicate. Default to False.
indexThen :: Nat → [a] → (a → Bool) → Bool
indexThen (N i) xs f = (¬ ∘ null) xs' ∧ head xs'
  where xs' = map f (drop i xs)
```

Fig. 3. Validity of positional programs

known from this single evaluation that *all possible refinements* of this test value will also satisfy (or fail to satisfy) the condition. If the partiality of a test value makes the condition undefined, the test value is refined at exactly the place needed for evaluation of the condition to proceed further.

In principle, Lazy SmallCheck might run *more* test cases than SmallCheck for the same condition — since it tests partial values as well as total ones. But in practice, where there is a structural condition that most tests do not satisfy, Lazy SmallCheck uses many fewer tests.

If we again test the property $\lambda p \rightarrow valid\ p \implies True$, but this time using Lazy SmallCheck, just 187 tests are needed to obtain the same 160 programs at depth two. That is just under 5% of the tests required under SmallCheck.

3   Canonicity

If we could only test a compiler using just two source programs, it would be a better test if the two programs really were quite distinct, not just insignificant variations of each other. The same argument applies even if we can use a large number of test programs. Resources are always limited. So we don't want to waste them by testing umpteen versions of essentially the same program.

We shall use several principles to define *canonical* programs. Each of these programs is a unique representative of a whole class of essentially equivalent programs. The principles of canonicity are discovered through the analysis of programs being generated.

3.1   Principles of Ordering and Complete Reference

The two programs below perform the same computation under the obvious iso-morphism between their datatypes. The only difference between them is the *ordering* of constructors, function definitions and case alternatives.

```
data D  =  A | B D D            data D  =  A D D | B
f x y   =  case x of            f x     =  case x of
           A     -> y                      A p q -> p
           B p q -> B p (g q y)  g x y    =  case x of
g x     =  case x of                       A p q -> A p (g q y)
           B p q -> p                       B     -> y
> g (f A (B A A))               > f (g B (A B B))
```

A canonical representative of both programs respects an ordering for each of these things. Assuming the standard, automatically derived instances of *Ord* for our AST datatypes, a canonical ordering predicate for programs is given in Figure 4.

```
canonicalOrder (Pro (Seq1 cons) _ (Seq eqns)) =
     -- Non-strict ordering of constructor arities
     orderedBy (≤) cons ∧par
     -- Strict lexicographic ordering of equations
     orderedBy (<) eqns ∧par
     -- Strict ordering of case-alternatives by constructor
     and [ orderedBy (<) [c | (c :→: _) ← alts]
         | (Lam _ (Case _ (Seq1 alts))) ← eqns]
  orderedBy :: (a → a → Bool) → [a] → Bool
  orderedBy f (x : y : zs) = f x y ∧ orderedBy f (y : zs)
  orderedBy _ _           = True
```

Fig. 4. Predicate for the ordering of constructors, equations and alternatives

The orderings over equations and alternatives are irreflexive; we forbid duplicate definitions. The ordering over constructor arities is not; we permit more than one constructor of the same arity.

The following programs are also in direct correspondence. There is a duality so far as the roles of the constructors A and B are concerned, and the arguments of function f are flipped.

```
data D = A | B              data D = A | B
f x y = case x of           f x y = case y of
        A -> A                      A -> x
        B -> y                      B -> B
> f B B                     > f A A
```

So here is a further ordering requirement in canonical programs. Constructors of equal arity must be *first used* in the program in the same order as they are declared in the datatype. And function arguments must be *first used* in the function body in the order given by their argument positions.

Further, for any program that declares *unused* constructors, arguments or pattern variables there is a simpler equivalent program without them. In a canonical program, all constructors and arguments are used.

Finally, a program with *unused function definitions* also has a smaller equivalent without them. In a canonical program, all functions can be reached by a static call-chain from the main expression. See §3.6 for further discussion of dead code.

After we impose all these ordering and complete-reference conditions, we have just two programs at depth two, generated by Lazy SmallCheck as a result of 109 tests. And at depth 3, instead of an overwhelming number of programs, just 4,413 programs are produced as a result of 24,373,980 tests.

Unorderable Equations. Consider the following programs that *do not* satisfy the equation-ordering condition.

```
data D = A | B A          data D = A | B A
f x = B (g x)             f x = B (g x)
g x = B (f x)             g x = B (f x)
> f A                     > g A
```

In the current positionally-referenced representation, these programs have *no canonical form*. Reversing the equation ordering simply gives the other program. Our solution for now is to *limit the number of top-level definitions to two* and change the referencing scheme as follows. Within a top-level definition reference is either recursive or else it references the other top-level definition: *Self* and *Other*. Within the main expression, we keep positional naming. i.e. 0 and 1.

As both of these reference models can be implemented with Boolean values, the *Red* constructor is changed to hold *Bool* instead of *Nat*. The definition of *valid* also needs to be changed to account for the new referencing scheme. The ordering predicates work without modification.

3.2   Principle of Depth Balance

To reach a rich space of small test programs, we need to generate function bodies at around depth four or five. But we do *not* need datatypes with four or five constructors, each with four or five arguments! Nor do we need multiple high-arity function declarations.

At depth n, the default syntactic generators give between one and n constructors. The constructors and functions each have $arity \leq n$. Not only is this signature space far richer than we need to express interesting programs — LISP has taught us that — but also the depth limits largely prevent *uses* of these declarations from being generated anyway.

Therefore, mirroring the top-level *two function limit*, the number of constructor declarations and the arities of declarations are capped at two. This could be implemented using a further condition but another approach will be outlined in §3.4.

3.3   Principle of Caller/Callee Demarcation

Wherever there is an application of a defined function, there may be different ways to split work between caller and callee. A canonical program should make this split only in standardised ways.

Both caller and callee should do *something*. The caller must do something: it cannot just be the application of the callee to some of the caller's arguments (or else any application of the caller could more simply be an application of the callee). The principle of complete reference excludes many cases, but we also exclude as a body any application of a function to exactly the same arguments.

```
data ProR   = ProR ExpR (Seq0'2 BodR)
data BodR   = SoloR ExpR | CaseR (AltR, AltR)
data ExpR   = VarR VarIdR | AppR DecIdR (Seq0'2 ExpR)
data VarIdR = ArgR Bool   | PatR Bool
data DecIdR = ConR Bool   | RedR Bool
data AltR   = NoAltR      | AltR ExpR
```

Fig. 5. Nonredundant representation of our core language

The callee must also do something: a function body cannot simply be one of the arguments (or else any application could be replaced by a subexpression). Again the principle of complete reference already excludes most cases, but we also exclude the identity.

Even in our original program representation, we had a form of caller/callee constraint: case expressions can only occur outermost in a function body. So the callee does the case distinction. In canonical programs, the caller computes the case subject: that is, a case subject is just an argument variable, and by the ordering principle, it must be the first argument.

This too could be implemented by a further condition, but we use another approach, as the following section explains.

3.4 Principle of Nonredundant Representation

It is pleasing that Lazy SmallCheck can prune away the 3,502 invalid or non-canonical programs of depth at most two by running only 109 tests, finally delivering for us the two interesting test programs. But the very high proportion of *Pro* values that fail the conditions does prompt a question: would a further change of representation enable us to generate fewer invalid or non-canonical programs in the first place?

We have already established that canonical case subjects are first arguments. So in our new representation the case subject can be omitted.

For a program to be valid, all uses of constructors or functions must match declared datatype and function arities. In a canonical program with complete reference, it follows that the datatype can be determined from the other parts of the program, and the arity of each function can be determined from its body. So instead of generating a datatype definition and function arities, and testing for valid and complete uses, we need only generate a main expression and function bodies.

The cap of two on the number of constructors and functions can also be encoded in the sequence representation types in programs, and in *Bool* index types for declarations. With function arities bounded by two a *Bool* index also suffices for argument variables. Figure 5 details the new representation.

Case-alternative patterns now reference constructors according to their position, doing away with the need for a separate ordering condition for alternatives.

The arity of functions can be deduced by finding the maximum argument in the function body. The datatype definition can be inferred by combining information about program constructor applications and the maximum pattern variable in constructor alternatives. Conditions are still used to prune away non-canonical programs that are not precluded by the nonredundant representation.

The change to a nonredundant representation dramatically reduces the number of tests required at each depth. At depth 3 (analogous to the previous representation's depth 4), only 25,393 tests are required to reduce a space of 2,371,256 programs to 11 canonical representatives. At depth 4, analogous to the previously unattainable depth 5, it takes 28,311,473 tests to find 423,582 canonical programs.

3.5   Principle of Live Computation

Most interesting functional programs are recursive. But some recursively defined functions can unproductively fail to terminate. For example, here are two programs generated at depth 4.

```
data D  =  A                    data D  =  A | B D
f       =  g A                  f       =  B f
g x     =  case x of            g x     =  case x of
           A -> f                          A   -> x
> f                                        B p -> g p
                                > g f
```

To exclude programs such as the one on the left, we add the condition that any recursive applications are either beneath a constructor, or else descend into the construction of a recursive argument. At depth 3, this simple termination condition does not reduce the number of programs produced but it does reduce the number of tests required to 19,099. At depth 4, only 74,414 canonical programs are now produced after 20,550,413 tests.

This still leaves some non-terminating programs such as the one on the right. (View D as Peano numerals, f as infinity and g as a semi-test for finite numbers.) A far more sophisticated condition [e.g. 1] would be needed to eliminate such programs yet allow useful recursion.

For now, we have decided to accept that some unproductive programs will remain. A more sophisticated condition would require significant extra machinery and adversely affect lazy pruning performance. However, property testing must allow for the possibility of an unproductive program.

3.6 Principle of Live Code

The following programs are among those generated at depth 3. They are indistinguishable in their execution as the B case alternatives are never used. Some form of data-flow analysis is needed to detect dead code.

```
data D = A | B        data D = A | B        data D = A | B
f x y = case x of     f x y = case x of     f x y = case x of
          A -> y                 A -> y                 A -> y
> f A B                          B -> x                 B -> A
                      > f A B                > f A B
```

Dynamic evaluation of candidate test programs, followed by a simple reachability analysis, detects dead code more accurately than reachability analysis alone. We must avoid unbounded computation arising from recursive applications, but to avoid unfolding all recursive calls would limit results too much. Our solution is *single-shot recursion*: on any call path we evaluate at most two applications of the same function.

The bounded evaluation traverses the abstract syntax tree in *normal order*, contrasting with the other *in-order* conditions. Validity checks can therefore be bypassed due to the use of Lazy SmallCheck's *parallel conjunction* operator. As validity is required for evaluation, a partial validity checker is integrated into the dead code checker.

Although the live-code condition supersedes the function-reachability and constructor-use of §3.1, it is still worth applying all these conditions. The combination of different traversal orders may prune failures sooner.

Eliminating programs with dead code results in another dramatic fall in tests; depth 3 requiring only 2,731 tests and depth 4 only 445,791 tests. Now just four canonical programs remain at depth 3. These are the constant A program and the following:

```
data D = A | B        data D = A           data D = A | B
f x = case x of       f x y = case x of    f x y = case x of
        A -> B                 A -> y                A -> y
> f A                  > f A A              > f A B
```

The leftmost program could be interpreted as partial inversion with D as the Boolean type. Both other programs are partial conjunction, where A is True and B is False, with different inputs. Alternatively, these could be viewed as partial disjunction where A is False and B is True.

At depth 4, we have just 64 programs that satisfy all these principles of canonicity and validity.

4 Performance

So far, we have discussed performance abstractly, with regard to the number of tests to reach a set of desirable programs. In this section, we shall also consider

Table 1. Performance of non-redundant representation at depth 3

Conditions	Execution time	Tests required	Remaining programs
Validity	2643ms	138,617	855
+ Ordering + Use	690ms	34,745	124
+ Caller/Callee	580ms	25,393	11
+ Live Computation	437ms	19,099	11
+ Live Code	72ms	2,731	4

execution time. All figures were obtained using GHC 7.0.3 on 2GHz dual-core PC with 4GB of RAM.

Table 1 shows performance figures when applying the various conditions at depth 3 of the non-redundant representation. The initial freely generated space contains 2,043,136 'programs'. Execution times are measured using the *Criterion* [9] benchmarking library, averaging 100 measurements and ensuring a 0.95 confidence interval. As each additional condition is applied, the number of tests required to reach a set of desirable programs falls. This trend is mostly mirrored by a fall in execution time. However, execution time does not fall quite as rapidly as the number of tests performed. The time per test lengthens as the number of conditions increases. In fact, the *mean execution time per test* increases by 38% from validity to the full suite of conditions for canonicity.

Enumerating all canonical programs at depth 4 takes approximately 15 seconds. At depth 5, it takes around 3 hours to produce the 310,003 canonical programs.

5   Applications

We use these canonical programs to investigate the correctness properties of language implementations and program optimisations. The first example produces a small program that exposes the differences between static binding and dynamic binding. The second investigates some correctness properties of compiler optimisations both in terms of semantic preservation and performance improvement.

5.1   Static vs. Dynamic Binding

Suppose we implement different semantics for our source language. One version uses *static binding*, evaluating arguments in the environment of the application call. The other uses *dynamic binding* where arguments are evaluated in the environment of the argument reference.

The generated programs are evaluated under each semantics up to a given maximum derivation-tree depth and the results are compared under equality. This property is defined as *prop_bind* in Figure 6. Testing discovers a small example program at depth 4, for which static binding and dynamic binding produce different results.

```
prop_bind :: Pro → Bool
prop_bind e = isJust static ∧ isJust dynamic ⟹ static ≡ dynamic
  where static   = evalFor 1000 False e ≫= return ∘ forceResult 5
        dynamic = evalFor 1000 True e ≫= return ∘ forceResult 5
```

Fig. 6. A mistaken equivalence between static and dynamic binding

```
data D = A | B D
f = g A A
g x y = case x of
          A   -> B y
          B p -> g p x
> g f f
```

Under static binding, the program returns B (B A) as we would usually expect. However, under the dynamic binding semantics, the program returns B A. In the recursive call to g, the environment contains $\{x \mapsto p, y \mapsto x, p \mapsto A\}$ when variable y is referenced.

5.2   Optimisations on a Sestoft Abstract Machine

Sestoft [13] details the derivation of several abstract machines of improving efficiency. These abstract machines evaluate expressions written in a core higher-order functional language. A simple transformation converts our core first-order language into a form that can be executed by the Sestoft Mark 2 abstract machine.

Our goal is to verify a simple program transformation that non-recursively inlines function applications. In this case, we wish to ensure not only *semantic equivalence* but also *optimisation of reduction steps*. These are formally defined as *prop_inline_sem* and *prop_inline_opt* respectively in Figure 7.

At depth 5, the semantic equivalence property is satisfied by all 310,003 canonical programs. However, the following counterexample is found for the optimisation property. If no inlining is performed then this program takes 44 steps to reduce to normal form. But if inlining is applied it takes 46 steps.

```
f x   = case x of
          A   -> B x
          B p -> g x p
g x y = case x of
          A -> f y
          B p -> x
> f (g A A)
```

```
prop_inline_sem :: ProR → Bool
prop_inline_sem p = isJust (haltState r0)  ⟹  haltState r0 ≡ haltState r1
   where r0 = (traceFor 1000 ∘ translate) p
         r1 = (traceFor 1000 ∘ translate ∘ opt_inline) p

prop_inline_opt :: ProR → Bool
prop_inline_opt p = isJust (haltState r0)  ⟹  length r0 ⩾ length r1
   where r0 = (traceFor 1000 ∘ translate) p
         r1 = (traceFor 1000 ∘ translate ∘ opt_inline) p

translate :: ProR → SestExpr
traceFor :: Int → SestExpr → [SestState]
haltState :: [SestState] → Maybe SestExpr
```

Fig. 7. Predicates for testing inlining transformation

The reason is as follows. In the original, g A A is only evaluated once but after inlining it is evaluated twice. The shared evaluation of x in the body of f is lost.

6   Further Work

Verifying Canonicalisation. We should like to verify that every interesting test program has a canonical equivalent. The program generating framework itself could be used to test the existence of canonical representatives for each *reasonable* program. Assuming that every program is represented by a canonical variant, we could write a function that transforms any given program into a canonical representative. We could check that the function satisfies this specification.

Increasing Coverage. Each canonical test program represents a class of programs performing equivalent computations but with different naming, ordering or abstraction boundaries, or with redundant parts. Every valid core program has an equivalent representative, and in that sense every core-program computation is represented in generated tests. This technique has proved very successful in reducing the exhaustive space of test programs.

But what if some desired property of a compiler, or other program-processor under test, fails only when a program is in some way non-canonical? If only canonical programs are tested, such potential failures will go undetected. One solution is to attach a post-processor to the canonical program generator. Given each canonical program, the post-processor picks an equivalent at random, not forgetting the possibility of picking the canonical program itself.

Extending the Core Language. The core language used in this paper lacks features found in other core representations of functional languages. For example, both *GHC External Core* [14] and *F-lite* [8] include primitive values and operations, (recursive) local definitions and higher-order functions.

The abstract syntax datatype, generator and validity checker could be extended to include these features. However, the search-space of generated programs would be greatly enlarged. Some further principles of canonicity would be essential for practical purposes.

Generalising the Framework. Although we have explained principles of canonicity in terms of our core language, the ideas are quite generic. In almost every programming language, or other complex structural representation, there are choices of names or positions, orderings and divisions between units, that do not fundamentally alter the computations or structures being described. There is also the possibility of parts that are in some sense redundant. So similar techniques might be applied successfully to generate test examples in quite different formalisms.

7   Related Work

The automatic generation of compiler test cases has long been an area of interest. A survey from the late 1990s [2] discusses and classifies a range of techniques. The papers cited generally use advanced generating grammars to ensure that only "semantically correct" (valid) programs are produced. A few authors generate test programs freely over context-free or EBNF grammars but with the stated aim of testing a compiler's syntax checker.

For testing functional programs, the QuickCheck work, starting with the award-winning paper at ICFP 2000 [4] has been hugely influential. QuickCheck is a library for property based testing based on the definition of type-based generators for *random* test values. A recent paper [10] describes the use of QuickCheck to generate random lambda terms for compiler testing. De Bruijn indexing [3] is used to avoid problems of equivalence up to renaming. Aside from the use of random lambda terms, as opposed to exhaustively enumerated small equational programs, another significant difference from the approach reported here is that Palka et al.[10] rely on a generating context including the signatures of pre-defined functions.

Other functional-programming researchers have looked into program enumeration. For example, Katayama [7] enumerates typed lambda terms. The motivation is to provide exhaustive search for appropriately typed expressions during program synthesis. Katayama highlights the advantages of a de Bruijn representation, and the importance of excluding "equivalent expressions which cause redundancy in the search space and multiple counting". In this work too, the generator generates terms applying a library of pre-defined functions, and one of the equivalance-avoiding techniques is to apply known simplification laws for these functions. But the discussion notes a need to do more to eliminate duplicate or equivalent solutions.

8 Conclusions

Our aim has been to enumerate valid and canonical programs for the purposes of compiler verification. We have shown that large spaces of freely generated terms can be pruned effectively to yield 'interesting' programs. Exploration of the search space indicates that Boolean programs such as partial inversion, conjunction and disjunction appear at depth 3. Canonical programs involving Peano numerals (e.g. addition) and lists (e.g. append) emerge at depth 6. This paper roughly mirrors the process by which the principles were discovered.

First, an algebraic data type for the abstract syntax is defined and a free generator is created using (Lazy) SmallCheck combinators. Through the observation of the resulting programs, conditions are defined to eliminate invalid and non-canonical programs. The representation is reconsidered to eliminate the redundancy that allows the invalid and non-canonical terms to arise. And so the procedure repeats. Implementation details are occasionally reevaluated to account for the interactions of the different conditions.

We have discovered several principles of canonicity for our first-order language and dramatically reduced the problem size. We expect that further investigation of the currently generated programs will reveal new principles of canonicity or more restrictive variations of existing conditions.

We applied our testing technique to investigate several properties relating to evaluation, compilation and optimisation. The results obtained are encouraging. However, more complex applications motivated our work: we wish to investigate the correctness and improvement properties of supercompilers. It remains to be seen what further refinements of our technique will be needed to succeed in this goal.

Acknowledgements. The authors would like to thank Michael Banks, Emma Maksymowicz and Chris Poskitt for their invaluable proof reading. They also extend their gratitude to the programme committee for their constructive feedback on earlier drafts. This research was supported, in part, by the UK's Engineering and Physical Sciences Research Council through the Large-Scale Complex IT Systems project, EP/F001096/1.

References

1. Abel, A.: Foetus — termination checker for simple functional programs (1998), http://www2.tcs.ifi.lmu.de/~abel/foetus.pdf
2. Boujarwah, A.S., Saleh, K.: Compiler test case generation methods: a survey and assessment. Information & Software Technology 39, 617–625 (1997)
3. de Bruijn, N.G.: Lambda calculus notation with nameless dummies, a tool for automatic formula manipulation, with application to the Church-Rosser theorem. Indagationes Mathematicae 75(5), 381–392 (1972)

4. Claessen, K., Hughes, J.: QuickCheck: a lightweight tool for random testing of haskell programs. In: Proceedings of the Fifth ACM SIGPLAN International Conference on Functional Programming, ICFP 2000, pp. 268–279. ACM (2000)
5. Dietz, P.F.: The GCL ANSI Common Lisp test suite (2008), http://en.scientificcommons.org/42309664
6. Jackson, D.: Software Abstractions: Logic, Language and Analysis, Revised edn. MIT Press (2012)
7. Katayama, S.: Systematic search for lambda expressions. In: Trends in Functional Programming, TFP 2005, vol. 6, pp. 111–126. Intellect Books (2007)
8. Naylor, M., Runciman, C.: The Reduceron reconfigured. In: Proceedings of the 15th ACM SIGPLAN International Conference on Functional Programming, ICFP 2010, pp. 75–86. ACM (2010)
9. O'Sullivan, B.: The criterion package, v0.5.1.1 (2011), http://hackage.haskell.org/package/criterion
10. Palka, M.H., Claessen, K., Russo, A., Hughes, J.: Testing an optimising compiler by generating random lambda terms. In: Proceedings of the Sixth IEEE/ACM Workshop on Automation of Software Test, AST 2011, pp. 91–97 (2011)
11. Partain, W.: The nofib benchmark suite of Haskell programs. In: Functional Programming, Workshops in Computing, Glasgow 1992, pp. 195–202. Springer (1992)
12. Runciman, C., Naylor, M., Lindblad, F.: SmallCheck and Lazy SmallCheck: automatic exhaustive testing for small values. In: Proceedings of the First ACM SIGPLAN Symposium on Haskell, Haskell 2008, pp. 37–48. ACM (2008)
13. Sestoft, P.: Deriving a lazy abstract machine. Journal of Functional Programming 7, 231–264 (1997)
14. Tolmach, A., Chevalier, T.: The GHC Team: An external representation for the GHC Core Language (for GHC 6.10) (2009), http://www.haskell.org/ghc/docs/6.10.4/html/ext-core/core.pdf

Generic Monadic Constructs
for Embedded Languages

Anders Persson[1,2], Emil Axelsson[1], and Josef Svenningsson[1]

[1] Chalmers University of Technology
[2] Ericsson
{anders.persson,emax,josefs}@chalmers.se

Abstract. We present a library of generic monadic constructs for embedded languages. It is an extension of Syntactic, a Haskell library for defining and processing generic abstract syntax. Until now, Syntactic has been mostly suited to implement languages based on pure, side effect free, expressions. The presented extension allows the pure expressions to also contain controlled side effects, enabling the representation of expressions that rely on destructive updates for efficiency. We demonstrate the usefulness of the extension by giving examples from the embedded language Feldspar which is implemented using Syntactic.

1 Introduction

A *domain specific language* (DSL) is a programming language dedicated to a particular domain. The purpose of a DSL is often to allow a problem or solution to be expressed more clearly and efficiently than a general purpose language would allow. Haskell has a long history of being a host language for embedded DSLs, where the DSL is implemented as a library in the host language [8,7].

One such language is Feldspar [5,4]. Feldspar is a domain specific language for programming performance sensitive embedded systems with focus on digital signal processing. The language is a *strongly typed language with pure semantics* and support for both scalar and vector computations. As is common for deeply embedded DSLs, a Feldspar program results in an intermediate representation or *abstract syntax tree* (AST). For code generation purposes, the AST is then translated into some other language, e.g. C or LLVM assembler, suitable for the target device and compiler. Other interpretations of the AST include, but are not limited to, evaluation, static profiling for memory use and pretty printing.

Different embedded languages often contain similar syntactic constructs. For example, most languages have a notion of variable binding, literals, conditional expressions, etc. In addition, most languages have similar functions for semantic interpretation and transformation. Examples of such functions include evaluation and constant folding. To assist the implementation of embedded languages and enable reuse of common implementation aspects, we have developed *Syntactic*.

Syntactic is a Haskell library [6,3] for defining generic abstract syntax, and a set of utilities for building embedded languages based on this syntax. By using

A. Gill and J. Hage (Eds.): IFL 2011, LNCS 7257, pp. 85–99, 2012.

an encoding of data types open to extension, Syntactic provides mechanisms for assembling individual constructs (e.g. literals, tuples, binding, etc) into larger languages. By basing an embedded language on Syntactic, the language becomes modular and open to extension with new syntax elements, front-end combinator libraries and backend interpretation and compilation functions.

1.1   Problem Description

Syntactic works best to implement languages based on pure expressions, i.e computations that are free of side effects. However, this purity makes it impossible to efficiently express algorithms that, for performance, rely on destructive updates of data. The problem manifests itself in both extra memory for storing intermediate results and extra execution time for copying data between intermediate storage locations. A sophisticated compiler might mitigate the problem somewhat by performing lifetime analysis on the data and optimizing the data structures. Still, the compiler can only apply the optimizations when conditions are right and it might be difficult for the programmer to predict when the optimizations will kick in. This is especially true in a large system where the parts are developed individually and conditions vary with the use site of a function. Furthermore, it is desirable to give the programmer more control of when certain values can be overwritten as long as it can be done while preserving the overall referential transparency provided by pure semantics.

As an example, consider the function iter. This Feldspar function generates a syntax tree by repeatedly applying the function f. Note that the first argument to iter is a regular Haskell value which is evaluated as part of the generation. Thus, iter 4 f is equivalent to f ∘ f ∘ f ∘ f.

```
import Feldspar
import Feldspar.Compiler

iter :: (Type a) ⇒ Length → (Data a → Data a) → Data a → Data a
iter 0 _ = id
iter n f = f ∘ iter (n-1) f

ex :: Data Int32 → Data Int32
ex = iter 4 (λx → x + x)
```

Using the Feldspar Compiler, we can generate the code below by evaluating icompile ex. Here, we can see that the result of each function application (v1, v2 and v3) is stored in its own location, even though the individual results are not needed later than the next statement. This extra storage becomes more problematic when the results are of a more complex type, e.g structures or arrays, where the cost of storing and copying cannot be neglected. Instead, we want the generated code to eliminate as many storage locations as possible and destructively update the remaining locations.

```
void ex(int32_t v0, int32_t * out)
{
    int32_t v1;
    int32_t v2;
    int32_t v3;

    v1 = (v0 + v0);
    v2 = (v1 + v1);
    v3 = (v2 + v2);
    (* out) = (v3 + v3);
}
```

A well-known method of expressing impure computations in a pure functional language is to use monads [15]. In this paper we present an extension to Syntactic that provides generic monadic constructs for use in deeply embedded languages. In order to add support for destructive updates in languages like Feldspar, we also provide specialized constructs for mutable references and arrays.

1.2 Contributions

This paper makes the following contributions:

- We show how to implement monadic combinators (in particular, `return` and (`>>=`)) as deeply embedded language constructs (section 3). By basing the implementation on the Syntactic framework, we make the constructs available to other languages based on Syntactic. This extension makes Syntactic applicable to a wider range of EDSLs.
- We avoid the common problem of defining a `Monad` instance for the embedded language by using a continuation monad wrapper around the embedded expressions (section 3.2). This allows us to use Haskell's `do`-notation and existing monadic combinators together with DSL programs. To our knowledge, this is a novel technique, and it has a great impact on the usability of the resulting DSLs.
- We show how to implement monadic language constructs, based on available Haskell types, to deal with destructive updates of data (section 4). These constructs give a pragmatic solution to the problem of expressing destructive updates in Feldspar programs.

It is worth noting that all of this was done without having to change the Syntactic framework or the existing Feldspar implementation. This serves as a great example of the modularity provided by Syntactic (see section 2.2).

The code in this paper is based on Syntactic, version 0.8 [3]. The Feldspar code is based on version 0.5 [2,1].

2 Introduction to Syntactic

When implementing deeply embedded DSLs in Haskell, a syntax tree is typically defined using a (generalized) algebraic data type [7,4,12]. As an example, consider a small expression language with support for literals and addition:

```
-- A simple expression langugage
data Expr₁ a where
    Lit₁ :: Num a ⇒ a → Expr₁ a
    Add₁ :: Num a ⇒ Expr₁ a → Expr₁ a → Expr₁ a
```

$Expr_1$ a is parameterized on the type of the value computed by the expression. It is easy to add a user friendly interface to this language by adding smart constructors and interpretation functions.

```
lit₁ :: Int → Expr₁ Int
lit₁ x = Lit₁ x

add₁ :: Expr₁ Int → Expr₁ Int → Expr₁ Int
add₁ x y = Add₁ x y

eval₁ :: Expr₁ Int → Int
eval₁ (Lit₁ x)   = x
eval₁ (Add₁ x y) = eval₁ x + eval₁ y
```

In this case, the smart constructors only serve to hide implementation details and constrain the type, but in later implementations they will also take care of some tedious wrapping.

The $eval_1$ function is just one possible interpretation of the expressions; we can extend the implementation with, say, pretty printing or program analysis. This can even be done without changing any existing code. However, adding a new construct to the language is not so easy. To extend the language with multiplication, we would need to add a constructor to the $Expr_1$ type as well as adding a new case to $eval_1$ (and other interpretations). Thus, with respect to language extension, a GADT representation of a language is not modular. This limitation is one side of the well-known *expression problem* [14].

There are several reasons why modularity is a desired property of a language implementation. During the development phase, it makes it *easier to experiment* with new language constructs. It also allows constructs to be developed and tested independently, *simplifying collaboration*. However, there is no reason to limit the modularity to a single language implementation. For example, Lit_1 and Add_1 are conceptually generic constructs that might be useful in many different languages. In an ideal world, language implementations should be assembled from a library of generic building blocks in such a way that only the truly domain-specific constructs need to be implemented for each new language.

The purpose of the Syntactic library [3] is to provide a basis for such modular languages. The library provides assistance for all aspects of an embedded DSL implementation:

- A generic AST type that can be customized to form different languages.
- A set of generic constructs that can be used to build custom languages.
- A set of generic functions for interpretation and transformation.
- Generic functions and type classes for defining the user interface of the DSL.

For more information about Syntactic, see our lecture notes from the CEFP summer school [6].

```
data AST dom a where
    Sym  :: Signature a ⇒ dom a → AST dom a
    (:$) :: Typeable a  ⇒ AST dom (a :→ b) → AST dom (Full a) → AST dom b

type ASTF dom a = AST dom (Full a)

newtype Full a  = Full { result :: a }
newtype a :→ b = Partial (a → b)

infixl 1 :$
infixr :→

class Signature a
instance Signature (Full a)
instance Signature b ⇒ Signature (a :→ b)
```

Listing 1. Type of generic abstract syntax trees in Syntactic

2.1 Using Syntactic

The idea of the Syntactic library is to express all syntax trees as instances of a very general type AST[1], defined in listing 1. Sym introduces a constructor from the domain dom, and (:$) applies such a constructor to one argument. By instantiating the dom parameter with different types, it is possible to use AST to model a wide range of algebraic data types. Even GADTs can be modeled.

To model our previous expression language using AST, we rewrite it as follows:

```
data NumDomain₂ a where
    Lit₂ :: Num a ⇒ a → NumDomain₂ (Full a)
    Add₂ :: Num a ⇒ NumDomain₂ (a :→ a :→ Full a)

type Expr₂ a = ASTF NumDomain₂ a
```

In this encoding, the types $Expr_1$ and $Expr_2$ are completely isomorphic (up to strictness properties). The correspondence can be seen by reimplementing our smart constructors for the $Expr_2$ language:

```
lit₂ :: Int → Expr₂ Int
lit₂ a = Sym (Lit₂ a)

add₂ :: Expr₂ Int → Expr₂ Int → Expr₂ Int
add₂ x y = Sym Add₂ :$ x :$ y
```

The implementation of $eval_2$ is left as an exercise to the reader. Note that, in contrast to Add_1, the Add_2 constructor is *non-recursive*. Types based on AST normally rely on (:$) to handle all recursion.

---

[1] The Typeable constraint on the (:$) constructor is from the standard Haskell module Data.Typeable, which, among other things, provides a type-safe cast operation. Syntactic uses type casting to perform certain syntactic transformations whose type-correctness cannot be verified by the type system. The Typeable constraint on (:$) leaks out to functions that construct abstract syntax, which explains the occurrences of Typeable constraints throughout this paper. It is possible to get rid of the constraint, at the cost of making certain AST functions more complicated.

2.2   Extensible Syntax

Part of the reason for using the AST type instead of a GADT is that it supports definition of generic traversals [6], which are the basis of the generic interpretation and transformation functions in Syntactic.

Another, equally important, reason for using AST is that it opens up for making our syntax trees extensible. We cannot that $Expr_2$ is closed in the same way as $Expr_1$: Adding a constructor requires changing the definition of $NumDomain_2$. However, the AST type is compatible with *Data Types à la Carte* [13], which is a technique for encoding open data types in Haskell.[2]

The idea is to create domains as co-products of smaller independent domains using the (:+:) type operator from Syntactic. To demonstrate the idea, we split $NumDomain_2$ into sub-domains and combine them into $NumDomain_3$, used to define $Expr_3$. The new type $Expr_3$ is again isomorphic to $Expr_1$.

```
data Lit₃ a where Lit₃ :: Num a ⇒ a → Lit₃ (Full a)
data Add₃ a where Add₃ :: Num a ⇒ Add₃ (a :→ a :→ Full a)

type NumDomain₃ = Lit₃ :+: Add₃

type Expr₃ a = ASTF NumDomain₃ a
```

To get extensible syntax we cannot use a closed domain, such as $NumDomain_3$, but instead use constrained polymorphism to abstract away from the exact shape of the domain. The standard way of doing this in Data Types à la Carte is to use the inj method of the (:<:) type class (provided by Syntactic). Using inj, the smart constructors for Lit₃ and Add₃ can be defined thus:

```
lit₃ :: (Lit₃ :<: dom, Num a) ⇒ a → ASTF dom a
lit₃ a = Sym (inj (Lit₃ a))

add₃ :: (Add₃ :<: dom, Num a, Typeable a)
        ⇒ ASTF dom a → ASTF dom a → ASTF dom a
add₃ x y = Sym (inj Add₃) :$ x :$ y
```

The definition of smart constructors can be automated with appSym from Syntactic. The following definitions of lit₃ and add₃ are equivalent to the ones above:

```
lit₃ = appSym ∘ Lit₃
add₃ = appSym Add₃
```

A constraint (Lit₃ :<: dom) can be read as "dom contains Lit₃". That is, dom should be a co-product chain of the general form (... :+: Lit₃ :+: ...).

The fact that we have now achieved a modular language can be seen by noting that the definitions of Lit₃/lit₃ and Add₃/add₃ are *completely independent*, and could easily be in separate modules. Any number of additional constructs can be added in a similar way.

---

[2] The original Data Types à la Carte uses a combination of type-level fixed-points and co-products to achieve open data types. Syntactic only adopts the co-products, and uses the AST type instead of fixed-points.

2.3 Syntactic Sugar

It is not very convenient to require all embedded programs to have the type AST. First of all, one might want to hide implementation details by defining a closed language:

```
newtype Expr4 a = Expr4 {unExpr4 :: ASTF NumDomain3 a}
```

Secondly, it is sometimes desirable to use more "high-level" or domain specific representations as long as these representations have a correspondence to an AST.

```
data Pair a where
  Pair :: Pair (a :→ b :→ Full (a,b))
data Select a where
  Sel1 :: Select ((a,b) :→ Full a)
  Sel2 :: Select ((a,b) :→ Full b)
```

Such high-level types are referred to as "syntactic sugar". Syntactic sugar is defined by the class below.

```
class Typeable (Internal a) ⇒ Syntactic a dom | a → dom where
    type Internal a
    desugar :: a → ASTF dom (Internal a)
    sugar   :: ASTF dom (Internal a) → a

instance Typeable a ⇒ Syntactic (ASTF dom a) dom where
    type Internal (ASTF dom a) = a
    desugar = id
    sugar   = id
```

In the Syntactic class the associated type Internal is a type function from the (sugared) user visible type a to its internal representation in the AST. Note that this type function does not need to be injective. It is possible to have several syntactic sugar types sharing the same internal representation.

As a simple example, the instances for Expr4 and (,) would look as follows:

```
instance Typeable a ⇒ Syntactic (Expr4 a) NumDomain3 where
    type Internal (Expr4 a) = a
    desugar = unExpr4
    sugar   = Expr4

instance (Pair :<: dom, Select :<: dom, Syntactic a dom, Syntactic b dom) ⇒
    Syntactic (a,b) dom where
      type Internal (a,b) = (Internal a, Internal b)
      desugar = uncurry $ sugarSym Pair
      sugar a = (sugarSym Sel1 a, sugarSym Sel2 a)
```

The sugarSym function from Syntactic extends the appSym function with support for syntactic sugar. Thus, the following declarations are equivalent:

```
pair1 a b = sugarSym Pair a b
pair2 a b = sugar $ appSym Pair (desugar a) (desugar b)
```

3 Monads in Syntactic

Monads, popularized by Wadler [15], provide ways of adding impure computations to languages with otherwise pure semantics. Such impure computations – effects – are desired when implementing functions that for performance require destructive updates. In this section we will show how to add an embedding of monadic computations to Syntactic.

As with other constructs in Syntactic, the monad embedding consists of two parts: a deep embedding representing the core syntax terms, and a set of library functions providing the programmer interface. To enable the use of Haskell's do-notation and existing monadic combinators together with DSL programs, the programmer interface is built on top of the Haskell continuation monad Cont (see section 3.2).

3.1 Deep Embedding

Monads in Haskell are types that are members of the Monad type class.

```
class Monad m where
    return :: a    → m a
    (>>=)  :: m a → (a → m b) → m b
    (>>)   :: m a → m b → m b
    fail   :: String → m a
```

This type class can be represented in Syntactic by the GADT below.[3]

```
data MONAD m a where
    Return :: MONAD m (a   :→ Full (m a))
    Bind   :: MONAD m (m a :→ (a → m b) :→ Full (m b))
    Then   :: MONAD m (m a :→ m b        :→ Full (m b))
```

The constructors are parameterized over the embedded monad m so that MONAD can represent different monads. An example of one monad is given in section 4.

As usual, we use appSym to turn the monad symbols into AST constructors.

```
ret = appSym Return
thn = appSym Then
```

However, Bind requires special care. A straightforward definition using appSym does not give us a very satisfying type:

```
bnd :: (MONAD m :<: dom, Typeable1 m, Typeable a, Typeable b)
    ⇒ ASTF dom (m a) → ASTF dom (a → m b) → ASTF dom (m b)
bnd = appSym Bind
```

The problem is the second argument. This is an expression that computes a function – but we do not have a way to construct such expressions. The solution chosen in Syntactic is to use *higher-order abstract syntax* (HOAS) [11] as a means to embed functions in a syntax tree, see listing 2.

---

[3] We omit the method fail, since we do not want to transfer its functionality to the embedded language. Exceptions can be implemented separately using the monadic support presented in this paper.

```
data HOLambda ctx dom a where
    HOLambda :: (Typeable a, Typeable b, Sat ctx a)
               ⇒ (ASTF (HODomain ctx dom) a → ASTF (HODomain ctx dom) b)
               → HOLambda ctx dom (Full (a → b))

type HODomain ctx dom = HOLambda ctx dom :+: Variable ctx :+: dom

lambda :: (Typeable a, Typeable b, Sat ctx a)
        ⇒ (ASTF (HODomain ctx dom) a → ASTF (HODomain ctx dom) b)
        → ASTF (HODomain ctx dom) (a → b)
lambda = appSym ∘ HOLambda

class Sat ctx a where
    data Witness ctx a
    witness :: Witness ctx a

instance ( Syntactic a (HODomain ctx dom), Syntactic b (HODomain ctx dom)
         , Sat ctx (Internal a)) ⇒
    Syntactic (a → b) (HODomain ctx dom) where
        type Internal (a → b) = Internal a → Internal b
        desugar f = lambda (desugar ∘ f ∘ sugar)
```

Listing 2. Higher-Order Abstract Syntax in Syntactic

To make a smart constructor based on HOAS for `Bind`, we first have to wrap the function argument with the combinator `lambda`:

```
bnd :: (MONAD m :<: dom, Typeable a, Typeable b, Typeable1 m, Sat ctx a)
     ⇒ ASTF (HODomain ctx dom) (m a)
     → (ASTF (HODomain ctx dom) a → ASTF (HODomain ctx dom) (m b))
     → ASTF (HODomain ctx dom) (m b)
bnd k f = appSym Bind k (lambda f)
```

Note that the second argument of `bnd` is an ordinary Haskell function from AST to AST, which leads to a type much closer to that of the ordinary (>>=) operator. Using the `Syntactic (a → b)` instance `bnd` can be expressed as `bnd = sugarSym Bind`.

The `Sat` class is used to parameterize over class constraints by associating them with a type `ctx`. This technique is inspired by restricted data types [9]. While the `Sat` class is not important in the implementation of monads, it is included in this paper to complete the presentation of HOAS in Syntactic.

The smart constructors – `ret`, `thn` and `bnd` – can be used to implement generic monad combinators like for example `liftM`.

```
-- Haskell implementation of liftM
liftM :: (Monad m) ⇒ (a → r) → m a → m r
liftM f m = do { x ← m; return (f x) }

-- Syntactic (deep) implementation of liftM
liftM_{deep} :: (MONAD m :<: dom, Typeable1 m, Typeable a, Typeable r, Sat ctx a)
             ⇒ (ASTF (HODomain ctx dom) a → ASTF (HODomain ctx dom) r)
             → ASTF (HODomain ctx dom) (m a) → ASTF (HODomain ctx dom) (m r)
liftM_{deep} f m = m 'bnd' λx → ret (f x)
```

Note how the use of higher-order syntax allows us to use an ordinary λ-abstraction to construct the continuation argument to `bnd`.

It would of course be nice if we could do without `liftM`$_{deep}$ and just use `liftM` for embedded programs. However, this is not directly possible, since we cannot make `AST` an instance of the `Monad` class. In the following sections, we will give a solution to this problem.

3.2   User Interface

For the monad extension, we wanted to use Haskell's existing `Monad` class as the interface. A `Monad` instance is valuable since it gives access to a wealth of combinators for monadic expressions and to the convenient `do`-notation.

A naive, but incorrect, implementation of the `Monad` instance is:

```
newtype Mon ctx dom m a = Mon { unMon :: ASTF (HODomain ctx dom) (m a) }


-- Incorrect implementation
instance (MONAD m :<: dom) ⇒ Monad (Mon ctx dom m) where
    return a = Mon $ ret a
    ma >>= f = Mon $ unMon ma 'bnd' (unMon ∘ f)
    ma >> mb = Mon $ unMon ma 'thn' unMon mb
```

However, that instance does not type-check for any of the methods. Consider (`>>=`) in Haskell, which has the type `Monad m ⇒ m a → (a → m b) → m b`. That signature is incompatible with the signature of the suggested implementation:

```
(MONAD m :<: dom, Sat ctx a, Typeable1 m, Typeable a, Typeable b)
⇒ Mon ctx dom m a
→ (ASTF (HODomain ctx dom) a → Mon ctx dom m b)
→ Mon ctx dom m b
```

This signature has two problems: (1) It constrains the type variables `a` and `b`, which are required to be parametrically polymorphic by (`>>=`), and (2) the value passed to the continuation has type `ASTF ... a` rather than just `a`, which would be required by (`>>=`).

A way around this problem would be to use a restricted monad [9]. However, such a solution would be incompatible with existing monad libraries in Haskell. Furthermore, it is not possible to use `do`-notation with restricted monads without the pervasive language extension `RebindableSyntax`.

3.3   Continuation Monad Wrapper

To work around the first problem above and make the parameter `a` polymorphic again, we introduce a continuation monad wrapper around the `AST`.

```
newtype MS ctx dom m a = MS { unMS :: forall r. Typeable r
                                    ⇒ Cont (ASTF (HODomain ctx dom) (m r)) a }
```

Here the Haskell Continuation Monad holds expressions that will eventually result in a syntax tree over the embedded monad `m`.

```
instance ( MONAD m :<: dom, Typeable1 m, Sat ctx (Internal a)
         , Syntactic a (HODomain ctx dom)
         ) ⇒
    Syntactic (MS ctx dom m a) (HODomain ctx dom) where
        type Internal (MS ctx dom m a) = m (Internal a)
        desugar a = runCont (unMS a) (sugarSym Return)
        sugar   a = MS $ cont (sugarSym Bind a)
```

Listing 3. Syntactic sugar for monads

The parameter `a` is polymorphic since the constraints imposed by the AST
type only affect the result `r` of the continuation monad. By encapsulating the
continuation monad in a `newtype` we can make the type parameter `r` universally
quantified and prevent it from leaking out to clients.

The `Monad` instance can be written as usual for a `newtype`.

```
instance Monad (MS ctx dom m) where
    return a = MS $ return a
    ma >>= f = MS $ unMS ma >>= unMS ∘ f
```

There is still one piece of the puzzle missing. While the `Monad` instance gives
us access the `do`-notation and monadic combinators, it is just a continuation
monad. However, since the side effect of our `MS` monad is to build an AST, we
need to convert each action into its corresponding syntax element. The syntactic
sugar in the next section will automate the process.

3.4   Monads as Syntactic Sugar

With the `Syntactic` instance in listing 3 we can convert between monadic computations and syntax trees.

The function `desugar` can build a syntax tree from an expression in the `MS`
monad by running the contuation-passing computation and returns the resulting
tree using `sugarSym Return` as the final continuation.

To construct a continuation-passing computation, `sugar` binds the result of
previous computations using `sugarSym Bind`.

As an illustration of how the continuation monad and the `Syntactic` instance
work together, we consider the following reduction of the expression

```
λx → desugar $ MS $ return x
```

Inline `desugar` from the `Syntactic (MS ...)` instance

```
λx → runCont (unMS (MS $ return x)) (sugarSym Return)
```

Simplify `unMS/MS` and inline `runCont`

```
λx → sugarSym Return x
```

Note that `runCont` applied the final continuation to the result of the computation
`return x`. We continue the reduction by inlining the definition of `sugarSym`.

```
λx → sugar $ appSym Return (desugar x)
```

Recall that for `Syntactic (ASTF dom a)` the definition of `sugar` is `id`.

```
λx → appSym Return (desugar x)
```

By inlining the definition of `appSym` the reduction is complete

```
λx → Sym (inj Return) :$ desugar x
```

Further examples of the sugared syntax will be shown in the context of the
`Mutable` monad in section 4.

4   Mutable Monad

With the monad feature added to Syntactic, it is now possible to extend it
further and embed specific monads into the AST type. To address our problem
with destructive updates we choose to implement a subset of the IO monad
from Haskell and the accompanying `Data.IORef` representing *mutable references*
in the IO monad. It is also possible to represent the mutable monad using the
state transformer monad from `Control.Monad.ST` and mutable references using
`Data.STRef`. The run function (`runST :: (forall s. ST s a) → a`) of the ST monad
has a universally quantified parameter `s` ensuring that the state does not leak out
of the monad, which increases safety. However, that implementation is slightly
more verbose and IO is sufficient to show mutability for this paper.

We add two constructs to our domain:

- `Mutable` represents a run function that will evaluate the mutations in sequence, returning the result as a pure value.
- `MutableRef` provides initialization, query and update of mutable references.

```
data Mutable a where
    Run    :: Mutable (IO a :→ Full a)

data MutableRef a where
    NewRef :: MutableRef (a :→ Full (IO (IORef a)))
    GetRef :: MutableRef (IORef a :→ Full (IO a))
    SetRef :: MutableRef (IORef a :→ a :→ Full (IO ()))

type MyDomain₆ = MONAD IO :+: Mutable :+: MutableRef :+: NumDomain₃
```

Then we define a monad `M` for mutable updates as a specialisation of the `MS` type
and close the language under `Data` to make type signatures nicer.

```
type M a = MS Poly MyDomain₆ IO a

newtype Data a = D { unD :: ASTF (HODomain Poly MyDomain₆) a }

instance Typeable a ⇒ Syntactic (Data a) (HODomain Poly MyDomain₆) where
    type Internal (Data a) = a
    desugar = unD
    sugar   = D
```

The context `Poly` is defined in `Syntactic` and denotes a fully polymorphic constraint.

Equipped with the `Syntactic` instance in listing 3, we create smart constructors and combinators with friendly types.

```
runMutable₆ :: (Typeable a) ⇒ M (Data a) → Data a
runMutable₆ = sugarSym Run

newRef₆ :: (Typeable a) ⇒ Data a → M (Data (IORef a))
newRef₆ = sugarSym NewRef

getRef₆ :: (Typeable a) ⇒ Data (IORef a) → M (Data a)
getRef₆ = sugarSym GetRef

setRef₆ :: (Typeable a) ⇒ Data (IORef a) → Data a → M (Data ())
setRef₆ = sugarSym SetRef

modifyRef₆ :: (Typeable a) ⇒ Data (IORef a) → (Data a → Data a) → M (Data ())
modifyRef₆ r f = getRef₆ r >>= setRef₆ r ∘ f
```

We can now rewrite the example function `iter` from the introduction, making use of mutable references to provide destructive updates. Note, to be able to use the Feldspar compiler, the example below is written using types and functions from Feldspar.

```
iter₆ :: (Type a) ⇒ Length → (Data a → Data a) → Data a → Data a
iter₆ n f i = runMutable $ do
    r ← newRef i
    go n r
    getRef r
  where
    go 0 _ = return ()
    go j r = modifyRef r f >> go (j-1) r

ex₆ :: Data Int32 → Data Int32
ex₆ = iter₆ 4 (λx → x + x)
```

Again, using the Feldspar Compiler we can generate the code by evaluating `icompile ex₆`. By virtue of the mutable references the calculation is now done in-place without the need for storing intermediate values.

```
void ex₆(int32_t v0, int32_t * out)
{
    int32_t e0;

    e0 = v0;
    e0 = (e0 + e0);
    e0 = (e0 + e0);
    e0 = (e0 + e0);
    (* out) = (e0 + e0);
}
```

5   Conclusion

We have shown an extension to the Syntactic library, enabling the representation of monadic computations in the generic AST type. Using the monad together with the constructs Mutable and MutableRef, we can model expressions with mutable references. By embedding the monads in a continuation monad we avoid the problem of creating a Monad instance, unlocking access to Haskell do-notation and monadic combinators. That the extensions were possible without changing the underlying Syntactic library or the target Feldspar language is a showcase of the modularity of these languages.

The monadic constructs and combinators in this paper are not specific to one language, but reusable by any language built using Syntactic, making Syntactic applicable for a wider range of EDSLs.

The monadic constructs in Syntactic can be reused to implement other monads and interfaces. The mutable arrays in Feldspar are similar to the mutable references presented in this paper.

We have also extended Feldspar with an experimental implementation of the Par monad from Control.Monad.Par, which is a monad for *deterministic parallelism* [10]. Future work includes studying the integration of different scheduling algorithms and code generation.

6   Related Work

To the best of our knowledge, the technique of embedding a monad syntacticly into an extensible EDSL presented in this paper is a novel technique. While others have embedded monads into the continuation monad, the technique has not been used in conjunction with Data Types à la Carte to define EDSLs.

Swierstra shows how to implement free monads on top of his Data Types à la Carte [13]. By limiting the available operations, the available side effects can be controlled at the type level. Since our work builds on Data Types à la Carte, we get the same control over available side effects. However, Swierstra's monad is not applicable to deeply embedded DSLs, as it does not include a deep embedding of the monadic combinators return and (>>=).

Hughes develops *restricted monads* in [9]. However, he does not create a proper Monad instance, but instead a WfMonad class which is parameterized on a dictionary. This makes the method incompatible with Haskell's do-notation and existing monad combinators.

Acknowledgements. This research is funded by Ericsson, Vetenskapsrådet, and the Swedish Foundation for Strategic Research. The Feldspar project is an initiative of and is partially funded by Ericsson Software Research and is a collaboration between Chalmers, Ericsson and ELTE University.

References

1. Feldspar compiler, http://hackage.haskell.org/package/feldspar-compiler
2. Feldspar language, http://hackage.haskell.org/package/feldspar-language
3. Syntactic library, http://hackage.haskell.org/package/syntactic
4. Axelsson, E., Claessen, K., Sheeran, M., Svenningsson, J., Engdal, D., Persson, A.: The Design and Implementation of Feldspar – an Embedded Language for Digital Signal Processing. In: Hage, J., Morazán, M.T. (eds.) IFL. LNCS, vol. 6647, pp. 121–136. Springer, Heidelberg (2011)
5. Axelsson, E., Dévai, G., Horváth, Z., Keijzer, K., Lyckegård, B., Persson, A., Sheeran, M., Svenningsson, J., Vajda, A.: Feldspar: A Domain Specific Language for Digital Signal Processing algorithms. In: Proc. Eighth ACM/IEEE International Conference on Formal Methods and Models for Codesign, MemoCode. IEEE Computer Society (2010)
6. Axelsson, E., Sheeran, M.: Feldspar: Application and Implementation. In: Zsók, V., Horváth, Z., Plasmeijer, R. (eds.) CEFP 2012. LNCS, vol. 7241, pp. 402–439. Springer, Heidelberg (2012)
7. Elliott, C., Finne, S., de Moor, O.: Compiling embedded languages. Journal of Functional Programming 13(3), 455–481 (2003)
8. Hudak, P.: Modular domain specific languages and tools. In: ICSR 1998: Proceedings of the 5th International Conference on Software Reuse, p. 134. IEEE Computer Society, Washington, DC (1998)
9. Hughes, J.: Restricted data types in Haskell. In: Proceedings of the 1999 Haskell Workshop (1999)
10. Marlow, S., Newton, R., Peyton Jones, S.: A monad for deterministic parallelism. In: Proceedings of the 4th ACM Symposium on Haskell, Haskell 2011, pp. 71–82. ACM, New York (2011), http://doi.acm.org/10.1145/2034675.2034685
11. Pfenning, F., Elliott, C.: Higher-order abstract syntax. In: Proceedings of the ACM SIGPLAN 1988 Conference on Programming Language Design and Implementation, PLDI 1988, pp. 199–208. ACM (1988)
12. Schrijvers, T., Peyton Jones, S., Sulzmann, M., Vytiniotis, D.: Complete and decidable type inference for GADTs. In: Proc. 14th ACM SIGPLAN International Conference on Functional Programming, pp. 341–352. ACM (2009)
13. Swierstra, W.: Data types à la carte. Journal of Functional Programming 18(4), 423–436 (2008)
14. Wadler, P.: The expression problem (1998), http://www.daimi.au.dk/~madst/tool/papers/expression.txt
15. Wadler, P.: Comprehending monads. In: Proceedings of the 1990 ACM Conference on LISP and Functional Programming, LFP 1990, pp. 61–78. ACM, New York (1990), http://doi.acm.org/10.1145/91556.91592

From Stack Traces to Lazy Rewriting Sequences

Stephen Chang[1], Eli Barzilay[1], John Clements[2], and Matthias Felleisen[1]

[1] Northeastern University, Boston, Massachusetts, USA
[2] California Polytechnic State University, San Luis Obispo, California, USA

Abstract. Reasoning about misbehaving lazy functional programs can be confusing, particularly for novice programmers. Unfortunately, the complicated nature of laziness also renders most debugging tools ineffective at clarifying this confusion. In this paper, we introduce a new lazy debugging tool for novice programmers, an algebraic stepper that presents computation as a sequence of parallel rewriting steps. Parallel program rewriting represents sharing accurately and enables debugging at the level of source syntax, minimizing the presentation of low-level details or the effects of distorting transformations that are typical for other lazy debuggers. Semantically, our rewriting system represents a compromise between Launchbury's store-based semantics and an axiomatic description of lazy computation as sharing-via-parameters. Finally, we prove the correctness of our tool by showing that the stepper's run-time machinery reconstructs the expected lazy rewriting sequence.

Keywords: lazy programming, debugging, lazy lambda calculus.

1   How Functional Programming Works

While laziness enables modularization [13], it unfortunately also reduces a programmer's ability to predict the ordering of evaluations. As long as programs work, this cognitive dissonance poses no problems. When a lazy program exhibits erroneous behavior, however, reasoning about the code becomes confusing, especially for novices. A programmer may look to a debugger for help, but the nature of laziness affects these tools as well, often forcing them to present evaluation in a distorted manner, with some debuggers ignoring or hiding laziness altogether.

In this paper, we present a new debugging tool for students of lazy programming, an algebraic stepper for Lazy Racket that explains computation via a novel rewriting semantics. Our key idea is to use substitution in conjunction with selective parallel reduction to simulate shared reductions. Shared expressions are identified semantically with labels and are reduced simultaneously in the program source. This enables a clean syntactic presentation of lazy evaluation that eliminates many of the drawbacks of previous syntax-based tools. Showing computation as a rewriting of the program source means that we do not need to apply complicated preprocessing transformations nor do we need extraneous low-level details to explain evaluation. In addition, our experience with the DrRacket stepper [6] for call-by-value Racket, as well as studies of other researchers [12,21], confirm that students find syntax-based tools more intuitive

A. Gill and J. Hage (Eds.): IFL 2011, LNCS 7257, pp. 100–115, 2012.

to use than graphical ones. This makes sense because programmers are already used to reasoning about their progams in terms of the source code.

Our rewriting semantics is also the appropriate basis for a correctness proof of the stepper. For the proof, we use a Haskell-like, thunk-based lazy language model, further enriched with continuation marks [6]—which help reconstruct the stepper sequence—and then exploit a proof strategy from Clements [5] to show that the implementation language bisimulates our lazy rewriting semantics.

Section 2 briefly introduces Lazy Racket and our stepper with examples. Section 3 presents our novel lazy rewriting system. Section 4 summarizes the implementation of Lazy Racket and presents a model of the lazy stepper, and Section 5 presents a correctness proof for the stepper.

2   Lazy Racket and Its Stepper

Lazy Racket programs are a series of definitions and expressions that refer to those definitions. Here is a simplistic example:

```
(define (f x) (+ x x))
(f (+ 1 2))
```

A programmer invokes the Lazy Racket stepper from the DrRacket IDE. Running the stepper displays the rewriting sequence for the current program. The steps are displayed aynchronously so the programmer can begin debugging before evaluation completes. Figure 1 shows a series of screenshots for the rewriting sequence of the above program. A green box highlights redexes on the left-hand side of a step and a purple box highlights contractums on the right-hand side.[1] The programmer can navigate the rewriting sequence in either the forward or backward direction.

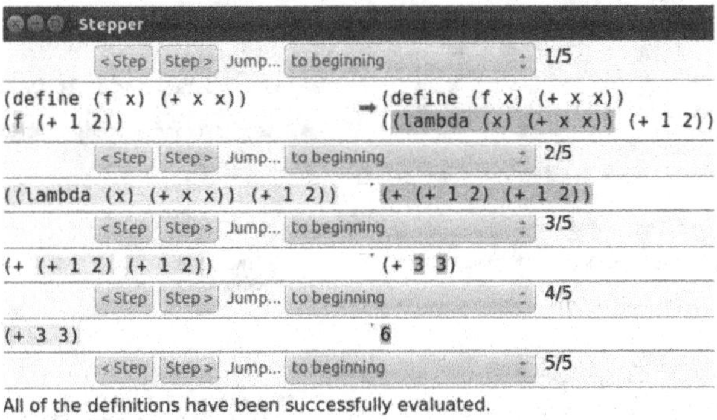

Fig. 1. Lazy Stepper, Example 1

In step 2, since arguments in an application are delayed, an unevaluated argument replaces each instance of the variable x in the function body. In step 3, since

---

[1] The tool utilizes colors though the printed figures may be in black and white.

arithmetic primitives are eager, the program requires the value of the argument for the first addition operand so it is forced. Simultaneously, all other shared instances of the argument are reduced as well. That is, *the stepper explains evaluation as an algebraic process using a form of parallel program rewriting.* Since the second operand refers to the same argument as the first one, by the time evaluation of the program requires a value for the second operand, a result is already available because the computed value of the first operand was saved. In short, no argument evaluation is repeated, satisfying the criteria for lazy evaluation.

A second example involves infinite lists:

```
(define (add-one x) (+ x 1))
(define nats (cons 1 (map add-one nats)))
(+ (second nats) (third nats))
```

The rewriting sequence for this program appears in Figure 2. Only the essential steps are shown. In step 4, since `cons` is lazy, its arguments are not evaluated until needed. However, while the contents of all thunks in the previous example were visible to the programmer, here an opaque `<Thunk#0>` represents the rest of `nats` because `nats` is currently being evaluated. The evaluation of `second` forces the `map` expression to produce a `cons` of two additional opaque thunks, `<Thunk#1>` and `<Thunk#2>`, because `map` is a libary function whose source is unknown. In step 5, `second` extracts `<Thunk#1>` from the list. In step 6, evaluation requires the value of `<Thunk#1>`, so it is forced. The ellipses on the left indicate forcing of an opaque thunk. In steps 6 and 7, the stepper simultaneously updates the `nats` definition with the result. It highlights only shared terms that are part of the current redex. This cleans up the presentation of the rewriting steps and makes lazy evaluation easier to follow in our tool. The remaining steps show the similar evaluation of the other addition operand and are thus omitted.

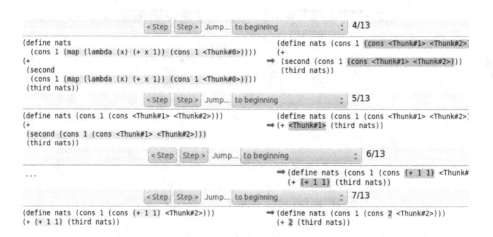

Fig. 2. Lazy Stepper, Example 2

3 Lazy Racket Semantics

Our key theoretical innovation is the lazy rewriting system, λ_{LR}, which specifies the exact nature of steps for our tool. The syntax of λ_{LR} is identical to the core of most functional programming languages and includes integers, strings, booleans, variables, abstractions, applications, primitives, lists, and a conditional:[2]

$$e = n \mid s \mid b \mid x \mid \lambda x.e \mid (e\ e) \mid (\mathtt{cons}\ e\ e) \mid \mathtt{null} \mid (p^1\ e) \mid (p^2\ e\ e) \mid (\mathtt{if}\ e\ e\ e)$$

$$n \in \mathbb{Z}, \quad s \in \mathrm{Strings}, \quad b = \mathtt{true} \mid \mathtt{false}, \quad p^1 = \mathtt{first} \mid \mathtt{rest}, \quad p^2 = + \mid - \mid * \mid /$$

To specify the semantics of λ_{LR}, we first extend e by adding a new expression:

$$e^{\mathrm{LR}} = e \mid e^{\mathrm{LR}\ell} \qquad \ell \in \mathrm{Labels}$$

The "labeled" expression, $e^{\mathrm{LR}\ell}$, consists of a tag ℓ and a subexpression e^{LR}. Labeled expressions are not part of the language syntax but are necessary for evaluation. Rewriting a labeled expression triggers the simultaneous rewriting of all other expressions with the same label. In our language, we require all expressions with the same label ℓ to be identical. We call this consistent labeling:

Definition 1. *A program is consistently labeled if, for all ℓ_1, ℓ_2, e_1^{LR}, e_2^{LR}, if $e_1^{\mathrm{LR}\ell_1}$ and $e_2^{\mathrm{LR}\ell_2}$ are two subexpressions in a program, and $\ell_1 = \ell_2$, then $e_1^{\mathrm{LR}} = e_2^{\mathrm{LR}}$.*

3.1 Rewriting Rules

To further formulate a semantics, we define the notion of values:

$$v = n \mid s \mid b \mid \lambda x.e^{\mathrm{LR}} \mid \mathtt{null} \mid (\mathtt{cons}\ e^{\mathrm{LR}\ell}\ e^{\mathrm{LR}\ell}) \mid v^\ell$$

Numbers, strings, booleans, λs, $\mathtt{null}$, and $\mathtt{cons}$ expressions where each element is labeled, are values. In addition, any value tagged with labels is also a value.

In the rewriting of λ_{LR} programs, evaluation contexts determine which part of the program to rewrite next. Evaluation contexts are expressions where a hole $[\,]$ replaces one subexpression:

$$E = [\,] \mid (E\ e^{\mathrm{LR}}) \mid (p^2\ E\ e^{\mathrm{LR}}) \mid (p^2\ v\ E) \mid (p^1\ E) \mid (\mathtt{if}\ E\ e^{\mathrm{LR}}\ e^{\mathrm{LR}}) \mid E^\ell$$

The $(E\ e^{\mathrm{LR}})$ context indicates that the operator in an application must be evaluated so that application may proceed. The p^1 and p^2 contexts indicate that primitives p^i are strict in all argument positions and are evaluated left to right. The $\mathtt{if}$ context dictates strict evaluation of only the test expression. Finally, the E^ℓ context dictates that a redex search goes under labeled expressions.

Evaluation of a λ_{LR} program proceeds according to the program rewriting system in Figure 3. It has two phases. A rewriting step begins when the progam is partitioned into a redex and an evaluation context and the redex is contracted according to the phase 1 rules. If the redex does not occur under a label, it is the only contracted part of the program. If the redex does occur under a label, then in phase 2, all other instances of that labeled expression are contracted in the same

---

[2] Cyclic structures are omitted for space but should be straightforward to add, see [9].

Phase 1:		$E[e^{\text{LR}}] \xmapsto{\ phase1\ }_{\text{LR}} E[e^{\text{LR}'}]$	
where:	e^{LR}	$e^{\text{LR}'}$	
	$((\lambda x.e_1^{\text{LR}})^{\vec{\ell}}\ e_2^{\text{LR}})$	$e_1^{\text{LR}}\{x := e_2^{\text{LR}\,\ell_1}\},\ \textbf{fresh}\ \ell_1$	β_{LR}
	$(p^2\ n_1{}^{\vec{\ell}}\ n_2{}^{\vec{\ell}})$	$(\delta\ (p^2\ n_1\ n_2))$	Prim
	$(\textbf{cons}\ e_1^{\text{LR}}\ e_2^{\text{LR}}),\ e_1^{\text{LR}}\text{ or } e_2^{\text{LR}}\text{ unlabeled}$	$(\textbf{cons}\ e_1^{\text{LR}\,\ell_1}\ e_2^{\text{LR}\,\ell_2}),\ \textbf{fresh}\ \ell_1, \ell_2$	Cons
	$((\textbf{first}\ \vert\ \textbf{rest})\ (\textbf{cons}\ e_1^{\text{LR}}\ e_2^{\text{LR}})^{\vec{\ell}})$	$e_1^{\text{LR}} \mid e_2^{\text{LR}}$	First | Rest
	$(\textbf{if}\ (\textbf{true}\ \vert\ \textbf{false})^{\vec{\ell}}\ e_1^{\text{LR}}\ e_2^{\text{LR}})$	$e_1^{\text{LR}} \mid e_2^{\text{LR}}$	If-t | If-f

Phase 2: If redex occurs under (nearest) label ℓ, where $E[\,] = E_1[(E_2[\,])^{\ell}]$, then:

$$E[e^{\text{LR}'}] \xmapsto{\ phase2\ }_{\text{LR}} E[e^{\text{LR}'}]\{\!\{\ell \Leftarrow E_2[e^{\text{LR}'}]\}\!\}$$

Fig. 3. The λ_{LR} Rewriting System

way. In phase 2, the evaluation context is further subdivided as $E[] = E_1[(E_2[\,])^{\ell}]$ where ℓ is the label nearest the redex, E_1 is the context around the ℓ-labeled expression, and E_2 is the context under label ℓ. Thus E_2 contains no additional labels on the path from the root to the hole. An "update" function performs the parallel reduction, where the notation $e_1^{\text{LR}}\{\!\{\ell \Leftarrow e_2^{\text{LR}}\}\!\}$ means "in e_1^{LR}, replace expressions under label ℓ with e_2^{LR}." The function is formally defined as follows:

$$e_1^{\text{LR}\,\ell}\{\!\{\ell \Leftarrow e_2^{\text{LR}}\}\!\} = e_2^{\text{LR}\,\ell}$$
$$e_1^{\text{LR}\,\ell_1}\{\!\{\ell_2 \Leftarrow e_2^{\text{LR}}\}\!\} = (e_1^{\text{LR}}\{\!\{\ell_2 \Leftarrow e_2^{\text{LR}}\}\!\})^{\ell_1},\ \ell_1 \neq \ell_2$$
$$(\lambda x.e_1^{\text{LR}})\{\!\{\ell \Leftarrow e_2^{\text{LR}}\}\!\} = \lambda x.(e_1^{\text{LR}}\{\!\{\ell \Leftarrow e_2^{\text{LR}}\}\!\})$$
$$(e_1^{\text{LR}}\ e_2^{\text{LR}})\{\!\{\ell \Leftarrow e_3^{\text{LR}}\}\!\} = (e_1^{\text{LR}}\{\!\{\ell \Leftarrow e_3^{\text{LR}}\}\!\}\ e_2^{\text{LR}}\{\!\{\ell \Leftarrow e_3^{\text{LR}}\}\!\})$$
$$(\_\ e_1^{\text{LR}}\ e_2^{\text{LR}}\ldots)\{\!\{\ell \Leftarrow e_3^{\text{LR}}\}\!\} = (\_\ e_1^{\text{LR}}\{\!\{\ell \Leftarrow e_3^{\text{LR}}\}\!\}\ e_2^{\text{LR}}\{\!\{\ell \Leftarrow e_3^{\text{LR}}\}\!\}\ldots)$$

In Figure 3, the β_{LR} rule specifies that function application occurs before the evaluation of arguments. To remember where expressions originate, the argument receives an unused label ℓ_1 before substitution is performed. The notation $e^{\text{LR}\,\vec{\ell}}$ represents an expression wrapped in one or more labels. During a rewriting step, labels are discarded from values because no further reduction is possible. Binary p^2 primitive applications are strict in their arguments, as seen in the Prim rule. The δ function interprets these primitives and is defined in the standard way (division by 0 results in a stuck state). The Cons rule shows that, if either argument is unlabeled, both arguments are wrapped with new labels. Adding an extra label around an already labeled expression does not affect evaluation because parallel updating only uses the innermost label. The First and Rest rules extract the appropriate component from a **cons** cell, and the If-t and If-f rules choose the first or second branch of the **if** expression.

A program rewriting step $\longmapsto_{\text{LR}}$ is the composition of $\xmapsto{\ phase1\ }_{\text{LR}}$ and $\xmapsto{\ phase2\ }_{\text{LR}}$. Program rewriting preserves the consistent labeling property.

Lemma 1. *If $e_1^{\text{LR}} \longmapsto_{\text{LR}} e_2^{\text{LR}}$ and e_1^{LR} is consistently labeled, then e_2^{LR} is as well.*

The rewriting rules are deterministic because any expression e^{LR} can be uniquely partitioned into an evaluation context and a redex. If e_1^{LR} rewrites to a expression e_2^{LR}, then e_1^{LR} rewrites to e_2^{LR} in a canonical manner. Thus an evaluator is defined:

$$\text{eval}_{LR}(e) \begin{cases} v, & \text{if } e \longmapsto\!\!\!\!\twoheadrightarrow_{LR} v \\ \bot, & \text{if, for all } e \longmapsto\!\!\!\!\twoheadrightarrow_{LR} e_1^{LR}, e_1^{LR} \longmapsto_{LR} e_2^{LR} \\ \text{error}, & \text{if } e \longmapsto\!\!\!\!\twoheadrightarrow_{LR} e_1^{LR}, e_1^{LR} \notin v, \nexists e_2^{LR} \text{ such that } e_1^{LR} \longmapsto_{LR} e_2^{LR} \end{cases}$$

where $\longmapsto\!\!\!\!\twoheadrightarrow_{LR}$ is the reflexive-transitive closure of $\longmapsto_{LR}$.

4 Lazy Stepper Implementation

Figure 4 summarizes the software architecture of our stepper. The first row depicts a λ_{LR} Lazy Racket rewriting sequence. To construct this rewriting sequence, the stepper first macro-expands a Lazy Racket program to a plain Racket program with `delay` and `force`. Then, annotations are added to the expanded program such that executing it emits a series of output values representing stack traces. The stepper reconstructs the reduction sequence for the unannotated Racket program from these stack traces. Finally, this plain Racket reduction sequence is synthesized to the desired Lazy Racket rewriting sequence.

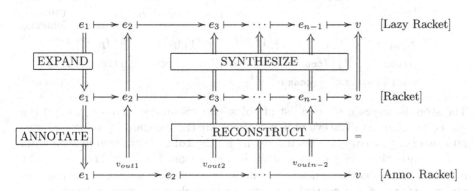

Fig. 4. Stepper Implementation Architecture

The correctness of the lazy stepper thus depends on two claims:

1. The reduction sequence of a plain Racket program can be reconstructed from the output produced by an annotated version of that program.
2. The rewriting sequence of a Lazy Racket program is equivalent to the reduction sequence of the corresponding Racket program, modulo macros.

The first point corresponds to the work of Clements [6] and is depicted by the bottom half of Figure 4. Indeed, the lazy stepper implementation mostly reuses the existing Racket stepper so we only explain the differences. The second point is depicted by the top half of Figure 4. The rest of the section formally presents the architecture in enough detail so that (1) our stepper can be implemented for any lazy programming language, and (2) so that we can prove its correctness.

4.1 Racket + delay/force

When the stepper is invoked on a Lazy Racket program, the source is first macro-expanded to a Racket program with delay and force strategically inserted. We model this latter language with λ_{DF}:

$$e^{\mathrm{RKT}} = n \mid s \mid b \mid x \mid \lambda x.e^{\mathrm{RKT}} \mid (e^{\mathrm{RKT}}\ e^{\mathrm{RKT}}) \mid (\mathtt{if}\ e^{\mathrm{RKT}}\ e^{\mathrm{RKT}}\ e^{\mathrm{RKT}}) \mid (\mathtt{cons}\ e^{\mathrm{RKT}}\ e^{\mathrm{RKT}}) \mid \mathtt{null}$$
$$\mid (p^1\ e^{\mathrm{RKT}}) \mid (p^2\ e^{\mathrm{RKT}}\ e^{\mathrm{RKT}}) \mid (\mathtt{delay}\ e^{\mathrm{RKT}}) \mid (\mathtt{force}\ e^{\mathrm{RKT}})$$

$$n \in \mathbb{Z}, \quad s \in \text{Strings}, \quad b = \mathtt{true} \mid \mathtt{false}, \quad p^1 = \mathtt{first} \mid \mathtt{rest}, \quad p^2 = + \mid - \mid * \mid /$$

The syntax of λ_{DF} is similar to λ_{LR} except that delay and force replace labeled expressions. A delay expression suspends evaluation of its argument in a thunk; applying force to a (nest of) thunk(s) evaluates it and memoizes the result.

The semantics of λ_{DF} combines the usual call-by-value world with store effects. We describe it with a CS machine [8]. The C stands for control string, and the S is a store. In our machine the control string may contain locations, i.e., references to delayed expressions in the store. In contrast to the standard CS machine, our store holds only delayed computations:

$$
\begin{array}{llll}
e^{\mathrm{DF}} = e^{\mathrm{RKT}} \mid \ell & \text{(Machine Expressions)} & c^{\mathrm{DF}} = E^{\mathrm{DF}}[e^{\mathrm{DF}}] & \text{(Control Strings)} \\
\mathcal{S}^{\mathrm{DF}} = \mathcal{P}_1^{\mathrm{DF}}, \dots, \mathcal{P}_n^{\mathrm{DF}} & \text{(Transition Sequences)} & \mathcal{P}^{\mathrm{DF}} = \langle c^{\mathrm{DF}}, \sigma \rangle & \text{(Machine States)} \\
\ell \in \text{Locations} & & \sigma = ((\ell, e^{\mathrm{DF}}), \dots) & \text{(Stores)} \\
& & & \text{(Evaluation Contexts)}
\end{array}
$$

$$E^{\mathrm{DF}} = [\,] \mid (E^{\mathrm{DF}}\ e^{\mathrm{DF}}) \mid (v^{\mathrm{DF}}\ E^{\mathrm{DF}}) \mid (\mathtt{if}\ E^{\mathrm{DF}}\ e^{\mathrm{DF}}\ e^{\mathrm{DF}}) \mid (p^2\ E^{\mathrm{DF}}\ e^{\mathrm{DF}}) \mid (p^2\ v^{\mathrm{DF}}\ E^{\mathrm{DF}})$$
$$\mid (\mathtt{cons}\ E^{\mathrm{DF}}\ e^{\mathrm{DF}}) \mid (\mathtt{cons}\ v^{\mathrm{DF}}\ E^{\mathrm{DF}}) \mid (p^1\ E^{\mathrm{DF}}) \mid (\mathtt{force}\ E^{\mathrm{DF}}) \mid (\mathtt{force}\ \ell\ E^{\mathrm{DF}})$$
$$v^{\mathrm{DF}} = n \mid s \mid b \mid \lambda x.e^{\mathrm{DF}} \mid (\mathtt{cons}\ v^{\mathrm{DF}}\ v^{\mathrm{DF}}) \mid \mathtt{null} \mid \ell \qquad \text{(Values)}$$

The store is represented as a list of pairs; ellipses means "zero or more of the preceding element". The evaluation contexts are the standard by-value contexts, plus two force contexts. The first resembles the force expression in a program and indicates the forcing of some arbitrary expression. The second force context is used when evaluating a delayed computation stored in location ℓ. Evaluation under a $(\mathtt{force}\ \ell\ [\,])$ context corresponds to evaluation under a label in λ_{LR}. This special second force context is non-syntactic, hence the need for defining separate machine expressions (e^{DF}) and control strings (c^{DF}) above.

The starting machine configuration for a Racket program e^{RKT} is $\langle e^{\mathrm{RKT}}, (\,) \rangle$ where the program is set as the control string and the store is initially empty. Evaluation stops when the control string is a value. Values are numbers, strings, booleans, abstractions, lists, or store locations. The CS machine transitions are specified in Figure 5. Every program e^{RKT} has a deterministic transition sequence because the left hand sides of all the transition rules are mutually exclusive and cover all possible control strings in the C register.

The by-value β_v transition is standard, as are the omitted transitions for if and the p^i primitive functions. The DELAY transition reduces a delay expression to an unused location ℓ and the suspended expression is saved at that location in the store. When the argument to a force expression is a location, the suspended expression at that location is retrieved from the store and plugged into a special

$$\longmapsto_{\mathrm{CS}}$$

$$\langle E^{\mathrm{DF}}[((\lambda x.e^{\mathrm{DF}})\ v^{\mathrm{DF}})], \sigma\rangle \quad \longmapsto_{\mathrm{CS}} \quad \langle E^{\mathrm{DF}}[e^{\mathrm{DF}}\{x := v^{\mathrm{DF}}\}], \sigma\rangle \quad \beta_v$$
$$\cdots$$
$$\langle E^{\mathrm{DF}}[(\mathtt{delay}\ e^{\mathrm{DF}})], \sigma\rangle \quad \longmapsto_{\mathrm{CS}}\ \langle E^{\mathrm{DF}}[\ell], \sigma[\![\ell \leftarrow e^{\mathrm{DF}}]\!]\rangle, \ell \notin \mathrm{dom}(\sigma)\ \ \mathrm{DELAY}$$
$$\langle E^{\mathrm{DF}}[(\mathtt{force}\ \ell)], \sigma\rangle \quad \longmapsto_{\mathrm{CS}}\ \langle E^{\mathrm{DF}}[(\mathtt{force}\ (\mathtt{force}\ \ell\ \sigma[\![\ell]\!]))], \sigma\rangle\ \ \mathrm{FORCE\text{-}DELAY}$$
$$\langle E^{\mathrm{DF}}[(\mathtt{force}\ \ell\ v^{\mathrm{DF}})], \sigma\rangle \quad \longmapsto_{\mathrm{CS}} \quad \langle E^{\mathrm{DF}}[v^{\mathrm{DF}}], \sigma[\![\ell \leftarrow v^{\mathrm{DF}}]\!]\rangle \qquad \mathrm{FORCE\text{-}UPDATE}$$
$$\langle E^{\mathrm{DF}}[(\mathtt{force}\ v^{\mathrm{DF}})], \sigma\rangle\ ,\ v^{\mathrm{DF}} \notin \mathrm{loc} \longmapsto_{\mathrm{CS}} \quad \langle E^{\mathrm{DF}}[v^{\mathrm{DF}}], \sigma\rangle \qquad\qquad \mathrm{FORCE\text{-}VAL}$$

Fig. 5. CS Machine Transitions

`force` evaluation context. This special context saves the store location of the forced expression so the store can be updated with the resulting value. The outer `force` context is retained in case there are nested `delay`s.

4.2   Continuation Marks

A stepper for a functional language needs access to the control stack of its evaluator to reconstruct the evaluation steps. One implementation technique is to grant complete, privileged access to the control stack. As Clements [6] argued, however, such privileged access is unnecessary and often undesirable, in part because the stepper would be tied to a specific language implementation.

Continuation marks enable the implementation of stack-accessing tools without granting privileged stack access. The stepper for Lazy Racket utilizes continuation marks to get a progam's stack trace and thus our implementation can be easily ported to any language that provides the two simple operations:

1. *store* a value in the current frame of the control stack,
2. *retrieve* all stored continuation marks.

The eager Racket stepper first annotates a source program with *store* and *retrieve* operations at appropriate points. Then, at each *retrieve* point, the stepper reconstructs a reduction step from the information in the continuation marks. The lazy stepper extends this model with `delay` and `force` constructs. The annotation and reconstruction functions are defined in Section 5.

4.3   Racket + delay/force + Continuation Marks

The language λ_{CM} extends λ_{DF} in a stratified manner and models the language for programs annotated with continuation marks:

$$e^{\mathrm{CM}} = e^{\mathrm{RKT}}\ |\ (\mathtt{ccm})\ |\ (\mathtt{wcm}\ e^{\mathrm{CM}}\ e^{\mathrm{CM}})\ |\ (\mathtt{output}\ e^{\mathrm{CM}})\ |\ (\mathtt{loc?}\ e^{\mathrm{CM}})$$

λ_{CM} adds four additional kinds of expressions to λ_{DF}. When a `wcm`, or "with continuation mark", expression is evaluated, its first argument is evaluated and stored in the current stack frame before its second argument is evaluated. A `ccm` expression evaluates to a list of all continuation marks currently stored in the stack. When reducing an `output` expression, its argument is evaluated and sent to an output channel; its result is inconsequential. The `loc?` predicate identifies locations and is needed by annotated programs.

4.4 CSKM Machine

One way to model continuation marks requires an explicit control stack. Hence, we first convert our CS machine to a CSK machine, where the evaluation context is separated from the control string, relocated to a new K register, and converted to a stack of frames. The conversion to a CSK machine is straightfoward [8]. In addition, we pair each context with a continuation mark m, which is stored in a fourth "M" register, giving us a CSKM machine. Here are all the continuations:

$$K^{\mathrm{CM}} = \mathtt{mt} \mid (\mathtt{app1}\ c^{\mathrm{CM}}\ K^{\mathrm{CM}}\ m) \mid (\mathtt{app2}\ v^{\mathrm{CM}}\ K^{\mathrm{CM}}\ m) \mid (\mathtt{if}\ c_1^{\mathrm{CM}}\ c_2^{\mathrm{CM}}\ K^{\mathrm{CM}}\ m)$$
$$\mid (\mathtt{prim2\text{-}1}\ p^2\ c^{\mathrm{CM}}\ K^{\mathrm{CM}}\ m) \mid (\mathtt{prim2\text{-}2}\ p^2\ v^{\mathrm{CM}}\ K^{\mathrm{CM}}\ m) \mid (\mathtt{prim1}\ p^1\ K^{\mathrm{CM}}\ m)$$
$$\mid (\mathtt{cons1}\ c^{\mathrm{CM}}\ K^{\mathrm{CM}}\ m) \mid (\mathtt{cons2}\ v^{\mathrm{CM}}\ K^{\mathrm{CM}}\ m) \mid (\mathtt{loc?}\ K^{\mathrm{CM}}\ m)$$
$$\mid (\mathtt{force}\ K^{\mathrm{CM}}\ m) \mid (\mathtt{force}\ \ell\ K^{\mathrm{CM}}\ m) \mid (\mathtt{wcm}\ c^{\mathrm{CM}}\ K^{\mathrm{CM}}\ m) \mid (\mathtt{output}\ K^{\mathrm{CM}}\ m)$$

The configurations of the CSKM machine are:

$$\begin{aligned} \mathcal{P}^{\mathrm{CM}} &= \langle c^{\mathrm{CM}}, \sigma, K^{\mathrm{CM}}, m\rangle\ \text{(Machine States)} & \mathcal{S}^{\mathrm{CM}} &= \mathcal{P}_1^{\mathrm{CM}}, \dots, \mathcal{P}_n^{\mathrm{CM}}\ \text{(Transition Seq.)} \\ c^{\mathrm{CM}} &= e^{\mathrm{CM}} \mid \ell \quad\quad\quad\text{(Control Strings)} & v^{\mathrm{CM}} &= v^{\mathrm{DF}} \quad\quad\quad\quad\quad\quad\quad\ \text{(Values)} \\ \sigma &= ((\ell, c^{\mathrm{CM}}), \dots) \quad\quad\text{(Stores)} & m &= \emptyset \mid v^{\mathrm{CM}} \quad\quad\quad\text{(Cont. Marks)} \end{aligned}$$

Control strings are again extended to include location expressions, values are the same as CS machine values, and stores map locations to control string expressions. The marks m are either empty or values.

The transitions for our CSKM machine are in Figure 6. For space reasons, we only include the transitions for the new constructs: wcm, ccm, output, and loc?. The other transitions are easily derived from the transitions for the CS machine [8]. To formally model output, we tag each transition, making our machine a labeled transition system [14]. When the machine emits output, the transition is tagged with the outputted value; otherwise, the tag is $\emptyset$.

$$\longmapsto_{\mathrm{CSKM}}$$

$\langle(\mathtt{wcm}\ c_1^{\mathrm{CM}}\ c_2^{\mathrm{CM}}), \sigma, K^{\mathrm{CM}}, m\rangle$	$\overset{\emptyset}{\longmapsto}_{\mathrm{CSKM}}$	$\langle c_1^{\mathrm{CM}}, \sigma, (\mathtt{wcm}\ c_2^{\mathrm{CM}}\ K^{\mathrm{CM}}\ m), \emptyset\rangle$	WCM:EXP
$\langle v^{\mathrm{CM}}, \sigma, (\mathtt{wcm}\ c^{\mathrm{CM}}\ K^{\mathrm{CM}}\ m), m'\rangle$	$\overset{\emptyset}{\longmapsto}_{\mathrm{CSKM}}$	$\langle c^{\mathrm{CM}}, \sigma, K^{\mathrm{CM}}, v^{\mathrm{CM}}\rangle$	WCM:VAL
$\langle(\mathtt{ccm}), \sigma, K^{\mathrm{CM}}, m\rangle$	$\overset{\emptyset}{\longmapsto}_{\mathrm{CSKM}}$	$\langle v^{\mathrm{CM}}, \sigma, K^{\mathrm{CM}}, \emptyset\rangle, v^{\mathrm{CM}}{=}\pi(K^{\mathrm{CM}}, m)$	CCM
$\langle(\mathtt{output}\ c^{\mathrm{CM}}), \sigma, K^{\mathrm{CM}}, m\rangle$	$\overset{\emptyset}{\longmapsto}_{\mathrm{CSKM}}$	$\langle c^{\mathrm{CM}}, \sigma, (\mathtt{output}\ K^{\mathrm{CM}}\ m), \emptyset\rangle$	OUT:EXP
$\langle v^{\mathrm{CM}}, \sigma, (\mathtt{output}\ K^{\mathrm{CM}}\ m), m'\rangle$	$\overset{v^{\mathrm{CM}}}{\longmapsto}_{\mathrm{CSKM}}$	$\langle 42, \sigma, K^{\mathrm{CM}}, m\rangle$	OUT:VAL
$\langle(\mathtt{loc?}\ c^{\mathrm{CM}}), \sigma, K^{\mathrm{CM}}, m\rangle$	$\overset{\emptyset}{\longmapsto}_{\mathrm{CSKM}}$	$\langle c^{\mathrm{CM}}, \sigma, (\mathtt{loc?}\ K^{\mathrm{CM}}\ m), \emptyset\rangle$	LOC:EXP
$\langle \ell, \sigma, (\mathtt{loc?}\ K^{\mathrm{CM}}\ m), m'\rangle$	$\overset{\emptyset}{\longmapsto}_{\mathrm{CSKM}}$	$\langle \mathtt{true}, \sigma, K^{\mathrm{CM}}, m\rangle$	LOC-T:VAL
$\langle v^{\mathrm{CM}}, \sigma, (\mathtt{loc?}\ K^{\mathrm{CM}}\ m), m'\rangle, v^{\mathrm{CM}}{\notin}\ell \overset{\emptyset}{\longmapsto}_{\mathrm{CSKM}}$		$\langle \mathtt{false}, \sigma, K^{\mathrm{CM}}, m\rangle$	LOC-F:VAL

Fig. 6. CSKM Machine Transitions

The starting state for a program e^{CM} is $\langle e^{\mathrm{CM}}, (\ ), \mathtt{mt}, \emptyset\rangle$; evaluation halts when the control string is a value and the control stack is mt. The transition sequence for a program is again deterministic.

The WCM:EXP transition sets the first argument as the control string and saves the second argument in a wcm continuation. In the resulting machine configuration, the M register is set to $\emptyset$ because a new frame is pushed onto the stack. When evaluation of the first wcm argument is complete, the resulting value is set as the new continuation mark, as dictated by the WCM:VAL transition, overwriting any previous mark. The CCM transition uses the π function to retrieve all continuation marks in the stack. The π function is defined as follows:

$$(\pi \; \mathtt{mt} \; m) = (\mathtt{cons} \; m \; \mathtt{null})$$
$$(\pi \; (\mathtt{app1} \; c^{\mathrm{CM}} \; K^{\mathrm{CM}} \; m) \; m') = (\mathtt{cons} \; m' \; (\pi \; K^{\mathrm{CM}} \; m))$$
$$(\pi \; (\mathtt{app2} \; v^{\mathrm{CM}} \; K^{\mathrm{CM}} \; m) \; m') = (\mathtt{cons} \; m' \; (\pi \; K^{\mathrm{CM}} \; m))$$
$$\cdots$$
$$(\pi \; (\mathtt{loc?} \; K^{\mathrm{CM}} \; m) \; m') = (\mathtt{cons} \; m' \; (\pi \; K^{\mathrm{CM}} \; m))$$

Only the first few cases are shown. The rest of the definition is similarly defined. The OUT:EXP transition sets the argument in an output expression as the control string and pushes a new output continuation frame onto the control stack. Again, the continuation mark register is initialized to $\emptyset$ due to the new stack frame. When the output expression is evaluated, the resulting value is emitted as output, as modeled by the tag on the OUT:VAL transition.

5   Correctness

Our algebraic stepper comes with a concise specification: the λ_{LR} rewriting system. Thus, it is relatively straightforward to state a correctness theorem for the stepper. Let ζ be a label-stripping function.

Theorem 1 (Stepper Correctness). *If for some Lazy Racket program e, the stepper shows the sequence $e, \zeta[\![e_1^{\mathrm{LR}}]\!], \ldots, \zeta[\![e_n^{\mathrm{LR}}]\!]$, then $e \longmapsto_{\mathrm{LR}} e_1^{\mathrm{LR}} \longmapsto_{\mathrm{LR}} \cdots \longmapsto_{\mathrm{LR}} e_n^{\mathrm{LR}}$.*

The theorem statement involves multistep rewriting because some steps, such as CONS, merely add labels and change nothing else about the term. The proof of the theorem consists of two lemmas. First, we show that a CS machine reduction sequence can be reconstructed from the output of an annotated version of that program running on a CSKM machine. Second, we prove that this reduction sequence is equivalent to the rewriting sequence of the original Lazy Racket program, modulo label assignment. The following subsections spell out the two lemmas and present proof sketches.

5.1   Annotation and Reconstruction Correctness

To state the first correctness lemma, we need three functions. First, $\mathcal{T}$ consumes CSKM steps and produces a trace of output values:

$$\mathcal{T}[\![\cdots \longmapsto_{\mathrm{CSKM}} \mathcal{P}_i^{\mathrm{CM}} \xrightarrow{v^{\mathrm{CM}}}_{\mathrm{CSKM}} \mathcal{P}_{i+1}^{\mathrm{CM}} \longmapsto_{\mathrm{CSKM}} \cdots]\!] = \ldots, v^{\mathrm{CM}}, \ldots \qquad \boxed{\mathcal{T} : \mathcal{S}^{\mathrm{CM}} \to v_1^{\mathrm{CM}}, \ldots, v_n^{\mathrm{CM}}}$$

Second, $\mathcal{A} : e^{\mathrm{RKT}} \to e^{\mathrm{CM}}$ annotates a Racket program and $\mathcal{R} : v_1^{\mathrm{CM}}, \ldots, v_n^{\mathrm{CM}} \to \mathcal{S}^{\mathrm{DF}}$ reconstructs a CS machine transition sequence from a list of output values.

Lemma 2 (Annotation/Reconstruction Correctness)
For any Racket program e^{RKT}, if $\langle e^{\text{RKT}}, (\,) \rangle \longmapsto_{\text{CS}} \cdots \longmapsto_{\text{CS}} \mathcal{P}^{\text{DF}}$, then:

$$\mathcal{R}[\![\mathcal{T}[\![\langle \mathcal{A}[\![e^{\text{RKT}}]\!], (\,), mt, \emptyset \rangle \longmapsto_{\text{CSKM}} \cdots \longmapsto_{\text{CSKM}} \mathcal{P}^{\text{CM}}]\!]]\!] = \langle e^{\text{RKT}}, (\,) \rangle \longmapsto_{\text{CS}} \cdots \longmapsto_{\text{CS}} \mathcal{P}^{\text{DF}}$$

Our annotation and reconstruction functions extend that of Clements [6]. Annotation adds `output` and continuation mark `wcm` and `ccm` operations to a program. For example, annotating the program $(+\ 1\ 2)$ results in the following:[3]

```
(let* ([t0 (output (cons Q[(+ 1 2)] (ccm)))]
       [v1 (+ 1 2)]
       [t1 (output (cons Q[v1] (ccm)))])
   v1)
```

Annotated programs utilize the quoting function, $\mathcal{Q}$, for converting an expression to a value representation. For example $\mathcal{Q}[\![(+\ 1\ 2)]\!] = (\texttt{list "+" 1 2})$. There is also an inverse function, $\mathcal{Q}^{-1}$, for reconstruction. The above annotated program evaluates to 3, outputting the values $\mathcal{Q}[\![(+\ 1\ 2)]\!]$ and $\mathcal{Q}[\![3]\!]$ in the process, from which the reduction sequence $(+\ 1\ 2) \to 3$ can be recovered. The `(ccm)` calls in the example return the empty list since there were no calls to `wcm`. There is no need for `wcm` annotations because the entire program is a redex.

Extending the example to $(+\ (+\ 1\ 2)\ 5)$ yields:

```
(let* ([v0 (wcm (list "prim2-1" "+" 5)
                (let* ([t0 (output (cons Q[(+ 1 2)] (ccm)))]
                       [v1 (+ 1 2)]
                       [t1 (output (cons Q[v1] (ccm)))])
                   v1))]
       [v2 (+ v0 5)]
       [t2 (output (cons Q[v2] (ccm)))])
   v2)
```

This extended example contains the first example as a subexpression and therefore, the annotated version of the program contains the annotated version of the first example. The $(+\ 1\ 2)$ expression now occurs in the context $(+\ [\ ]\ 5)$ and the `wcm` expression stores an appropriate continuation mark. The `"prim2-1"` label indicates that the hole is in the left argument position. The first `output` expression now produces the output value $(\texttt{list}\ \mathcal{Q}[\![(+\ 1\ 2)]\!]\ (\texttt{list "prim2-1" "+" 5}))$, which can be reconstructed to the expression $(+\ (+\ 1\ 2)\ 5)$. Reconstructing all outputs produces $(+\ (+\ 1\ 2)\ 5) \to (+\ 3\ 5) \to 8$.

The context information stored in continuation marks is used to reconstruct machine states and the reconstruction and annotation functions defined in Figures 7 and 8 demonstrate how this works for `force` and `delay` expressions. If a forced expression e^{RKT} does not evaluate to a location, the annotations are like those for the above examples. If e^{RKT} evaluates to a location, additional continuation marks (Figure 7, boxes 1 and 2) are needed to indicate the presence of `force` contexts during the evaluation of the delayed computation. An additional `output` expression (box 3) is also needed so that steps showing the removal of both the `(force [ ])` and `(force ℓ [ ])` contexts can be reconstructed. With

---

[3] For clarity, we use some syntactic sugar here (`let*` and `list`).

(rest (ccm)) (box 5), we ensure that the (force ℓ [ ]) context is not part of the reconstructed expression. The location $v0$ (box 4) is included in the output so the store can be properly reconstructed. The "val" tag directs the reconstruction function to use the value $\mathcal{Q}[\![v2]\!]$ from the emitted location-value pair during reconstruction.

$$\mathcal{A}[\![(\texttt{force } e^{\text{RKT}})]\!] \;=$$

$$\boxed{\mathcal{A} : e^{\text{RKT}} \rightarrow e^{\text{CM}}}$$

```
(let* ([v0 (wcm (list "force") A[[eᴿᴷᵀ]])]
       [v1 (if (not (loc? v0))
               v0
               (wcm (list "force")₁
                    (wcm (list "force" v0)₂
                         (let* ([v2 (force v0)] ; v0 is location
                                [t0 (output₃ (cons (list "val" v0₄ Q[[v2]])
                                                   (rest (ccm))₅))])
                              v2))))]
       [t1 (output (cons Q[[v1]] (ccm)))])
  v1)
```

$$\mathcal{A}[\![(\texttt{delay } e^{\text{RKT}})]\!] \;=$$

```
(let* ([t0 (output (cons Q[[(delay eᴿᴷᵀ)]] (ccm)))]
       [ℓ (alloc)]
       [t1 (output (cons (list "loc" ℓ Q[[eᴿᴷᵀ]]₆) (ccm)))])
  (delay A[[eᴿᴷᵀ]]))
```

Fig. 7. Annotation function for delay and force

The annotation of a delay expression requires predicting the location of the delayed computation in the store. We therefore assume we have access to an alloc function that uses the same location-allocating algorithm as the memory management system of the machine.[4] In addition to the location, the delayed expression itself (box 6) is also included in the output, to enable reconstruction of the store. The "loc" tag directs the reconstruction function to use the location from the emitted location-value pair when reconstructing the control string.

The reconstruction function in Figure 8 consumes a list of values, where each value is a sublist and reconstructs a CS machine state from each sublist. The first element of every v_i^{CM} sublist represents a (quoted) expression that is plugged into the context represented by the rest of the sublist. The store is reconstructed by retrieving all the location-value pairs in all the sublists up to the current one. The arguments to the store-reconstruction function $\mathcal{R}_S$ may contain duplicate entries for a location, so a location-value pair is only included in the resulting store if it does not occur in any subsequent arguments.

---

[4] Since labels are displayed as sharing, this unrealistic assumption is acceptable.

$$\mathcal{R}[\ldots, v_i^{\mathrm{CM}}, \ldots] = \ldots, \langle \mathcal{R}_E[\![(\texttt{rest } v_i^{\mathrm{CM}})]\!][\mathcal{R}_C[\![(\texttt{first } v_i^{\mathrm{CM}})]\!]], \qquad \boxed{\mathcal{R} : v_1^{\mathrm{CM}}, \ldots, v_n^{\mathrm{CM}} \to \mathcal{S}^{\mathrm{DF}}}$$
$$\mathcal{R}_S[v_1^{\mathrm{CM}}, \ldots, v_i^{\mathrm{CM}}]\rangle, \ldots$$

$$\mathcal{R}_E[\![(\texttt{cons (list "force") } v^{\mathrm{CM}})]\!] = (\texttt{force } \mathcal{R}_E[\![v^{\mathrm{CM}}]\!]) \qquad \boxed{\mathcal{R}_E : v^{\mathrm{CM}} \to E^{\mathrm{DF}}}$$
$$\mathcal{R}_E[\![(\texttt{cons (list "force") } \ell) \; v^{\mathrm{CM}})]\!] = (\texttt{force } \ell \; \mathcal{R}_E[\![v^{\mathrm{CM}}]\!])$$

$$\mathcal{R}_C[\![(\texttt{list "val" } \ell \; v^{\mathrm{DF}})]\!] = \mathcal{Q}^{-1}[v^{\mathrm{DF}}] \qquad \boxed{\mathcal{R}_C : v^{\mathrm{CM}} \to e^{\mathrm{DF}}}$$
$$\mathcal{R}_C[\![(\texttt{list "loc" } \ell \; v^{\mathrm{DF}})]\!] = \ell$$
$$\text{otherwise, } \mathcal{R}_C[v^{\mathrm{DF}}] = \mathcal{Q}^{-1}[v^{\mathrm{DF}}]$$

$$\mathcal{R}_S[\![(\texttt{cons (list } s \; \ell \; v^{\mathrm{DF}'}) \; \_), v_{rest}^{\mathrm{DF}}, \ldots] \qquad \boxed{\mathcal{R}_S : v_1^{\mathrm{CM}}, \ldots, v_n^{\mathrm{CM}} \to \sigma}$$

$$= \begin{cases} (\texttt{cons } (\ell, \mathcal{Q}^{-1}[v^{\mathrm{DF}'}]) \; \mathcal{R}_S[v_{rest}^{\mathrm{DF}}, \ldots]), & \text{if } \ell \notin \texttt{dom}(\mathcal{R}_S[v_{rest}^{\mathrm{DF}}, \ldots]) \\ \mathcal{R}_S[v_{rest}^{\mathrm{DF}}, \ldots] & \text{if } \ell \in \texttt{dom}(\mathcal{R}_S[v_{rest}^{\mathrm{DF}}, \ldots]) \end{cases}$$
$$\mathcal{R}_S[v^{\mathrm{DF}}, v_{rest}^{\mathrm{DF}}, \ldots] = \mathcal{R}_S[v_{rest}^{\mathrm{DF}}, \ldots], \qquad \text{if } (\texttt{first } v^{\mathrm{DF}}) \neq (\texttt{list } s \; \ell \; v^{\mathrm{DF}'})$$

Fig. 8. Reconstruction function for `delay` and `force`

The proof of lemma 2 extends Clements's proof [5, Section 3.4] with cases for `delay` and `force`. The original cases must cope with the additional store, but this is straightforward.

5.2   Lazy Racket Correctness

The φ function in Figure 9 macro-expands a Lazy Racket program. Because source terms don't include labels, φ is undefined for labeled terms. Its partial inverse, φ^{-1}, defined in Figure 10, synthesizes an unlabeled Lazy Racket program from a (CS machine representation of a) Racket program.

Lemma 3 states Lazy Racket's correctness in terms of φ, φ^{-1}, the label-stripping function ζ, and the λ_{LR} rewriting system. That is, every CS machine sequence has an equivalent λ_{LR} rewriting sequence, modulo φ^{-1} and ζ.

$$\varphi[\lambda x.e] = \lambda x.\varphi[e] \qquad \boxed{\varphi : e \to e^{\mathrm{RKT}}}$$
$$\varphi[\![(e_1 \; e_2)]\!] = ((\texttt{force } \varphi[e_1]) \; (\texttt{delay } \varphi[e_2]))$$
$$\varphi[\![(\texttt{cons } e_1 \; e_2)]\!] = (\texttt{cons (delay } \varphi[e_1]) \; (\texttt{delay } \varphi[e_2]))$$
$$\varphi[\![(\texttt{if } e_1 \; e_2 \; e_3)]\!] = (\texttt{if (force } \varphi[e_1]) \; \varphi[e_2] \; \varphi[e_3])$$
$$\varphi[\![(p^n \; e \; \ldots)]\!] = (p^n \; (\texttt{force } \varphi[e]) \; \ldots)$$
$$\text{otherwise, } \varphi[e] = e$$

Fig. 9. Macro-expanding Lazy Racket to plain Racket

$$\varphi^{-1}[\![c^{\mathrm{DF}}]\!]\sigma = e, \text{ where } \langle e, \_\rangle = \bar{\varphi}[\![c^{\mathrm{DF}}]\!]\sigma \qquad \boxed{\varphi^{-1} : c^{\mathrm{DF}} \times \sigma \to e}$$

$$\boxed{\bar{\varphi} : c^{\mathrm{DF}} \times \sigma \to \langle e, \sigma\rangle}$$

$$\bar{\varphi}[\![\lambda x.e^{\mathrm{DF}}]\!]\sigma = \langle \lambda x.e, \sigma\rangle, \qquad \text{where } \langle e, \sigma\rangle = \bar{\varphi}[\![e^{\mathrm{DF}}]\!]\sigma$$

$$\bar{\varphi}[\![(c_1^{\mathrm{DF}}\ c_2^{\mathrm{DF}})]\!]\sigma = \langle (e_1\ e_2), \sigma''\rangle, \qquad \text{where } \langle e_1, \sigma'\rangle = \bar{\varphi}[\![c_1^{\mathrm{DF}}]\!]\sigma,\ \langle e_2, \sigma''\rangle = \bar{\varphi}[\![c_2^{\mathrm{DF}}]\!]\sigma'$$

$$\bar{\varphi}[\![(p^2\ c_1^{\mathrm{DF}}\ c_2^{\mathrm{DF}})]\!]\sigma = \langle (p^2\ e_1\ e_2), \sigma''\rangle, \qquad \text{where } \langle e_1, \sigma'\rangle = \bar{\varphi}[\![c_1^{\mathrm{DF}}]\!]\sigma,\ \langle e_2, \sigma''\rangle = \bar{\varphi}[\![c_2^{\mathrm{DF}}]\!]\sigma'$$

$$\bar{\varphi}[\![(\mathtt{cons}\ c_1^{\mathrm{DF}}\ c_2^{\mathrm{DF}})]\!]\sigma = \langle (\mathtt{cons}\ e_1\ e_2), \sigma''\rangle, \text{where } \langle e_1, \sigma'\rangle = \bar{\varphi}[\![c_1^{\mathrm{DF}}]\!]\sigma,\ \langle e_2, \sigma''\rangle = \bar{\varphi}[\![c_2^{\mathrm{DF}}]\!]\sigma'$$

$$\bar{\varphi}[\![(p^1\ c^{\mathrm{DF}})]\!]\sigma = \langle (p^1\ e), \sigma'\rangle, \qquad \text{where } \langle e, \sigma'\rangle = \bar{\varphi}[\![c^{\mathrm{DF}}]\!]\sigma$$

$$\bar{\varphi}[\![(\mathtt{if}\ c_1^{\mathrm{DF}}\ e_2^{\mathrm{DF}}\ e_3^{\mathrm{DF}})]\!]\sigma = \langle (\mathtt{if}\ e_1\ e_2\ e_3), \sigma''\rangle, \text{where } \langle e_1, \sigma'\rangle = \bar{\varphi}[\![c_1^{\mathrm{DF}}]\!]\sigma,\ \langle e_2, \sigma'\rangle = \bar{\varphi}[\![e_2^{\mathrm{DF}}]\!]\sigma'$$
$$\langle e_3, \sigma'\rangle = \bar{\varphi}[\![e_3^{\mathrm{DF}}]\!]\sigma'$$

$$\bar{\varphi}[\![(\mathtt{delay}\ e^{\mathrm{DF}})]\!]\sigma = \bar{\varphi}[\![e^{\mathrm{DF}}]\!]\sigma$$

$$\bar{\varphi}[\![\ell]\!]\sigma = \bar{\varphi}[\![\sigma[\ell]]\!]\sigma$$

$$\bar{\varphi}[\![(\mathtt{force}\ c^{\mathrm{DF}})]\!]\sigma = \bar{\varphi}[\![c^{\mathrm{DF}}]\!]\sigma$$

$$\bar{\varphi}[\![(\mathtt{force}\ \ell\ c^{\mathrm{DF}})]\!]\sigma = \langle e, \sigma'[\ell \leftarrow e]\rangle, \qquad \text{where } \langle e, \sigma'\rangle = \bar{\varphi}[\![c^{\mathrm{DF}}]\!]\sigma$$

$$\text{otherwise, } \bar{\varphi}[\![e^{\mathrm{DF}}]\!]\sigma = \langle e^{\mathrm{DF}}, \sigma\rangle$$

Fig. 10. Synthesizing Lazy Racket from plain Racket

Lemma 3 (LR Correctness). *For all Lazy Racket programs e and Racket programs c^{DF} such that $\langle \varphi[\![e]\!], (\ )\rangle \longmapsto\!\!\!\twoheadrightarrow_{\mathrm{CS}} \langle c^{\mathrm{DF}}, \sigma\rangle$, there exists a Lazy Racket program e^{LR} such that $e \longmapsto\!\!\!\twoheadrightarrow_{\mathrm{LR}} e^{\mathrm{LR}}$ and $\varphi^{-1}[\![c^{\mathrm{DF}}]\!]\sigma = \zeta[\![e^{\mathrm{LR}}]\!]$.*

Proof (Sketch). We prove the lemma by induction on the number of CS machine steps. For the base case, the lemma holds because $\varphi^{-1}[\![\varphi[\![e]\!]]\!](\ ) = e$. Otherwise, we proceed by case analysis on the last transition step. For each case, we prove correct synthesis of evaluation contexts and redexes separately.   □

6   Related Work

Researchers have developed many debugging tools for lazy languages. However, few of these tools show laziness during evaluation or do so in a intuitive manner. Some tools present declarative traces [19,18,24,26] that show a reduction sequence for each expression in the program but removes all notions of temporal ordering of the reductions, a key element to understanding lazy evaluation.

Declarative tools are popular because researchers struggle to portray laziness operationally. The most basic operational tool records a trace of function calls during evaluation [15]. Unlike declarative debuggers, these tools explain the lazy evaluation of expressions relative to other expressions; however, the complexity of laziness often makes such tools confusing. In reaction, some researchers developed stack tracing tools that approximate a call-by-value language [1,20].

Operational-style tools similar to ours show the step-by-step evaluation of lazy programs. Unfortunately, many of these hide the laziness during evaluation as well [3,7,12]. Snyder [23] developed a tool that resembles ours in that it reconstructs reduction sequences from an annotated program. It uses graph combinators, however, and the tool is only able to reconstruct an approximation of the source code. Lapalme and Latendresse [16] developed a tool that, like ours, inserts "breakpoints" to generate a sequence of reductions but they do not mention how the steps are determined, nor do they show actual examples. The GHCi debugger [17] shows laziness while stepping through a program, but presents it in terms of the low-level implementation. This produces steps that both users and the authors of the tool consider confusing. Foubister [10] and Taylor [25] developed graph reduction stepper tools, but programmers prefer textual tools [12,21], especially for teaching novices.

Gibbons and Wansbrough [11] created a lazy stepper based on the call-by-need calculus of Ariola and Felleisen [2]. While the calculus is useful for reasoning about equivalences of lazy expressions, it can be confusing to use for reasoning about lazy executions for three reasons. First, the calculus includes administrative transformation steps that do not represent real computation the way substitution does. Second, to express sharing, the calculus never resolves function calls and instead retains all arguments long after they become superfluous. Third, the calculus dereferences variables one at a time, which can be confusing since all instances of a particular variable are supposed to represent just one expression. Watson's tool [27] manages to eliminate the administrative steps and the persistent arguments at the expense of explicit sharing. Shared terms are held in a implicit store so programmers are forced to remember those terms. An argument seemingly reappears as each variable is dereferenced, which can potentially be confusing. Penney [22] improves Watson's visualization using "where" clauses to explicitly show shared terms but tracking such clauses as the number of placeholders accumulate seems like it would be difficult. No tool uses full substitution and parallel rewriting steps to represent laziness.

Finally, few tools come with formal models and correctness proofs for their architecture. Chitil and Luo [4] developed a model for the declarative Hat debugger's trace generator and show that the evaluation steps can be reconstructed from the information in the traces. Watson also provides formal definitions for his transformations [27], and uses a standard store-based operational semantics for the rewriting steps.

References

1. Allwood, T.O., Peyton Jones, S., Eisenbach, S.: Finding the needle: stack traces for GHC. In: Proc. 2nd Symp. on Haskell, pp. 129–140 (2009)
2. Ariola, Z.M., Felleisen, M., Maraist, J., Odersky, M., Wadler, P.: The call-by-need λ calculus. In: Proc. 22nd POPL, pp. 233–246 (1995)
3. Augustson, M., Reinfelds, J.: A visual miranda machine. In: Proc. Software Education Conference SRIG-ET, pp. 233–246 (1995)

4. Chitil, O., Luo, Y.: Structure and properties of traces for functional programs. In: Proc. 3rd Intl. Works. Term Graph Rewriting, pp. 39–63 (2006)
5. Clements, J.: Portable and High-level Access to the Stack with Continuation Marks. Ph.D. thesis, Northeastern University (2006)
6. Clements, J., Flatt, M., Felleisen, M.: Modeling an Algebraic Stepper. In: Sands, D. (ed.) ESOP 2001. LNCS, vol. 2028, pp. 320–334. Springer, Heidelberg (2001)
7. Ennals, R., Peyton Jones, S.: HsDebug: debugging lazy programs by not being lazy. In: Proc. Works. on Haskell, pp. 84–87 (2003)
8. Felleisen, M., Findler, R.B., Flatt, M.: Semantics Engineering with PLT Redex. MIT Press (2009)
9. Felleisen, M., Friedman, D.P.: A syntactic theory of sequential state. Theor. Comput. Sci. 69(3), 243–287 (1989)
10. Foubister, S.P.: Graphical Application and Visualisation of Lazy Functional Computation. Ph.D. thesis, University of York (1995)
11. Gibbons, J., Wansbrough, K.: Tracing lazy functional languages. In: Proc. CATS, pp. 11–20 (1996)
12. Goldson, D.: A symbolic calculator for non-strict functional languages. Comput. J. 37(3), 177–187 (1994)
13. Hughes, J.: Why functional programming matters. Comput. J. 32(2), 98–107 (1989)
14. Keller, R.: Formal verification of parallel programs. Commun. ACM 19(7) (1976)
15. Kishon, A.: Theory and Art of Semantics-Directed Program Execution Monitoring. Ph.D. thesis, Yale University (1992)
16. Lapalme, G., Latendresse, M.: A debugging environment for lazy functional languages. LISP and Symbolic Computation 5(3), 271–287 (1992)
17. Marlow, S., Iborra, J., Pope, B., Gill, A.: A lightweight interactive debugger for Haskell. In: Proc. Works. on Haskell, pp. 13–24 (2007)
18. Naish, L.: Declarative debugging of lazy functional programs. In: Proc. 16th ACSC (1993)
19. Nilsson, H., Fritzson, P.: Algorithmic debugging for lazy functional languages. In: Proc. 4th PLIPL, pp. 385–399 (1992)
20. O'Donnell, J.T., Hall, C.V.: Debugging in applicative languages. LISP and Symbolic Computation 1(2), 113–145 (1988)
21. Patel, M.J., du Boulay, B., Taylor, C.: Effect of format on information and problem solving. In: Proc. 13th Conf. of the Cognitive Science Society, pp. 852–856 (1991)
22. Penney, A.: Augmenting Trace-based Functional Debugging. Ph.D. thesis, University of Bristol, Australia (1999)
23. Snyder, R.M.: Lazy debugging of lazy functional programs. New Generation Computing 8, 139–161 (1990)
24. Sparud, J., Runciman, C.: Tracing lazy functional computations using redex trails. In: Proc. 9th PLILP, pp. 291–308 (1997)
25. Taylor, J.P.: Presenting the Lazy Evaluation of Functions. Ph.D. thesis, Queen Mary and Westfield College (1996)
26. Wallace, M., Chitil, O., Brehm, T., Runciman, C.: Multiple-view tracing for Haskell: a new hat. In: Proc. Works. on Haskell, pp. 151–170 (2001)
27. Watson, R.D.: Tracing Lazy Evaluation by Program Transformation. Ph.D. thesis, Southern Cross University, Australia (1997)

Model Based Testing
with Logical Properties versus State Machines

Pieter Koopman, Peter Achten, and Rinus Plasmeijer

Institute for Computing and Information Sciences (ICIS),
Radboud University Nijmegen, The Netherlands
{pieter,p.achten,rinus}@cs.ru.nl

Abstract. Model-based testing of single functions is usually based on logical properties as specification. In practice it appears to be rather hard to develop a sufficiently strong set of properties to spot all errors. For model-based testing of state based systems one usually employs a state machine as model and a conformance relation between this specification and the software under test. For (abstract) data types we can use both ways of model-based testing. In this paper we compare the specification effort required to make a model that is able to find issues and the number of tests needed to find issues for some well-known data types. Our examples show that it can be easier to write state based specifications. Moreover, state based testing of data types finds more implementation issues and is very efficient.

1   Introduction

Many polymorphic abstract data types, adts, are used to store items in one way or another. Typical examples of such a storage structure are files, search trees, lists, and queues. In a functional programming language the interface of such an adt is just a set of functions. In order to test the implementation of such an adt two different approaches can be used. First, we can state logical properties about functions in the interface, or combinations of these functions. Second, we can treat the actual contents of the adt as state in a model-based conformance test. In this paper we compare these approaches based on the effort needed to make a specification for an effective model-based test and the error detection power of the associated tests.

In the world of functional programming languages the model-based testing approach based on logical properties is best known. This is mainly due to the success of QuickCheck [6]. Such a test tool is typically a library offering a domain specific language to state logical properties. Model-based test tools founded on logical properties try to falsify properties by finding a counterexample. This is done by generating test data of the desired type and evaluating the property for these values. When the property evaluates to false for one of the test values used the property is falsified, otherwise it passes the test.

Another popular approach to model-based testing is based on state transition models and a conformance relation between the model and the system under

A. Gill and J. Hage (Eds.): IFL 2011, LNCS 7257, pp. 116–133, 2012.

test, sut. This is used when the reaction of the system depends on the history. A model can be a Finite State Machine, fsm, an Extended State Machine, esm, or other transition system. A fsm is by definition finite and deterministic. A generalization of a fsm is an esm which can have an infinite number of states or is nondeterministic. A model-based test tool for models with a state tries to show nonconformance of the sut and the model. To find nonconformance the test tool applies inputs allowed by the model to the sut, and checks if the corresponding output from the sut is accepted by the model.

When we want to test a single function, logical properties are the technique to be used. When we have to test a system with a state a conformance based test tool is our friend. So, at first glance it seems obvious to test polymorphic data types by stating logical properties about the functions in the interface. However, the separation of kinds of model-based testing applicable is not as clear as it might look. For many adts we can specify properties about individual functions in the interface, or combinations of those functions. The internal representation of an abstract data type cannot be inspected. Hence we usually state a property about a combination of functions in the interface. Cracking open the abstract type is undesirable. It is better to model the properties of an adt independent of its internal representation. Those logical properties are tested by a property based test tool. On the other hand we can model the adt by a state machine where the transitions are just applying the functions in the interface. The state of the sut is just the adt itself. In this paper we compare these two approaches to test abstract data types. We focus on the effort needed to create an appropriate specification and the error detecting power of the tests.

In this paper we use the model-based test tool G∀st [11] which is distributed as a Clean library. It implements model-based testing with logic properties as well as conformance tests. One distinguishing property of G∀st compared to QuickCheck is that it uses a systematic generation of test cases instead of pseudo random generation. Moreover G∀st uses a *generic, type-driven* generation algorithm that is able to enumerate the values of any algebraic data type. The generic generation of test cases has as advantages that the user can request the compiler to derive the generation of the values from a new type instead of coding this herself. For sufficiently small finite types this allows proofs by exhaustive testing.

In Sections 2 and 3 we review the logical property based approach and the state based approach respectively. Next we apply both approaches to two case studies: a smart $O(1)$ implementation of queues in Section 4 and AVL trees in Section 5. We list the observations in Section 6 and discuss related work in Section 7. Finally we draw conclusions in Section 8.

2   Logical Property Based Testing

Model based testing with logical properties is introduced in functional programming by Claessen and Hughes with QuickCheck [6]. Due to its success, this approach is ported to many languages[1] and many variants were developed.

---

[1] See http://en.wikipedia.org/wiki/QuickCheck

Functions are used as representation of terms in first order logic. Function arguments are treated as universally quantified variables. Typical examples of expressions in first order logic are De Morgan's law: $\forall p, q \in \mathbb{B} . \neg(p \wedge q) = (\neg p) \vee (\neg q)$, and a property that states that the absolute value of any integer is greater or equal to zero $\forall i \in \mathbb{Z} . \mathrm{abs}(i) \geq 0$. In G∀st this is expressed as:

```
pDeMorgan :: Bool Bool → Bool
pDeMorgan p q = not (p && q) == not p || not q
```

```
pAbs :: Int → Bool
pAbs i = abs·i ≥ 0
```

Logical property based test tools try to falsify such properties by generating arguments of the desired type and evaluating the properties for those arguments. To ensure termination the test tools use a maximum number of tests. Typical default values for this parameter are between 100 (e.g. QuickCheck) and 1000 (e.g. G∀st) test cases. If no counterexample is found the property passes the tests.

Testing the properties above yields Proof by exhaustive testing for pDeMorgan. Since there are only four different tests possible, systematic generation is less work and gives stronger test results: Proof instead of just Pass. Testing pAbs yields the counterexample −2147483648, the minimum 32-bit integer, in the fifth test. Since values like 0, 1, -1, maxint and minint are critical test values for many properties about integers, G∀st generates them in the beginning of the test suite.

3   State Machine Based Testing

Outside the functional programming community model-based testing is usually based on a conformance relation for transition systems [17]. Since this is less common in functional programming we elaborate the description a little. We use again the tool G∀st now for state based testing.

Various machine models are used by state based test tools. In G∀st the specification is an esm. The difference of an esm with a Mealy machine is that the number of states, inputs, and outputs can be infinite. Moreover, they can be nondeterministic.

The states of the model in G∀st are members of some arbitrary data type S. Similarly, there are data types I for inputs and O for outputs. A transition is of the form $s \xrightarrow{i/o} t$, where s, t are states, i is an input which triggers the transition, and o is a, possibly empty, list of outputs. Since the specification can be nondeterministic, it is possible that there are multiple transitions from a given start state, s, with the same input, i, and different outputs o or target states t. A specification is *partial* if there is no transition specified for one or more reachable state and input combinations. A specification is *deterministic* if there is at most one target state for every combination of state and input. In G∀st we encode state machines by functions of the (synonym) type Spec.

```
:: Spec s i o := s i → [Trans o s]
:: Trans o s  = Pt [o] s | Ft ([o]→[s])
```

Since the specification can be nondeterministic there is a list of transitions for a given state and input. G∀st has two kinds of transitions. Either we list the outputs and the target state, Pt [o] s, or we give a function that yields the target states given the list of outputs, Ft ([o]→[s]). The later option is needed to specify systems that allow huge numbers of different outputs on a transition.

We illustrate the representation of state transition systems in G∀st with a small example of a cash system that accepts button inputs and produces a list of coins representing the current value. In its initial state, Init, it ignores all buttons except B0. The Run state is parameterized by the amount of money. M-buttons decrease the amount of money, while P buttons increase it. We use a function and a Ft transition to accept any list of coins with the correct value. The class value yields the obvious integer value of buttons and coins.

```
::  Button = M100 | M10 | M1 | B0 | P1 | P10 | P100
::  Coin   = C1 | C2 | C5 | C10 | C20 | C50 | C100 | C200
::  State  = Init | Run Int

cashSpec :: State Button → [Trans Coin State]
cashSpec Init      B0 = [Pt [] (Run 0)]
cashSpec Init      b  = [Pt [] Init]
cashSpec (Run n) b
    | m ≥ 0
        = [Ft λl → if (value l = m) [Run m] []]
        = [Pt [] (Run n)]
where m = value b + n
```

A trace σ is a sequence of inputs and associated outputs from a given state. The empty trace, ϵ, connects a state to itself: $s \overset{\epsilon}{\Rightarrow} s$. We write $s \overset{\sigma}{\Rightarrow}$ to indicate $\exists u . s \overset{\sigma}{\Rightarrow} u$ and $s \overset{i/o}{\longrightarrow} \equiv \exists u . s \overset{i/o}{\longrightarrow} u$.

The inputs allowed in a state s are $init(s) \equiv \{i | \exists o.s \overset{i/o}{\longrightarrow}\}$. The states after applying trace σ in state s are given by s after $\sigma \equiv \{t | s \overset{\sigma}{\Rightarrow} t\}$. Operations like init, and after are overloaded for sets of states. Note that there are infinitely many traces and an infinitely long trace if the state machine contains a loop, that is $\exists s, \sigma . s \overset{\sigma}{\Rightarrow} s$, even if the machine is a fsm.

For *conformance* between a model and a sut the observed output of the sut should be allowed by the model for each input i in the init after every trace σ. Formally, conformance of the sut to the specification spec is defined as:

$$\text{sut } conf \text{ spec} \equiv \forall \sigma \in \text{traces}_{\text{spec}}(s_0).\forall i \in \text{init}(s_0 \text{ after}_{\text{spec}} \sigma)\forall o \in [O].$$

$$(t_0 \text{ after}_{\text{sut}} \sigma) \overset{i/o}{\longrightarrow} \Rightarrow (s_0 \text{ after}_{\text{spec}} \sigma) \overset{i/o}{\longrightarrow}$$

Here s_0 is the initial state of the specification and t_0 is the initial state of the sut. Note that this conformance relation compares inputs and outputs. The actual states of the sut are never used, hence the sut is treated as a black box. Comparing inputs and outputs of the model and the sut implies that they have to use identical types of inputs and outputs. The states however, can be of completely different types.

Testing state based machines is built on this conformance relation. Model-based testing checks the conformance relation for a finite number of finite traces. Since there can be infinitely many or infinitely long traces, testing conformance is in general an approximation of the relation *conf*.

Instead of generating traces of the specification and verify whether they are accepted by the sut the test algorithm of G∀st, testConf, maintains the after states of the current trace. It determines for n transitions on a single trace *on-the-fly* [20,21] whether the observed behaviour of the sut is conform to the model. If there are no after states testing has determined nonconformance. If the number of steps to do is zero, testing this trace is terminated without any conformance problems. Otherwise we choose an arbitrary input that is accepted by the specification in one of the current states, apply it to the sut and observe the corresponding output. The new set of states for the specification is the set of states that is obtained after the transition $\xrightarrow{i/o}$. The algorithm continues testing with one step less and the new set of states.

```
:: Verdict = Pass | Fail

testConf :: Int [S] T → Verdict
testConf n [] t = Fail
testConf 0 ss t = Pass
testConf n ss t
    | isEmpty inputs = Pass
    | otherwise      = testConf (n−1) (after ss i o) t2
where inputs = init ss
      i       = elemFrom inputs
      (o,t2) = sut t i
```

In order to test conformance we evaluate testConf N $[s_0]$ t_0 for M traces. When there is a *test goal* (some specific behaviour) we use this to select the input i from the current init, otherwise the test system selects a pseudo random element. The real implementation of this algorithm in G∀st is more involved since it is parameterized by the sut and spec, has to collect the trace, guide input selection, allow pseudo random input selection, etc. When a trace is found that proves nonconformance, the trace is shown together with the intermediate model states on the trace. The sut is treated as a black box, hence its states cannot be shown.

In order to use model-based testing for abstract data types with a state machine as specification, the sut must behave as a state machine. For the sut we construct a very simple machine that stores the actual adt as its state. For the specwe use a state machine with a state that contains enough information to check the transitions. Such a state is typically a naïve implementation of the interface offered by the adt, or an abstraction of it.

In the next sections we show case studies of model-based testing based on logical properties and the conformance relation.

4   Model Based Testing of Queues

The first case study is an abstract data type for FIFO queues. The assumption is that we have some smart amortized $O(1)$ implementation of queues [4,12] that makes it worthwhile to test.

```
:: Queue a

newQueue  ::  Queue a
enqueue   ::  a (Queue a) → Queue a
dequeue   ::    (Queue a) → (a, Queue a)
isEmptyQ  ::    (Queue a) → Bool
head      ::    (Queue a) → a
```

Note that dequeue and head are partial functions. They should not be applied to an empty queue, since that invokes a runtime error.

It is of course very well possible to design an interface for a queue without partial functions, e.g., the functions dequeue and head can for instance yield a Maybe a rather than an a. We deliberately chose partial functions for demonstrational purpose. For logical properties it is simple to avoid application of partial functions to illegal arguments, in a state based approach this involves restrictions on the allowed transitions.

4.1   Logical Property Based Testing of Queues

The properties of FIFO queues that we test are combinations of queue manipulations and check a relation between the elements stored and retrieved. It is easy to create more properties of this kind.

p0 A new queue produced by newQueue is empty.

p1 Inserting a single element in a new (empty) queue results in a non-empty queue, and the element obtained by dequeing that non-empty queue should be the same element, and the resulting queue should be empty again.

p2 When we dequeue an element from a queue with two elements, the obtained element is the first element enqueued. This property distinguishes a stack from a queue.

p3 This is an extended version of **p2**. First we enqueue two elements in an empty queue. The first element obtained by dequeueing is the first element enqueued. The second element obtained by dequeueing should be the last element enqueued.

p4 When we enqueue a list of elements and dequeue elements until the queue is empty, we should obtain the same list of elements.

p5 In this property we first enqueue elements x and y. Next we dequeue an element a which should be equal to x. We continue by enqueuing element z and dequeuing element b. This element b should be equal to y.

These properties can be phrased in G∀st for any type t under the class restriction that we have equality for the elements. For a polymorphic property G∀st cannot detect the type to be used in the tests. It is sufficient to test polymorphic functions with one well chosen type, see also [3].

On one hand we want a small type to prevent redundant tests. On the other hand the type must be sufficiently large to include all relevant situations, see [10]. In all tests executed in the remainder of the paper we use the type T7:

```
:: T7 = C0 | C1 | C2 | C3 | C4 | C5 | C6
```

The seven elements guarantee that we can construct fully filled search trees with all different elements of depth 2 in the second case study. With trees of depth 2 we expect to encounter all relevant recursion patterns. For queues a smaller type, like Bool, will also do.

We request the compiler to derive the generation of the test values for T7 by **derive** ggen T7. This has two advantages: we do not have to specify it manually, and everything will continue to work well when we change this type for one reason or another.

```
p0 :: Bool
p0 = isEmptyQ newQueue

p1 :: t → Bool | Eq t
p1 x = not (isEmptyQ q) && a = x && isEmptyQ q2
where q       = enqueue x newQueue
      (a, q2) = dequeue q

p2 :: t t → Bool | Eq t
p2 b c = fst (dequeue (enqueue c (enqueue b newQueue))) = b

p3 :: t t → Bool | Eq t
p3 x y = a = x && b = y
where (a, q2) = dequeue (enqueue y (enqueue x newQueue))
      (b, q3) = dequeue q2

p4 :: [t] → Bool | Eq t
p4 l = elements (enqueueList l) = l
elements q = if (isEmptyQ q) [] (let (e,q2) = dequeue q in [e: elements q2])
enqueueList l = foldl (swap o enqueue) newQueue l

p5 :: t t t → Bool | Eq t
p5 x y z = a = x && b = y
where (a, q1) = dequeue (enqueue y (enqueue x newQueue))
      (b, q2) = dequeue (enqueue z q1)
```

The test results of these logical properties are discussed in table 1 after the introduction of the state based model of queues.

4.2   State Machine Based Testing of Queues

Although the adt Queue is a collection of interface functions, it is quite easy to turn it into a state machine. The state of the constructed machine is the queue that is used in the interface functions.

Since the test system needs a data type as input for the state machine we define the data type Qcmd that mirrors the functions that manipulates queues. The constructer, newQueue will be tested when it is used to create the initial queue of the trace.

```
:: Qcmd a = EnQ a | DeQ | IsEmpty | Head
```

The queue state machine, qstm, holds a queue as state and applies the function corresponding to the Qcmd to this queue. The output of the machine is either a Boolean (for isEmptyQ), or a queue element of type t (for dequeue and head).

```
qstm :: (Queue t) (Qcmd t) → ([Either Bool t], Queue t)
qstm q (EnQ a) = ([], enqueue a q)
qstm q DeQ     = ([Right a], q2) where (a, q2) = dequeue q
qstm q Head    = ([Right (head q)], q)
qstm q IsEmpty = ([Left (isEmptyQ q)], q)
```

```
:: Either a b = Left a | Right b
```

For the specification we naïvely use a list of elements to model the queue. The complexity of this model is worse than the desired amortized $O(1)$ behaviour of Queue, but that does not affect the test results. Manipulating the queue model is just a little bit slower than necessary.

```
specQ :: [T] (Qcmd T) → [Trans (Either Bool T) [T]]
specQ q       (EnQ a) = [Pt [] (q++[a])]
specQ [a:x] DeQ       = [Pt [Right a] x]
specQ [a:x] Head      = [Pt [Right a] [a:x]]
specQ q     IsEmpty = [Pt [Left (isEmpty q)] q]
specQ q     c         = []
```

The last alternative of this specification, specQ q c = [], is somewhat special. It states that nothing is specified for all cases not covered by the previous alternatives. In particular it states here that nothing is defined for applying dequeue or head to an empty queue. Since nothing is specified for this combination of state and input, the testing algorithm will not try the input DeQ or Head for the state with an empty queue. Formally DeQ and Head are not in the init of the state []. It is easy to see that the simple model spec specifies the required behaviour for *all* allowed queue manipulations. The combination of transitions used in the actual tests is determined by the test tool.

Although it is easy to check whether the state machine covers all manipulating functions in the interface of the adt in all relevant situations, it is not necessary to include everything. Conformance testing works fine with a partial specification. A specification is partial if it does not cover the complete behaviour of the sut, see Section 3. Here the functions head and dequeue will not be used with an empty queue model. Since head and dequeue queue are partial functions it missing cases are not relevant. By omitting those transition from the model everything is allowed. Whenever everything is allowed testing is useless, hence those transitions will not occur in the tests.

Table 1. Test results for queues

	Q	Q1	Q2	Q3	Q4	Q5	Q6
P0	Proof 1	Proof 1	Proof 1	Proof 1	Proof 1	Proof 1	Proof 1
P1	Proof 7	Proof 7	Proof 7	Proof 7	Proof 7	Proof 7	Issue 1
P2	Proof 49	Proof 49	Proof 49	Issue 2	Proof 49	Proof 49	Proof 49
P3	Proof 49	Proof 49	Proof 49	Issue 2	Proof 49	Proof 49	Issue 2
P4	Passed 1000	Passed 1000	Issue 4	Issue 6	Passed 1000	Passed 1000	Issue 2
P5	Proof 343	Issue 2	Proof 343	Issue 3	Proof 343	Proof 343	Issue 3
Conf	Passed 100000	Issue 15	Issue 15	Issue 11	Issue 12	Issue 52	Issue 12

4.3   System under Test

In order to determine the capabilities to find issues of both testing approaches
we constructed an implementation of this queue using two lists of elements as
suggested by [4,12]. The first list contains elements in the right order, the second
list contains the rest of the queue in reversed order. The idea is to add elements
to the front of the second list on enqueue and extract elements from the front of
the first list for dequeueing. When the first list is empty the entire second list is
reversed and becomes the new first list.

```
:: Queue a = Q [a] [a]
```

We also constructed 6 incorrect queue implementations. Five implementations
contain typical small programming errors such as:

```
enqueue :: a (Queue a) → Queue a
enqueue a (Q f t) = Q [] [a:t]
```

It is obvious that the queue loses its front elements when we enqueue an element.
In a correct implementation we have to replace [] by f. Implementation Q5
implements a correct bounded queue.

4.4   Test Results

The obtained test results are show in Table 1. The first column gives the property
tested. In this table Proof n implies a proof by exhaustive testing after n tests.
Such proof holds obviously only for the type T7 used in the actual tests. A
polymorphic property proven for one type of arguments, does not necessarily
holds for all arguments if there are type restrictions. Without type restrictions
the proof holds for every argument if the current type is large enough [19]. The
weaker result Passed n indicates that the property passed n tests successfully. We
used maximally 1000 test cases for each property, which is the default in G∀st.
For conformance testing the default is 100 traces of maximal 1000 transitions.
The result Issue n indicates that an issue was found in executing test case n.

In fact, p4 was added after the first round of tests. After the initial tests we
observed that incorrect implementations Q2, Q4, and Q5 passed the tests with logical properties successfully. Even with this additional property, implementations
Q4 and Q5 still pass the tests.

The tests with the state based model spots issues in all incorrect implementations quickly. At most 52 transitions are needed to show nonconformance of the incorrect implementations. This number is of course somewhat dependent on the pseudorandom order of transitions chosen. By varying the seed for pseudorandom generation we were not able to create significant changes in this number of transitions needed to find the issue.

The issue for Q4 is found after the input trace: [IsEmpty, EnQ C0, EnQ C2, EnQ C3, Head, EnQ C0, EnQ C0, EnQ C4, IsEmpty, EnQ C4, DeQ, Head] . This indicates that the implementation of head is incorrect in a state obtained by executing the this sequence of transitions. It is no surprise that this error was not indicated by testing with logical properties: there is no property stating anything about this function. It appears that we need to store at least 3 elements and to dequeue before the function head fails. The erroneous definition is:

```
head  :: (Queue a) → a
head (Q []  t) = last t
head (Q f  _) = last f
```

When we know this, it can be revealed by testing the property

```
p6 :: T T T → Bool
p6 x y z = head (snd (dequeue (enqueueList [x,y,z]))) = y
```

4.5 Algebraic Queue Properties

One might wonder if the somewhat disappointing issue detecting power of testing with logical properties is due to an insufficient set of properties. When we know the errors in the implementation, it is possible to state properties that reveal them. In general however, we do not know if there are issues at all, let alone the nature of the problems. Queues are well studied (mathematical) objects. This has resulted in algebraic properties describing the desired behaviour of queues, see e.g. [8,9]. Algebraic rules for our queues are:

$$isEmptyQ \ newQueue = True$$
$$isEmptyQ \ (enqueue \ x \ q) = False \tag{1}$$
$$head \ (enqueue \ x \ q) = \text{if } q == newQueue \text{ then } x \text{ else } head \ q \tag{2}$$
$$dequeue \ (enqueue \ x \ q) = \text{if } q == newQueue \text{ then } (x, \ q) \text{ else } (y, \ enqueue \ x \ q_2) \tag{3}$$
$$\text{where } (y, \ q_2) \ = \ dequeue \ q \tag{3}$$

We can transform these algebraic rules directly into testable properties. The first axiom is implemented by p0. Properties corresponding to the other axioms are:

```
pA1 :: t (Queue t) → Bool
pA1 t q = not (isEmptyQ (enqueue t q))

pA2 :: t (Queue t) → Bool | Eq t
pA2 x q = head (enqueue x q) = if (isEmptyQ q) x (head q)
```

Table 2. Test results for algebraic properties of queues with two different generators

gen1	Q	Q1	Q2	Q3	Q4	Q5	Q6
pA1	Passed 1000	Passed 1000	Passed 1000	Passed 1000	Passed 1000	Passed 1000	Passed 1000
pA2	Passed 1000	Passed 1000	Passed 1000	Passed 1000	Passed 1000	Passed 1000	Passed 1000
pA3	Passed 1000	Issue 7	Issue 2	Issue 8	Passed 1000	Passed 1000	Issue 1
gen2	Q	Q1	Q2	Q3	Q4	Q5	Q6
pA1	Passed 1000	Passed 1000	Passed 1000	Passed 1000	Passed 1000	Passed 1000	Passed 1000
pA2	Passed 1000	Passed 1000	Passed 1000	Passed 1000	Passed 1000	Passed 1000	Passed 1000
pA3	Passed 1000	Issue 7	Issue 2	Issue 4	Passed 1000	Passed 1000	Issue 1

```
pA3 :: t (Queue t) → Bool | Eq t
pA3 x q = dequeue (enqueue x q) == if (isEmptyQ q) (x, q) (y, enqueue x q2)
where (y,q2) = dequeue q
```

Note that these properties quantify over queues rather than individual elements to store in the queues. If the implementation of the queue is known we can simply derive the generic generation of queues. Without breaking the abstraction barrier of the abstract queue implementations, we can generate the infinite list of queues by systematically inserting elements in the queue.

```
ggen{|Queue|} xs s = qs
where qs = [newQueue: [enqueue x q \\ (x, q) ← diag2 (xs s) qs]]
```

The argument xs is the generator for queue elements and s is the generator state. By diag2 we mix new queue elements and generated queues in a fair way. As an alternative we can generate lists and enqueue all their elements:

```
ggen{|Queue|} xs s = map enqueueList (ggen{|*→*|} xs s)
```

We tested the algebraic properties with both generators called gen1 and gen2 respectively. The results are very similar to the test results with the ad hoc properties. The correct implementation, Q, passes all tests. For the incorrect implementations Q1, Q2, Q3, and Q6 issues are found very quickly, but the incorrect implementations Q4 and Q5 pass the tests. By increasing the number of test cases (to at least 2626), or using a more advanced generator, it is possible to find issues with pA3 in Q5. The error in Q4 cannot be detected by testing these properties, it will never occur in the prescribed used of the queue.

4.6   Review of Queue Test Results

As first conclusion from this case study is that it is hard to determine if a given set of logical properties is enough to find issues in each implementation with simple programming errors. The second conclusion is that it is much easier to see that a state based specification covers all relevant transitions. The test results show that the random walk finds issues quickly.

5   Model Based Testing of AVL Trees

The second case study is the AVL variant of self-balancing binary search trees [1]. These are search trees where the difference in height of sibling subtrees is at most one. We used this as an exercise for students in our functional programming course. To detect the error spotting power of our specification we use 30 of their solutions as sut. We add the implementation used to demonstrate those trees, a quickly patched version of the AVL trees used in the Clean libraries to implement mappings, and our own implementation of this adt as sut.

The students had to implement the following interface for AVL trees:

```
:: AVLTree a

mkAVLLeaf        ::          AVLTree a
mkAVLNode        :: a → AVLTree a
isMemberAVLTree  :: a (AVLTree a) → Bool       | Eq, Ord a
insertAVLTree    :: a (AVLTree a) → AVLTree a  | Eq, Ord a
deleteAVLTree    :: a (AVLTree a) → AVLTree a  | Eq, Ord a
isAVLTree        ::   (AVLTree a) → Bool        | Eq, Ord a
```

The last function in this interface is rather nonstandard. It checks the internal correctness of the adt. It was introduced to enforce the students to think about correctness of their implementation and to enable them to test it. The function isAVLTree is very convenient in any test of this data type and we will heavily use it. In fact this function is the only way to distinguish a proper AVL tree implementation, from any other implementation providing a correct implementation of the interface without advanced measurements of time and space consumption. In order to test the correct implementation of this predicate we also made a reference implementation isAVLTreeR for each sut. Our first property states that they have the same result for all trees. For black box testing we really need such a predicate to distinguish AVL trees from any other container type with the appropriate interface.

5.1 Logical Property Based Testing of AVL Trees

We can test an implementation of this interface very similar to the queue implementation of Section 4. We state logical properties about single function applications in the interface and combinations of those functions. Based on the experience with testing queues we included more properties over list of elements and properties that consider combinations of insert and delete operations.

```
// check comparelsAVL for arbitrary instances of the data type AVLTree T
pIsAVL :: Property
pIsAVL = comparelsAVL For (ggen{|*|} genState)

// both implementations of the correctness predicate should yield same result
comparelsAVL :: (AVLTree T) → Bool
comparelsAVL t = isAVLTreeR t == isAVLTree t

// after inserting e in an empty tree, the tree should contain it
pAVL0 :: T → Bool
pAVL0 e = isMemberAVLTree e (insertAVLTree e mkAVLLeaf)
```

```
// all single element trees should contain the element used in constructing it
pAVL1 :: T → Bool
pAVL1 e = isMemberAVLTree e (mkAVLNode e)

// every tree contains the inserted element
pAVL2 :: T (AVLTree T) → Bool
pAVL2 e t = isMemberAVLTree e (insertAVLTree e t)

// all generated AVL-trees obey the constraints checked by isAVLTreeR
pAVL3 :: (AVLTree T) → Bool
pAVL3 t = isAVLTreeR t

// any tree constructed from a list of elements contains an element iff it is in the list
pAVL4 :: T [T] → Bool
pAVL4 e l = isMemberAVLTree e t = isMember e l
where t  = foldr insertAVLTree mkAVLLeaf l

// a deleted element is in the AVL-tree iff there were multiple inserts
pAVL5 :: T [T] → Bool
pAVL5 e l = isMemberAVLTree e t2 = (length (filter ((=) e) l) > 1)
where t  = foldr insertAVLTree mkAVLLeaf l
      t2 = deleteAVLTree e t

// each AVL-tree is valid after removing an element
pAVL6 :: T (AVLTree T) → Bool
pAVL6 e t = isAVLTreeR (deleteAVLTree e t)

// each AVL-tree is valid after removing a list of elements
pAVL7 :: [T] (AVLTree T) → Bool
pAVL7 l t = isAVLTreeR (foldr deleteAVLTree t l)
```

Properties such as pAVL2 impose a slight complication, because G∀st has to generate AVL-trees. For generating valid AVL-trees we cannot rely on the generic algorithm. This algorithm can construct type correct instances of the data type, but generic generation has no notion on the constraints on AVL-trees. However, we can construct AVL-trees by inserting the elements of a list of randomly created elements one by one in an empty tree. We manually specify this in the following instance of the generation algorithm ggen of G∀st.

```
:: AVLTreeT :== AVLTree T

ggen{|AVLTreeT|} s = map (foldr insertAVLTree mkAVLLeaf) (ggen{|*|} s)
```

We can test the correctness of the generated trees by a property like pAVL3.

5.2   State Machine Based Testing of AVL Trees

Analogous to the first case study, we proceed by creating a naïve specification that uses straightforward unsorted lists to model the behaviour of AVL-trees. Of course many operations on the list are $O(n)$ instead of $O(\log n)$ as required

Table 3. Test results for AVL-trees

	1	2	3	5	9	13	14	16	22	30	32	33
pIsAVL	CE 4	CE 3	Pass	Pass	CE 4	CE 3	CE 2	CE 2	Pass	CE 4	Pass	Pass
pAVL0	Proof 7	Proof 7	Proof 7	Proof 7	Proof 7	Proof 7	Proof 7	Proof 7	Proof 7	Proof 7	Proof 7	Proof 7
pAVL1	Proof 7	Proof 7	Proof 7	Proof 7	Proof 7	Proof 7	Proof 7	Proof 7	Proof 7	Proof 7	Proof 7	Proof 7
pAVL2	Pass	Pass	Pass	Pass	Pass	Pass	Pass	Pass	Pass	Pass	Pass	Pass
pAVL3	Pass	CE 3	Pass	Pass	Pass	CE 3	CE 2	CE 2	CE 16	CE 6	Pass	Pass
pAVL4	Pass	Pass	Pass	Pass	Pass	Pass	Pass	Pass	Pass	CE 247	Pass	Pass
pAVL5	Pass	Pass	CE 4	CE 4	Pass	CE 4	CE 5	Pass	CE 22	CE 163	Pass	Pass
pAVL6	CE 23	CE 7	Pass	Pass	CE 974	CE 4	CE 2	CE 7	CE 93	CE 22	Pass	Pass
pAVL7	CE 47	CE 4	Pass	Pass	Pass	CE 4	CE 2	CE 2	CE 121	CE 16	Pass	Pass
Conf	CE 41	CE 2	CE 60	CE 60	CE 45	CE 2	CE 2	CE 1	CE 9	CE 22	CE 8899	Pass

for the AVL-trees. Again this does not harm the behaviour, it only slows down the tests. The type Cmd mimics the operations on AVL-trees.

```
:: Cmd a = Ins a | Del a | Mem a
```

The function stm turns an AVLTree into a state machine that accepts these commands and applies the corresponding functions to the AVL-tree. After each operation that can change the tree there is a Boolean in the output that indicates whether the new tree is still a valid AVL-tree. Since this invokes isAVLTree each time it might be useful, there is no reason to add it as a separate transition by adding it to Cmd.

```
stm :: (AVLTree T) (Cmd T) → ([Bool], AVLTree T)
stm avl (Ins a) = ([isAVLTree avl2], avl2) where avl2 = insertAVLTree a avl
stm avl (Del a) = ([isAVLTree avl2], avl2) where avl2 = deleteAVLTree a avl
stm avl (Mem a) = ([isMemberAVLTree a avl], avl)
```

In the specification we mimic the behaviour of AVL-trees by a simple list of elements. The specification requires True in the output when stm checks the correctness of AVL-trees.

```
specAVL :: [T] (Cmd T) → [Trans Bool [T]]
specAVL list (Ins a) = [Pt [True] [a:list]]
specAVL list (Del a) = [Pt [True] (removeMember a list)]
specAVL list (Mem a) = [Pt [isMember a list] list]
specAVL list _       = []
```

5.3   Test Results

We had 33 implementations of AVL-trees available that can be used as sut. It appears that it is not easy to implement this adt correctly. Only 12 implementations execute the test without runtime errors. Typical runtime errors are caused by missing cases, or invoking (double) rotations to trees that cannot be rotated in that way. Implementations with runtime errors are excluded from the tests.

The test results are listed in Table 3. Due to layout constraints the number of successful tests, 1000, is omitted in this table. We also write CE, for CounterExample, instead of Issue. It is somewhat remarkable that only 5 implementations pass the test for a correct implementation of the function isAVLTree checking the constraints of the AVL-trees. This makes stand alone testing of these implementations unnecessarily hard.

Table 3 shows that implementing AVL-trees correctly is quite hard, only implementation 33 passes all tests. The results of logical property based testing and conformance based testing are rather similar. Only implementation 32 contains an issue that is found by conformance testing of state machines, but is not spotted by the logical properties. This implementation is the naïvely changed implementation of a dynamic mapping from keys to values. In the original implementation inserting a value with the same key replaces the previous mapping of this key to a value. In AVL-trees this value is added for the second time to the tree. The error is due to the naïve adaptation of this data type to AVL-trees, we cannot blame the original mapping. The issue is exposed by some sequences of insert and delete. A small example is [Ins C4, Ins C4, Ins C3, Del C4, Ins C3, Ins C3, Ins C6, Ins C4, Ins C0, Ins C0, Ins C0, Del C6].

The students had to implement simple unit tests for their implementations. This probably explains why the simple properties pAVL0, pAVK1, and pAVL2 find no issues. The test results in Table 3 show clearly that those unit tests were insufficient to yield correct implementations. Often a small number of test cases or transitions are enough to show an issue or nonconformance. However, there are also examples that require several hundreds of test cases, or thousands of transitions. Since all tests for any of the implementations in Table 3 are executed within a few seconds, there is no reason to decrease the default number of tests or transitions in G∀st.

6   Observations

Model-based testing based on logical properties and state based conformance testing effectively spots issues. In both case studies we found more errors using the state based approach. This is not a fundamental restriction of the logical property based approach. It just indicates that our set of properties was not strong enough. Without detailed study of the internals of the adt it is undecidable if a set of logical properties is sufficient. For state based specifications it is easy to determine if every transition is covered by the model in all relevant states.

The state based models needed in the conformance tests are very concise and can be constructed almost mechanically from the interface of the adt. Often there is just one transition in the model for each function in the interface. Only the state to be used in such a model requires some real design decisions.

When an issue is found during the test execution there are two potential candidates to blame: the model and the sut. In our experience it turns out to be easier to interpret the issues found by conformance based testing than the issues found with logical property based testing. There are two reasons for this. First, G∀st shows the trace leading to the issue including all states of the model on this trace. This aids in seeing what the model prescribes. Second, in state based conformance testing there is only one concise model while logical property based testing uses a set of logical properties. One often needs pen and paper or an automated execution to determine the source of the issue. Although issues can be caused by the model and the sut, the vast majority of errors appear to be in the sut. This is an encouraging result, we want that testing is an easy way to determine and improve the quality of a sut and not that a lot of effort and a sut are needed to make a correct model.

The proofs by exhaustive testing of logical properties are a stronger test result than the pass obtained for conformance testing. Only for finite state machines a proof is possible under strong assumptions on the sut. Nevertheless, the default pseudorandom walk in conformance testing proves to be very effective.

7   Related Work

There are many variants of QuickCheck, such as [16] and [5]. Those test tools are based on logical properties and generate test cases based on the property to test. Hence they suffer from the same problem as logical property based testing in G∀st: it only works reliably if we have a sufficiently strong set of properties. This paper illustrates that developing such a set of properties is a lot of work and not trivial. Bernardy et al have a schema to construct an optimal monomorphic instance for a polymorphic property [3]. In this approach testing remains dependent on the set of logical properties.

Many automatic test tools outside functional programming only execute the specified tests automatically, they do not generate a test suite. JUnit, and its ports to other languages, is the best known example. In those tools there is no clear separation between properties and test values, there is just a collection of individual tests to be executed. In [2] Arts et al. specify a model-based way to generate tests for data types. These tests are based on logical properties, while this paper shows that tests based on state machines are more effective.

There are several related notions of conformance of state machine, e.g. [17]. Most of these relations have also been implemented, e.g. [18]. Many of these implementations require either finite state machines, or impose severe restrictions on the data types used (e.g. only byte-sized integers). The availability of arbitrary data types and values as state, input and output is crucial for the state based tests of abstract data types used in this paper. Most tools have limited power to handle data types.

In the object oriented world there are some trace based test tools. T2 [15] generates traces on the fly based on a class definition in Java. There are optionally special methods in such a class to check their correctness. This is called *in-code* specification. Jartege [13] generates test traces and executes them afterwards. Constraints stated in JML are checked during the execution of the generated traces. Randoop [14] uses on-the-fly testing with traces of method applications. The correctness is optionally specified by some Java classes. In our approach the external specification is leading in trace generation and checking. In this paper the subjects of tests are abstract types in Clean. There is no reason why this approach cannot be used for types, or classes, in other languages accessed via the foreign function interface of Clean. Definitions such as isAVL from Section 5 act very similar to the in-class specifications of those Java tools.

In [7] Claessens and Hughes discuss testing of queues in a monadic setting. They do not focus on the error detecting capabilities.

8   Conclusion

There are two approaches to model-based testing. In one approach the models are logical properties. The test system tries to falsify these properties by generating test values for the universally quantified variables in those properties and evaluating the property for those variables. In the other approach the model is a state machine. The test system tries to show nonconformance of the sut and the model by applying inputs from the init of the model to the sut and check whether the observed output is allowed by the system.

The logical property based approach is used for systems without a state, typically pure functions or combinations of those functions. The conformance based approach is used for systems with a state, that is systems where the reaction on an input depends on the history.

In this paper we have compared these two approaches to test (polymorphic) abstract data types. Our results show that it is easier to make a state based model than to develop a complete set of logical properties. It is hard to determine when the set of logical properties is complete. If we do not know the details of the implementation of the adt, it is even impossible to decide if a given set of properties is powerful enough. Due to deficiencies in the set of logical properties the conformance based approach performs better in our case studies. The state based models are more concise than the set of logical properties. For these reasons we advocate the use of conformance based testing for algebraic data types. This works only if the conformance based test tool can handle data types flexibly, and many existing tools are not able to do this. Out test tool G∀st is very well suited for this purpose.

The ability to generate proofs by exhaustive testing for properties over finite domains in G∀st can yield more confidence than just a successful test. In the conformance based approach this is only possible for finite state machines and severe restrictions on the sut [11].

The combined approach is very effective in our examples. Since G∀st provides model-based testing based on logical properties as well as conformance testing, it is an excellent tool for testing an adt. The user gets best of both worlds in a single framework.

References

1. Adelson-Velskii, G., Landis, E.: An algorithm for the organization of information. Soviet Mathematics Monthly 3, 1259–1263 (1962)
2. Arts, T., Castro, L.M., Hughes, J.: Testing Erlang data types with Quviq Quickcheck. In: Proceedings of the 7th ACM SIGPLAN Workshop on ERLANG, ERLANG 2008, pp. 1–8. ACM, New York (2008)
3. Bernardy, J.-P., Jansson, P., Claessen, K.: Testing Polymorphic Properties. In: Gordon, A.D. (ed.) ESOP 2010. LNCS, vol. 6012, pp. 125–144. Springer, Heidelberg (2010)
4. Burton, F.W.: An efficient functional implementation of FIFO queues. Inf. Process. Lett. 14(5), 205–206 (1982)

5. Christiansen, J., Fischer, S.: EasyCheck — Test Data for Free. In: Garrigue, J., Hermenegildo, M.V. (eds.) FLOPS 2008. LNCS, vol. 4989, pp. 322–336. Springer, Heidelberg (2008)

6. Claessen, K., Hughes, J.: QuickCheck: a lightweight tool for random testing of Haskell programs. In: Proceedings of the 5th International Conference on Functional Programming, ICFP 2000, pp. 268–279. ACM, Montreal (2000)

7. Claessen, K., Hughes, J.: Testing monadic code with quickcheck. SIGPLAN Not. 37, 47–59 (2002)

8. Feijs, L.M.G., Jonkers, H.B.M.: Formal Specification and Design. Cambridge University Press (1992)

9. Guttag, J.V., Horning, J.J.: The algebraic specification of abstract data types. Acta Informatica 10, 27–52 (1978)

10. Koopman, P., Plasmeijer, R.: Effective test set generation for model-based testing (submitted for publication)

11. Koopman, P., Plasmeijer, R.: Fully Automatic Testing with Functions as Specifications. In: Horváth, Z. (ed.) CEFP 2005. LNCS, vol. 4164, pp. 35–61. Springer, Heidelberg (2006)

12. Okasaki, C.: Purely Functional Data Structures. Cambridge University Press (1998)

13. Oriat, C.: Jartege: A Tool for Random Generation of Unit Tests for Java Classes. In: Reussner, R., Mayer, J., Stafford, J.A., Overhage, S., Becker, S., Schroeder, P.J. (eds.) QoSA 2005 and SOQUA 2005. LNCS, vol. 3712, pp. 242–256. Springer, Heidelberg (2005)

14. Pacheco, C., Ernst, M.D.: Randoop: feedback-directed random testing for Java. In: Companion to the 22nd ACM SIGPLAN Conference on Object-oriented Programming Systems and Applications Companion, OOPSLA 2007 (2007)

15. Prasetya, W., Vos, T., Baars, A.: Trace-based reflexive testing of OO programs with T2. In: Proceedings of the 2008 International Conference on Software Testing, Verification, and Validation, pp. 151–160. IEEE Computer Society (2008)

16. Runciman, C., Naylor, M., Lindblad, F.: Smallcheck and lazy Smallcheck: automatic exhaustive testing for small values. SIGPLAN Not. 44, 37–48 (2008)

17. Tretmans, J.: Testing Concurrent Systems: A Formal Approach. In: Baeten, J.C.M., Mauw, S. (eds.) CONCUR 1999. LNCS, vol. 1664, pp. 46–65. Springer, Heidelberg (1999)

18. Tretmans, J., Brinksma, E.: TorX: automated model based testing. In: Hartman, A., Dussa-Zieger, K. (eds.) Proceedings of the 1st European Conference on Model-Driven Software Engineering, MDSE 2003, Nurnberg, Germany (2003)

19. Voigtländer, J.: Much ado about two (pearl): a pearl on parallel prefix computation. In: Proceedings of the 35th Annual ACM SIGPLAN-SIGACT Symposium on Principles of Programming Languages, POPL 2008, pp. 29–35. ACM, New York (2008)

20. de Vries, R., Tretmans, J.: On-the-fly conformance testing using SPIN. Software Tools for Technology Transfer, STTT 2(4), 382–393 (2000)

21. van Weelden, A., Oostdijk, M., Frantzen, L., Koopman, P., Tretmans, J.: On-the-fly formal testing of a smart card applet. In: Sasaki, R., Qing, S., Okamoto, E., Yoshiura, H. (eds.) Proceedings of the 20th International Information Security Conference, SEC 2005, Makuhari Messe, Chiba, Japan, pp. 564–576. Springer (May 2005); Also available as Technical Report NIII-R0428

Property-Based Testing and Verification: A Catalog of Classroom Examples*

Rex Page

University of Oklahoma, Norman OK 73019

Abstract. For the past a decade, John Hughes of Chalmers University and Quviq has pioneered property-based testing in debugging industrial software. Three undergraduate courses at the University of Oklahoma have paralleled this work, but on the pedagogical side and with the additional goal of verification of properties by mathematical proof, using both paper-and-pencil methods and mechanized logic. An essential part of both efforts, and probably the most important part, is the formalization in predicate logic of the expectations of software developers. This is central to engineering software quality in the defect dimension. This report discusses property-based testing in course work and provides some examples from the classroom. Hughes has observed that software properties useful for testing functional software often (1) compare the results of different ways of computing the same thing or (2) check that forward and inverse transformations restore the original data. What percentage of useful software properties fall into these categories? Our collection of examples from course records may help shed some light on how closely pedagogy on property-based testing matches observations of relative frequencies of various categories of properties in industry and may also serve as an educational aid in learning to use property-based testing effectively in software development.

1 Property-Based Testing in the Classroom

Students in the computer science program at the University of Oklahoma are required to take three courses in which expected software behaviors are expressed as formulas in predicate logic. In one of the courses (applied logic), the focus is on paper-and-pencil proofs that the properties hold. In the others (a two-course sequence in software engineering), the focus is on software development, including testing and verification. For the past three years, all three courses have included project experience with automated testing on random data generated by the DoubleCheck tool in the Dracula programming environment [1], a facility similar to QuickCheck [2], but for software expressed in ACL2 [3], which includes a programming language based on Common Lisp.

Used in its native form, the ACL2 mechanized logic requires properties to be expressed as theorems, and programmers can sometimes succeed in getting

---

* Partially supported by National Science Foundation Award Number 1016532.

A. Gill and J. Hage (Eds.): IFL 2011, LNCS 7257, pp. 134–147, 2012.

ACL2 to verify those theorems by mathematical proof. In some cases ACL2 fully automates the proof process. For more complex properties, ACL2 needs help in the form of lemmas or hints about proof strategy.

The Dracula environment acts as an interface to the ACL2 programming language and logic, adding to it a testing environment with generators for random data. On request, Dracula converts DoubleCheck properties to ACL2 theorems and submits them to the mechanized logic for verification. Students can carry out testing based on formal predicates about behaviors they expect in software they are developing. When testing convinces them that their software works properly, they have the option to proceed to full, mechanized verification of the theorems expressed in those predicates. Property-based testing with random data becomes part of the software development process, and full verification also plays a role.

For example consider the following DoubleCheck test for the associativity of list concatenation.

```
(defproperty append-assoc :repeat 1000
  (xs :value (random-list-of (random-symbol))
   ys :value (random-list-of (random-symbol))
   zs :value (random-list-of (random-symbol)))
  (equal (append xs (append ys zs))
         (append (append xs ys) zs)))
```

Dracula checks the property specified by the equation at the end of the definition against a thousand random choices for the lists involved in the equation. (The :repeat specification controls the number of tests, which defaults to fifty if unspecified.) Dracula selects both the lengths of the lists and the symbols comprising their elements from independent, random distributions. Programmers can control those distributions through special directives or by writing their own generators. The random data generators provided by DoubleCheck are adequate for most of the testing students do in their course work, but some software engineering course projects call for the design of generators.

When asked to prove that the associative property of concatenation holds for all choices of the lists, Dracula converts the property definition to the following theorem and submits it to the ACL2 mechanized logic.

```
(defthm append-assoc-thm
  (equal (append xs (append ys zs))
         (append (append xs ys) zs)))
```

The theorem is a copy of the predicate specified in the DoubleCheck property, without consideration of the kinds of data it specifies. However, the specified property can restrict the test in certain ways, and when it does this, the restrictions are incorporated in the theorem as hypotheses in an implication. For example, nthcdr is an intrinsic ACL2 operator that delivers a list like its second argument, but without an initial segment of elements, the length of which is specified by the first argument. Predicates about nthcdr, to be proven as ACL2 theorems, must restrict the first argument to the natural numbers. A property definition can specify such a restriction through a :where clause, as in the following definition.

```
(defproperty nthcdr-len
  (n  :value (random-integer)
      :where (natp n)
   xs :value (random-list-of (random-symbol)))
  (<= (len (nthcdr n xs)) n))
```

When random test data is restricted by a :where clause, Dracula includes the restriction as a hypothesis in an implication that has the specified property as its conclusion. When there are multiple :where clauses, their logical conjunction forms the hypothesis. If asked to call for a proof that the length property of nthcdr holds for all data, Dracula would submit the following theorem to the ACL2 mechanized logic.

```
(defthm nthcdr-len-thm
  (implies (natp n)
           (<= (len (nthcdr n xs)) n)))
```

Through :where restrictions and other annotations, DoubleCheck provides full access to the mechanized logic of ACL2. Dracula also allows direct definition of ACL2 theorems, which are submitted to the mechanized logic without modification, but students generally find it convenient to stay within the DoubleCheck property-definition syntax because they usually go through the testing stage before attempting full verification of properties as theorems.

We find that as students proceed through courses using Dracula and DoubleCheck, they gradually evolve from the point of view that testing software components is a matter of running a few tests on selected, specific cases to the conclusion that, while running thousands of random tests based on formal predicates may not provide full guarantees, it goes much further in that direction than the one-off tests they previously relied on. They also gain an appreciation of the difference between testing a program and knowing for certain some of the properties of a program.

We are now in the process of cataloging property-based testing examples from lectures, homework projects, and examinations, expressing them in the common framework provided by Dracula, and, in many cases, using the ACL2 mechanized logic to carry out proofs of the properties. This report describes some of the examples and categories, specifies a few in detail, presents some preliminary data about categories of property-based tests appearing in the examples, and comments on the distribution of those examples across the observed categories.

2 Property Categories and Examples

John Hughes has for years used property-based testing in industrial environments [4] [5] [6] [7] [8]. He has found that, while industrial software testing usually calls for checking output against post-conditions on models of state, tests of functional programs most often fall into one of two categories: (1) comparing the results of computing a value in two different ways (function equality tests)[1] (2) checking that an inverse function reproduces the original input when applied to the results of the forward computation (round-trip tests) [9].

We have categorized so far about half of over 300 properties defined in logic and software engineering courses over the past decade. About a quarter of these properties are either not characterized (miscellaneous) or can be viewed as type specifications, a category that would not arise for properties expressed in statically typed languages. About one in eight fall into a special kind of function equality that we refer to as property preservation, such as preservation of length by functions that rearrange lists into increasing order.

2.1   Function Equality Properties

The property expressing the associativity of append (Section 1) is an example of a function equality test. Figure 1 samples typical function equality tests from lectures in my software engineering courses over the past decade.

The first three tests in Figure 1 involve only intrinsic functions in ACL2:

```
(defproperty cdr-reduces-len-by-1
  (xs :value (random-list-of (random-symbol))
      :where (consp xs))
  (= (len(cdr xs))
     (- (len xs) 1)))
(defproperty cons-as-append
  (x  :value (random-symbol)
   xs :value (random-list-of (random-symbol)))
  (equal (append (list x) xs)
         (cons x xs)))
(defproperty law-of-added-exponents
  (m :value (random-integer)
     :where (integerp m)
   n :value (random-integer)
     :where (integerp n)
   x :value (random-integer)
     :where (and (acl2-numberp x) (/= x 0)))
  (= (expt x (+ m n)) (* (expt x m) (expt x n))))
```

---

[1] Hughes uses the term "commutative diagram" to describe this type of test because in his experience such a test usually involves an abstract data type with corresponding transformations between concrete and abstract versions of the same data. One route on the diagram transforms concrete data and then moves the result to the abstract domain. The other route moves the data to the abstract domain, then transforms it. Our term, "function equality", connotes a somewhat broader category of tests.

1. removing the first element of a non-empty list reduces its length by 1
2. inserting an element at the beginning of a list is a special case of concatenation
3. law of added exponents
4. conventional exponentiation and the Russian peasant algorithm
5. the nth element of the product of a scalar and a vector is the same as the product of the scalar and the nth element of the vector
6. evaluating a polynomial conventionally and by Horner's rule
7. the first element of a list is the last element of its reverse
8. various tail recursions match a corresponding nested recursion (list reversal or Fibonacci numbers, for example)
9. the number of elements in a flattened tree is the number of nodes in the tree
10. the sum of the numbers in a list constructed from n copies of a number x is the product of n and x
11. DeMorgan's laws for lists of Booleans
12. various Boolean identities, such as the absorption laws
13. associative law of concatenation
14. demultiplexing a list splits it into its even-indexed and odd-indexed elements
15. multiplexing two lists puts the elements of one of them in even-indexed positions in the result list and the elements of the other in the odd-indexed positions
16. the low-order bit in the binary representation of an even number is zero
17. inserting n zeros at the low-order end of a binary numeral produces the numeral of a number 2^n times larger
18. the length of a binary numeral with no leading zeros is the ceiling of the base-2 logarithm of the next integer after the one the numeral denotes
19. a ripple-carry binary adder delivers the sum of the input numerals
20. a shift-and-add binary multiplier delivers the product of the input numerals

Fig. 1. Function Equality Properties (43%): (f x) = (g x)

Other tests express relationships among functions defined by the programmer.

```
(defun s*v (s v)  ; (s*v_1 s*v_2 s*v_3 ... )
  (if (consp v)
      (cons (* s (first v))
            (s*v s (rest v)))
      v))
(defproperty s*v-elements
  (s  :value (random-integer)
   v  :value (random-list-of (random-integer))
      :where (consp v)
   n  :value (random-between 0 (1- (len v)))
      :where (and (natp n) (< n (len v))))
  (= (nth n (s*v s v)) (* s (nth n v))))
```

The ACL2 mechanized logic fully automates all but a few the proofs of all of the function equality properties in Figure 1. However, some of the proofs (the law of exponents for example) depend on theorems of numeric algebra imported from a standard ACL2 library.

2.2   Round-Trip Properties

Many property-based tests involve first encoding some information, then decoding it with an inverse operator. A classic example of such a property applies the list-reversal operator twice. Since reverse is its own inverse, two applications in succession reproduce the original list. Figure 2 samples typical round-trip properties from course work.

1. double reverse
2. use linear encryption to encrypt a message, then decrypt it
3. compute the quotient and remainder, given a divisor and dividend, then reconstruct the dividend from the quotient, remainder, and divisor
4. convert a number to a binary numeral, then back to a number
5. convert a binary numeral with no leading zeros to a number, then back to a binary numeral
6. convert a number to a binary numeral, insert some leading zeros, then convert back to a number
7. a list is the concatenation of its first n elements and its remaining elements
8. demultiplex a list of signals into the even-numbered and odd-numbers ones, then multiplex them to reproduce the original list
9. multiplex two lists that contain the same number of signals, then demultiplex to reproduce the original lists
10. $log_2(2^n) = n$
11. pad a list to a specified length, then compute its length
12. chop a list to a specified length, then compute its length
13. concatenate two lists, then reproduce the second list by dropping the number of elements in the first from the beginning of the concatenation
14. concatenate two lists, then reproduce the first list by extracting the number of elements it contains from the beginning of the concatenation
15. split a list into contiguous sublists of a specified length, then append all the sublists together
16. extract the packets in a list that are separated by a given delimiter, then reconstruct the list from the packets
17. insert a key into a search tree, then extract the key

Fig. 2. Round-Trip Properties (17%): $(f\ (g\ x)) = x$

The following linear encryption and decryption functions set the stage for an examination of the second example from the list of round-trip properties in Figure 2. This particular encryption method simply adds adjacent numbers in a list of integers in the range 0 through $m - 1$ using arithmetic modulo m. It inserts a fixed number at the end of the list to encode the last element.

If the numbers were, for example, ASCII character codes, the encoding would handle text messages. More complex linear encodings that transform adjacent pairs with a two-by-two matrix of coefficients could be handled similarly.

```
(defun encrypt-pair (m x x-nxt)
  (mod (+ x x-nxt) m))
(defun decrypt-pair (m x-encrypted y-decrypted)
  (mod (- x-encrypted y-decrypted) m))
(defun encrypt (m xs) ; linear encryption
  (if (consp (cdr xs))
      (cons (encrypt-pair m (car xs) (cadr xs))
            (encrypt m (cdr xs)))
      (list (encrypt-pair m (car xs) (1- m)))))

(defun decrypt (m ys)
  (if (consp (cdr ys))
      (let* ((decrypted-cdr (decrypt m (cdr ys))))
        (cons (decrypt-pair m (car ys) (car decrypted-cdr))
              decrypted-cdr))
      (list (decrypt-pair m (car ys) (1- m)))))
```

With these definitions decrypt inverts encrypt. The following property implements a round-trip test of this fact.

```
(defun codep (m x)
  (and (natp x) (< x m)))
(defun code-listp (m xs)
  (and (natp m) (> m 1)
       (if (consp xs)
           (and (codep m (car xs)) (code-listp m (cdr xs)))
           (null xs))))
(defproperty decrypt-inverts-encrypt
  (m  :value (+ (random-natural) 2)
   n  :value (random-natural)
   xs :value (random-list-of (random-between 0 (- m 1)))
   :where (and (natp m) (> m 1)
               (consp xs) (code-listp m xs)))
  (equal (decrypt m (encrypt m xs)) xs))
```

This example reinforces the importance of running many tests and the value
of verification by mathematical proof. If a bug is inserted in the test, allowing
the values in the message to range up to $m + 1$ instead of $m - 1$, DoubleCheck
runs almost 700 tests before uncovering the error. Serious testing usually requires
thousands of tests, and careful consideration of the distribution of random values
generated by the tests may also be necessary.

The ACL2 mechanized logic succeeds in fully automating the proof of the
inversion property for this linear encryption/decryption implementation when
given access to some algebraic properties of modular arithmetic that are supplied
in a standard library. Again, the :where clause states the hypothesis in the
implication being verified, and the equation at the end of the property definition
specifies the conclusion. An error in the value specification for random test data

does not affect the theorem, since Dracula uses only :where clauses and the Boolean formula specifying the property to generate the theorem it submits to the mechanized logic.

The mechanized logic fully automates the proofs of all the round-trip properties in Figure 2 except the last three. It needs a little help to work its way through the properties of the list-splitting and packets functions and substantial help to verify search tree properties.

2.3 Other Categories of Properties

Function equality, round-trip, and the properties we think of as preserving some characteristic of the input are all characterized by equations: (f x) = (g x), (f (g x)) = x, and (p (f x)) = (p x), respectively. All three categories could be viewed as versions of function equality, in a sense. We view them as distinct categories because we think they provide useful guidelines to students looking for properties that express testable expectations of the software they develop.

Two examples of preservation properties involve list concatenation. Concatenation preserves total length of the input lists and also preserves the elements that occur in the input.

```
(defproperty append-preserves-len
   (xs :value (random-list-of (random-symbol))
    ys :value (random-list-of (random-symbol)))
   (= (len (append xs ys)) (+ (len xs) (len ys))))
(defproperty append-conserves-elements
   (x  :value (random-symbol)
    xs :value (random-list-of (random-symbol))
    ys :value (random-list-of (random-symbol)))
   (iff (member-equal x (append xs ys))
        (or (member-equal x xs) (member-equal x ys))))
```

Sorting functions, reverse, various forms of list merge, whether order-preserving or simple, two-way multiplexing (lock-step selection from one list or the other) are other operations that preserve length and list elements. Figure 3 summarizes the idea of preservation properties with such examples.

1. various "conservation of list-length" properties (for example, length of the list delivered by a sorting function is the same as the length of the input list; similar statements about concatenation, reverse, multiplexing, demultiplexing, and ordered merge)
2. various "conservation of values" properties (for example, a value is in the list delivered by a sorting function if and only if it is in the input list; similar properties for concatenation, reverse, multiplexing, demultiplexing, and ordered merge)
3. the cosine of the angle between two vectors is not affected by multiplying all the elements of one of the vectors by the same scalar

Fig. 3. Preservation Properties (14%): (p (f x)) = (p x)

Since formulas in ACL2 are untyped, it is often useful to define properties to test expectations about type. Figure 4 displays some properties of this kind.

Finally, some properties that we have found useful in the classroom do not seem to fall into any of the categories we have described. Figure 5 describes some of these miscellaneous properties.

1. the length of a list is a natural number
2. the square of a rational number is non-negative
3. the sum (or product) of two positive numbers is positive
4. the inner product of vectors of rational numbers is a rational number
5. the maximum (or minimum) of a list of rational numbers is a rational number
6. a permutation generator delivers a list of lists
7. quicksort delivers an ordered list (same goes for insertion sort and merge-sort)

Fig. 4. Type Properties (14%)

1. the maximum (or minimum) of a list is an element of the list
2. no element of a list is greater than (less than) its maximum (minimum)
3. demultiplexing a list with more than one element produces two shorter lists
4. a suffix (or prefix) of a list cannot be longer than the list
5. removing a positive number of elements from a non-empty list makes it shorter
6. the square of the inner product of two vectors does not exceed the square of the product of their norms
7. the cosine of the angle between two different vectors is strictly less than 1

Fig. 5. Miscellaneous Properties (12%)

3   Tips for Converting Properties to Theorems

Property-based tests are Boolean formulas with value specifications for random data generation. Expressing software expectations as Boolean formulas focuses attention on correctness issues, and that, by itself, has a positive affect on software reliability. A mechanized logic like ACL2 offers an opportunity to go beyond testing to verification of properties by mathematical proof. Guiding the mechanized logic through this extra step often requires substantial effort, but there are some things that can be done to facilitate the verification process and help students succeed with mechanized proofs.

Many of our observations about facilitating verification are specific to the ACL2 theorem prover. Consequently, they will be of greatest value to people using the ACL2 system, especially within the Dracula environment. Other theorem provers will require other tricks. However, part of the following discussion includes a conjecture about the potential usefulness of some of these ideas in other systems of mechanized logic.

3.1   Dealing with Data Types

The ACL2 logic requires all functions to be total. That is, they must specify values for all kinds of input. Value specifications in tests usually restrict themselves to data within the expected domain of operations. For example, suppose add is a function designed to compute the sum of two binary numerals, and nat is a function that converts binary numerals to numbers. If binary numerals are represented by lists of zeros and ones, the following function equality test would make sense.

```
(defproperty add-computes-sum-of-binary-numerals
  (xs :value (random-list-of (random-between 0 1))
   ys :value (random-list-of (random-between 0 1)))
  (= (nat (add xs ys))
     (+ (nat xs) (nat ys))))
```

One then might want to prove the corresponding theorem.

```
(defthm add-computes-sum-thm
  (= (nat (add xs ys))
     (+ (nat xs) (nat ys))))
```

This might or might not be a theorem. It depends on details in the representation of binary numerals. If nat and add require their arguments to be lists of zeros and ones, as they are in the value specifications of the add-computes-sum property, then the theorem will need a hypothesis constraining the arguments to lists of zeros and ones.

```
(defthm add-computes-sum-thm-with-type-constraints
  (implies (and (bit-listp xs) (bit-listp ys))
           (= (nat (add xs ys))
              (+ (nat xs) (nat ys)))))
```

That seems reasonable, especially to people accustomed to statically typed languages, but it means that every theorem whose proof cites this one (theorems about a a shift-and-add multiplier for example) will have to confirm the hypotheses. That can lead to a tangle of complications as the system grows.

One way to reduce complexity, making it easier to build a theory, is to reduce the number of required hypotheses by designing functions that interpret unexpected data in ways that are consistent with the desired theory.[2] For example, the following definition of nat interprets lists of zeros and ones as binary numerals. It assumes that the low-order bit comes first, then the 2s bit, 4s bit, and so on up to the high-order bit.

```
(defun nat (xs) ; number from little-endian binary numeral
  (if (consp xs)
      (if (equal (car xs) 1)
          (+ 1 (* 2 (nat (cdr xs))))
          (* 2 (nat (cdr xs))))
      0))
```

---

[2] I learned this trick from Ruben Gamboa. He says he learned it from Robert Boyer.

In addition to dealing with the expected data (lists of zeros and ones), this definition interprets any ACL2 data structure as a binary numeral, and it does so in a way that is consistent with its interpretation of the expected form of input. The trick this example employs is to denote one-bits by the number 1. Anything other than the number 1 denotes a zero-bit. Furthermore, the arguments may take any form, not just lists. This definition of nat interprets any atom in the same way that it interprets the empty list (namely, as a numeral for the number zero).

This typeless approach makes the theorem hold without hypotheses. When Dracula submits the add-computes-sum property to ACL2 in the form of the corresponding theorem (add-computes-sum-thm, above), the mechanized logic proves it, given the definition of nat that interprets 1's as one-bits and everything else as zero-bits.

If we go on to define a function mul that computes the product of two binary numerals by a shift-and-add algorithm, a proof that the multiplication function works properly avoids a complicated nest of hypothesis verification. The proof goes through, unfettered. It's not so easy when the definitions place restrictions on the form of the arguments.

```
(defthm mul-computes-product-of-binary-numerals
  (= (nat (mul xs ys))
     (* (nat xs) (nat ys))))
```

Many modern programming languages incorporate type consistency theorems in the compilation process. The mechanized logic of ACL2 can verify type consistency along with more advanced properties, but the programmer must attend to all of these issues in the development process. The ACL2 logic requires total functions to improve its success in finding proofs without always relying on detailed assistance from the programmer ([3], page 89). Reasoning about types in the development process is part of the price paid for the effectiveness of ACL2.

However, I suspect that reducing the network of hypotheses in a collection of related properties would simplify verification, even in typeful systems. For example, in a statically typed system, one might constrain numerals to be lists of integers, but not to lists of zeros and ones. The integer zero could represent a zero-bit, and any other integer could represent a one-bit. The type system would implicitly verify the list-of-integers constraint automatically, so a theorem prover could ignore that part and the chosen bit-representation semantics would avoid unnecessary hypotheses. Of course, in this case, using lists of Booleans to represent numerals might be a better choice. That would relegate the entire network of hypotheses to the domain of type consistency and leave the theorem prover free to operate without verifying additional constraints.

3.2   Verifying Termination

Since ACL2 requires all functions to be total, it must verify termination before admitting a function to its logic. Its ability to do this is impressive, but making use of certain idioms can simplify the process.

Count Down. For example, ACL2 is always able to admit functions whose termination depends on an inductive parameter that is a natural number counting down to a particular value. It is often not successful if the counting goes the other direction. As a result, most ACL2 programmers define such functions in ways that take advantage of the strengths of ACL2 in this area. For example the following code defines two functions that deliver a list of integers between given lower and upper limits. However, one of the functions (`between-partial`) fails when its arguments are complex numbers or non-numeric values.

```
(defun between-partial (m n) ; (m m+1 ... n)
  (if (<= m n)
      (cons m (between-partial (+ m 1) n))
      nil))
(defun between-append (m n xs) ; (append (m m+1 ... n) xs)
  (if (posp n)
      (between-append m (- n 1) (cons (+ m n) xs))
      (cons m xs)))
(defun between (m n) ; (m m+1 ... n)
  (between-append m (- n m) nil))
```

Even if the definition of `between-partial` is converted to a total function by choosing the non-recursive formula when one or both of its arguments are not integers, ACL2 fails to admit it because ACL2 is not good at finding a workable induction measure when the count goes up instead of down. Rearranging the definition so that the count goes down plays to the strengths of ACL2.

In addition, the function must be made total by dealing with non-numeric values for the parameters. This example uses the predicate `posp`, which is true for integers exceeding zero and false for all other inputs, including non-numeric values, to accomplish the goal of defining a function that terminates, regardless of what values are supplied as arguments.

Induction on Suffixes and Proof Guidance. Another pattern that facilitates proofs of termination arises when a list in an inductive reference is shortened by applying the `cdr` function. When the shortening operation has, instead, the form (`nthcdr n xs`), where n is a positive integer, ACL2 needs a little help. The following theorem, which ACL2 succeeds in proving when an induction strategy is suggested, is often helpful when `nthcdr` is the operator that makes the induction work.

```
(defthm nthcdr-shortens-lists
  (implies (and (posp n) (consp xs))
           (< (len (nthcdr n xs)) (len xs)))
  :hints (("Goal" :induct (len xs)))))
```

ACL2 applies this theorem to prove termination of the following function, which constructs a list from every n^{th} element of its second argument. In this case ACL2 automatically uses the theorem about `nthcdr` in the termination proof even without the :use hint in the definition. The hint is included here primarily to illustrate its form. ACL2 occasionally needs a directive like this to find its way to a proof.

```
(defun every-nth (n xs) ; (x_1 x_n+1 x_2n+1 ...)
  (declare (xargs
    :measure (len xs)
    :hints (("Goal" :use (:instance nthcdr-shortens-lists)))))
  (if (and (consp xs) (posp n))
      (cons (car xs) (every-nth n (nthcdr n xs)))
      xs))
```

To succeed, students need to follow a few guidelines in designing functions. In addition to the guidelines already discussed, clean code helps a lot, but that is always a worthwhile goal, so the fact that ACL2 encourages it is a plus. Nested recursion simplifies reasoning more often then tail recursion, so that is another useful heuristic. When tail recursion is needed for efficient computation, it is sometimes helpful to write two versions of a function, one with nested recursion and one with tail recursion, prove them to be equal in the extensional sense, then use one for computation and the other for reasoning.

When the ACL2 logic needs guidance, hints suggesting an induction strategy and/or theorems that might be useful in the proof are often sufficient. The ACL2 system includes directives for dozens of other kinds of guidance, but students can go a long way with nothing beyond these two.

When numbers are involved, importing prepackaged bundles of theorems about numeric algebra often gets the theorem prover around road blocks. ACL2 refers to such bundles as "books". The "arithmetic-3/top" book provides many theorems about the associative, commutative, and distributive laws of addition and multiplication, linear inequalities, and the like, and "arithmetic-3/floor-mod/floor-mod" provides theorems useful when reasoning about formulas that employ modular arithmetic.

Surprisingly little specialized knowledge is needed to use ACL2 productively. One reason for choosing ACL2 in a course where both property-based testing and full verification play a role, but are not the only topics of study, is that ACL2 so often succeeds in verifying properties with little or no help. That makes it possible to introduce verification without spending the entire course bringing students up to speed on guiding the mechanized logic.

4   Summary and Future Work

Properties for testing that correspond to neither function equality nor round-trip tests may express expectations that bear on correctness or consistency with the environments in which the software components are used.

We have categorized 146 of over 300 properties defined in courses over the past decade. Sixty-three fell into the function equality category, 25 were round-trip properties, 21 preservation properties, 20 type properties, and 17 miscellaneous properties. The Hughes categories (function equality and round-trip) comprise 60% of the classroom examples in our current database. This expands to 74% when preservation properties are recognized as a special case of function equality properties and not placed in a separate category. In this view the prominence of function equality and round-trip properties in software development is to some extent confirmed by our experience in the classroom.

A catalog of course projects that has many descriptions of software properties can be found in the "20 Projects" web site [10]. We have an ongoing effort to extend this to a database of properties from course work, including property definitions from lectures, projects, and examinations. The database will include function definitions and formal property statements in Dracula/ACL2 logic. We anticipate over 300 property specifications and over 200 function definitions, indexed by category and web accessible.

We also plan to apply the ACL2 mechanized logic to these properties and to develop the lemmas and hints required for mechanized proof of the properties. We hope that this database will be useful in future educational efforts and will help students learn to formulate useful properties.

Acknowledgments. The author thanks Marco T. Morazán for suggesting a section on tips for full verification of properties and John Hughes for helpful discussions of property categories. Caleb Eggensperger and Allen Smith provided valuable assistance in developing and categorizing example properties.

References

1. Eastlund, C.: Doublecheck your theorems. In: Proceedings of the 8th International Workshop on the ACL2 Theorem Prover and its Applications, pp. 42–46 (2009)
2. Classen, K., Hughes, J.: QuickCheck: A lightweight tool for random testing of Haskell programs. In: Proceedings of the 5th ACM SIGPLAN International Conference on Functional Programming, pp. 268–279 (2000)
3. Kaufmann, M., Manolios, P., Moore, J.S.: Computer-Aided Reasoning: An Approach. Kluwer Academic Publishers (2000)
4. Arts, T., Hughes, J., Johansson, J., Wiger, U.: Testing telecoms software with QuviQ QuickCheck. In: Proceedings of the 2006 ACM SIGPLAN Workshop on Erlang, pp. 2–10 (2006)
5. Derrick, J., Walkinshaw, N., Arts, T., Earle, C.B., Cesarini, F., Fredlund, L.-A., Gulias, V., Hughes, J., Thompson, S.: Property-Based Testing - The ProTest Project. In: de Boer, F.S., Bonsangue, M.M., Hallerstede, S., Leuschel, M. (eds.) FMCO 2009. LNCS, vol. 6286, pp. 250–271. Springer, Heidelberg (2010)
6. Claessen, K., Palka, M., Smallbone, N., Hughes, J.: Finding race conditions in Erlang with QuickCheck and PULSE. In: Proceedings of the 14th ACM SIGPLAN International Conference on Functional Programming, pp. 149–160 (2009)
7. Claessen, K., Smallbone, N., Hughes, J.: QuickSpec: Guessing formal specifications using testing. In: Proceedings of the 4th International Conference on Tests and Proofs, pp. 6–21 (2010)
8. Hughes, J., Norell, U., Sautret, J.: Using temporal relations to specify and test an instant messaging server. In: Proceedings of the 32nd International Conference on Software Engineering, pp. 95–102 (2010)
9. Hughes, J., Bolinder, H.: Testing a database for race conditions with QuickCheck. In: Proceedings of the 10th ACM SIGPLAN Erlang Workshop, pp. 72–77 (2011)
10. Page Rex. 20 projects (2008),
   http://www.cs.ou.edu/~rlpage/SEcollab/20projects/

Describing and Optimising Reversible Logic Using a Functional Language

Michael Kirkedal Thomsen

DIKU, Department of Computer Science, University of Copenhagen
shapper@diku.dk

Abstract. This paper presents the design of a language for the description and optimisation of reversible logic circuits. The language is a combinator-style functional language designed to be close to the reversible logical gate-level. The combinators include high-level constructs such as ripples, but also the recognisable inversion combinator f^{-1}, which defines the inverse function of f using an efficient semantics.

It is important to ensure that all circuits descriptions are reversible, and furthermore we must require this to be done statically. This is ensured by the type system, which also allows the description of arbitrary sized circuits. The combination of the functional language and the restricted reversible model results in many arithmetic laws, which provide more possibilities for term rewriting and, thus, the opportunity for good optimisation.

1 Introduction

Reversible computation is based on computational models that are both forward and backward deterministic. A motivation for using such models dates back to 1961 when Landauer [21] showed that, theoretically, the energy necessary for a computation is *not* correlated with the number of computations performed (as was the general belief), but *instead* with the amount of information that is discarded. If one deletes information in a computing device, the device must dissipate a small amount of heat to account for the information loss. This theoretical result have been experimentally verified very recently [8].

In theory, this *Landauer limit* accounts only for a small fraction of the total energy usage of a computation in a device. However, this limit is a strict *lower bound* on the dissipation and the actual amount is proportional to the signal energy used to represent the erased information [19]. In practice, the signal energy is much higher than the Landauer limit and, thus, so is the energy to be dissipated by information loss. Furthermore, the principle applies to each logic gate in the device (as well as high-level programming language), so with the current circuit miniaturisation the fraction of the total energy usage is increasing.

In general all injective (computable) functions can be computed in a reversible way and all non-injective functions can be embedded such that they also can be computed reversibly [3,7]. In some cases such embeddings can be efficient; *e.g.* addition $(+(a,b) = c)$ can be embedded by saving one of the inputs

A. Gill and J. Hage (Eds.): IFL 2011, LNCS 7257, pp. 148–163, 2012.

$(+(a, b) = (c, b))$. Some injective functions are widely used today. A good example is loss-less multimedia encodings, where an inverse transform always exists. Reversible implementations of both the fast Fourier transform and cosine transforms have been investigated [15].

Today, reversible logic circuits are designed either by hand or by use of circuit synthesis approaches, and both of these approaches have clear drawbacks. While efficient hand-made designs of small regular circuits have been demonstrated (such as adders and ALUs [31,33]), the restriction of reversibility quickly causes the design of larger circuits to be complex and error-prone. Algorithms for reversible logic synthesis, on the other hand, are by necessity a compromise between algorithm execution speed (exact synthesis is infeasible for larger circuits), logic depth (leading to increased delay), and logic width (adding many extra undesired wires) of the generated circuits (cf. [34]).

There is therefore a need to look at the problem of reversible circuit design from a programming language perspective, in order to exploit the inherent properties of a higher-level description and thereby generate more efficient designs. Here, especially function inversion (f^{-1}) comes to mind, but also the use of simple guaranteed reversible constructs (*reversible updates*) and local use of temporary lines (also called *ancillae lines*).

This paper proposes a language designed to be close to the reversible logical gate-level used to describe (and possibly implement) reversible circuits. At the same time it has the features of a functional language, enabling circuit optimisation using simple algebraic laws. The language is point-free and the design and much of its notation is inspired by Backus' FP language [5] and its language extension μFP [28], which were designed for VLSI implementations. The combinator style used makes writing the descriptions more cumbersome compared to higher-level design languages, but enables easier reasoning about the circuits. This language is therefore suitable as a domain-specific intermediate language for a reversible logic design flow.

Using a domain-specific language to describe logic circuits is far from a new idea, and modern ASIC and VLSI designs would not be possible without computer-aided design tools. Some of the most widely used languages for describing circuits are imperative (*e.g.* VHDL, Verilog, and SystemC) but there also exists a wide range of functional languages designed specifically for describing hardware. Functional programming has been argued to be "a perfect match" for hardware design [29] and the results presented here suggest that this is also true for descriptions of reversible hardware.

Organisation. In the following section we explain the basics of reversible logic as needed for this work. In Sec. 3 we describe the language and in Secs. 4 and 5, we show applications of the language to reversible binary adders and loss-less encoding. Sec. 6 describes future work, and we conclude in Sec. 7.

$$A \longrightarrow\!\!\!\times\!\!\!\longrightarrow \overline{A}$$

Fig. 1. Not gate   Fig. 2. Feyn gate   Fig. 3. Toff gate   Fig. 4. Fred gate

2   Reversible Computation

This section introduces the main concepts of reversible logic used throughout the paper.

A few reversible languages have been developed and to the author's knowledge the most widely used is the reversible imperative language Janus [22,37]. Also a first approach to a general-purpose functional language has very recently been proposed [36]. Closer to the logic level is a small description language (based on the Janus syntax) designed to aid with reversible logic synthesis [35]. Finally, the implementation of monads for quantum computing in Haskell [1] is worth mentioning.

Here, we shall characterise reversibility in terms of *local invertibility* [37], meaning that all gates and operations must have an easy inverse (*e.g.* plus with minus as its inverse). Furthermore, we only use a class of operations called *reversible updates* [4] that, by definition, guarantee reversibility of the operations, in that it is only possible to augment a value a with a value that does not depend on a. The benefit is that we can easily check if descriptions are indeed reversible, and quickly find the *inverse* of such descriptions. On the other hand, the possible atomic reversible operations *are* restricted, but not so much that it results in loss of expressiveness: the language can still describe the functionality of all possible reversible logic circuits.

2.1   Reversible Logic

In this paper we use the formalism of Toffoli, Fredkin [18, 32] and Barenco et al. [6] to describe *reversible logic circuits*.

A *reversible gate* is defined as a bijective boolean function from n to n values. There exists many of these gates, but we restrict ourselves to the following basic reversible logic gates [6]:

- The Not gate (Fig. 1) is the only gate from conventional logic that is reversible.
- The *Feynman gate* (Feyn, Fig. 2), or controlled-not gate, negates the input A iff the control C is true.
- The *Toffoli gate* (Toff, Fig. 3), or controlled-controlled-not gate, negates the input A iff both controls C_1 and C_2 are true.
- The *Fredkin gate* (Fred, Fig. 4), or controlled-swap gate, swaps the two inputs A and B iff the control C is true.

A *reversible circuit* is then a acyclic network of reversible gates, where *fan-out* is not permitted.

As one of the central goals of reversible circuits is to avoid information destruction, the number of auxiliary bits used is an important non-standard characteristic of reversible circuits. We say that a *garbage* bit is a non-constant output line that is not part of the desired result, but is required for logical reversibility, and an *ancilla* bit (usually used as a *scratch* variable) is a bit-line that is assured to be constant at both input and output. The distinction between the two is important, as garbage bits accumulate over the computation (which is likely to lead to information destruction), while ancillae can be reused with each new computation of the circuit.

2.2   Implementation of Reversible Logic

Reversible computation is related to other emerging technologies such as quantum computation [17,26], optical computing [12], and nanotechnologies [24] that use a similar or slightly extended set of gates. First implementations and fabrications of reversible logic in CMOS technology have also been accomplished (e.g. [27]). These exploit the fact that reversible logic is particularly suitable (1) when it comes to reuse of signal energy (in contrast to static CMOS logic that sinks the signal energy with each gate) and (2) when using *adiabatic switching* [2,20] to switch transistors in a more energy efficient way. In fact, SPICE simulations of reversible circuits have shown that such implementations have the potential to reduce energy consumption by a factor of 10 [14, 16]. Actual implementation of circuit designs, however, is not considered in this paper.

3   The Language

In the following section we will present the language for describing combinatorial reversible logic circuits. The language is designed to be close to actual reversible logic; using a point-free combinator style functional language gives a close correspondence to the often-used diagram notation for reversible logic (*e.g.* see Fig. 12). The syntax of the language is shown in Fig. 5, and a (slightly simplified) type system is shown in Fig. 6.

The design and much of the notation is inspired by the FP language [5] and its language extension μFP [28]. It should be noted, however, that this language only supports reversible combinational circuits and does not include a state-construct as in μFP; there are currently no physical implementations of reversible memory, mainly because of the constraint to use only combinatorial circuit constructs. Most research on the design of reversible logic circuits focusses on combinational circuits, although abstract approaches to reversible memory [25] and interfacing circuits with static volatile memory [10] have been investigated. It is, however, possible to extend the language with memory constructs, if desired.

3.1   Reversibility and Local Invertibility

A very important property of the language is to guarantee reversibility of the described circuits or functions. There are many possible approaches to ensure

$$
\begin{aligned}
D ::= &\ (\textbf{Def}\ funcName = R)^* & \text{function definition}\\
R ::= &\ \textsf{Id} & \text{identity gate}\\
&\ \textsf{Not} \mid \textsf{Feyn} \mid \textsf{Toff} \mid \textsf{Fred} & \text{basic reversible gates}\\
&\ \textsf{Flip} \mid \textsf{Rup} \mid \textsf{Rdn} \mid \{n_1, n_2, \dots\} & \text{permutations}\\
&\ \textsf{Zip} \mid \textsf{Split} \mid \textsf{Concat} & \text{reordering}\\
&\ funcName & \text{function use}\\
&\ R; R \mid [R, R] & \text{composition}\\
&\ R\ ?\ (R, R) & \text{general conditional}\\
&\ R\ ?\ R \mid R\ !\ R & \text{special conditionals}\\
&\ \alpha R \mid \backslash R \mid /R & \text{map, ripples}\\
&\ R^{-1} & \text{inverse}
\end{aligned}
$$

Fig. 5. Syntax of the language

this. In the reversible imperative language Janus [22,37], programs are only to some extent guaranteed to be reversible. This is because Janus includes general conditional and loop statements where reversibility can only be guaranteed at run-time by performing assertion checks. If an assertion check fails during program execution, the interpreter throws an error; the program computes a partial function.

This approach is not suitable when describing circuits, so in the proposed language, reversibility is instead guaranteed by the following properties:

1. No cyclic circuits are possible. This is guaranteed by the composition functions' forms in the language design. With serial and parallel composition (Sec. 3.4) circuit components can only be combined in the width or depth of the circuits.
2. No fan-in or fan-out. Serial composition is possible only with circuits of the same type. The language is point-free so assignment of one input-wire to multiple output-wires (and *vice versa*) is not possible.
3. All basic constructs and function forms are reversible. That is, they all have the same number of inputs and outputs and implement bijective functions.
4. The language does not feature general recursion. Instead, it includes combinators (*ripples*) that recurse over the width of the inputs.

While these properties guarantee that the language is reversible, they do not ensure that it is easy to find the inverse of a given circuit. To ensure an efficient way of finding inverse circuits we enforce the principle of *local invertibility* [37]. This means that all atoms and function forms must have a simple inverse that is defined similarly to the original term. We shall see in Sec. 3.7 that they all have a simple inverse form, and even that many atoms are self-inverse. Thus, in effect, a reversible circuit description is a list of function definitions in the language that is well-typed.

$$\boxed{\tau ::= \; \texttt{w} \mid \tau * \tau \mid n \times \tau} \qquad\qquad \boxed{n ::= \; \mathsf{Nat} \mid \mathsf{X}}$$

Reversible gates:

$$\frac{}{\mathsf{Id} : \tau \to \tau} \qquad\qquad \frac{}{\mathsf{Not} : \texttt{w} \to \texttt{w}} \qquad\qquad \frac{}{\mathsf{Feyn} : \texttt{w} * \texttt{w} \to \texttt{w} * \texttt{w}}$$

$$\frac{}{\mathsf{Toff} : \texttt{w} * \texttt{w} * \texttt{w} \to \texttt{w} * \texttt{w} * \texttt{w}} \qquad\qquad \frac{}{\mathsf{Fred} : \texttt{w} * \texttt{w} * \texttt{w} \to \texttt{w} * \texttt{w} * \texttt{w}}$$

Permutations:

$$\frac{}{\pi_n : \tau_1 * ... * \tau_n \to \pi_n(\tau_1 * ... * \tau_n)} \qquad\qquad \frac{}{\mathsf{Rup} : \tau_1 * \tau_2 * ... * \tau_n \to \tau_2 * ... * \tau_n * \tau_1}$$

$$\frac{}{\mathsf{Flip} : \tau_1 * ... * \tau_n \to \tau_n * ... * \tau_1} \qquad\qquad \frac{}{\mathsf{Rdn} : \tau_1 * ... * \tau_n * \tau_m \to \tau_m * \tau_1 * ... * \tau_n}$$

Wire grouping:

$$\frac{}{\mathsf{Zip} : n \times m \times \tau \to m \times n \times \tau}$$

$$\frac{}{\mathsf{Split} : n \times \tau \to \underbrace{\tau * ... * \tau}_{n \text{ in total}}} \qquad\qquad \frac{}{\mathsf{Concat} : \underbrace{\tau * ... * \tau}_{n \text{ in total}} \to n \times \tau}$$

Compositions:

$$\frac{f : \tau \to \tau'' \qquad g : \tau'' \to \tau'}{f \, ; g : \tau \to \tau'} \qquad\qquad \frac{f : \tau_1 \to \tau_1' \qquad g : \tau_2 \to \tau_2'}{[f,g] : \tau_1 * \tau_2 \to \tau_1' * \tau_2'}$$

Conditionals:

$$\frac{f : \tau_1 \to \tau_1' \qquad \tau_1' \in \{\texttt{w}, \tau * \texttt{w}\} \qquad (g;h) : \tau_2 \to \tau_2'}{f \; ? \; (g,h) : \tau_1 * \tau_2 \to \tau_1 * \tau_2'}$$

$$\frac{f \; ? \; (g, \mathsf{Id}) : \tau \to \tau_1'}{f \; ? \; g : \tau \to \tau'} \qquad\qquad \frac{f \; ? \; (g, g^{-1}) : \tau \to \tau}{f \; ! \; g : \tau \to \tau}$$

Apply-to-all and ripples:

$$\frac{f : \tau \to \tau'}{\alpha f : n \times \tau \to n \times \tau'} \qquad\qquad \frac{f : \tau_1 * \tau_2 \to \tau_1 * \tau_2'}{\backslash f : \tau_1 * (n \times \tau_2) \to \tau_1 * (n \times \tau_2')}$$

Application and inversion:

$$\frac{\Gamma(funcName) : \tau \to \tau'}{\vdash_\Gamma funcName : \tau \to \tau'} \qquad\qquad \frac{f : \tau' \to \tau}{f^{-1} : \tau \to \tau'}$$

Fig. 6. Type system. A similar rule to $\backslash f$ exists for $/f$. Γ is a mapping from function names to code.

3.2 The Type System in Short

Types in the language (Fig. 6) define grouping structure of wires. The only atom type is $\texttt{w}$, which denotes one single bit-wire, while there are two grouping structures. The first is $\tau * \tau'$, which denotes a pair. The second is $n \times \tau$, which a denotes a list of length n containing only τ's. Here n is either a natural number or a meta variable, *i.e.* making it possible to describe arbitrary sized circuits. All constructs are then a mapping from one type to another, where reversibility ensures that the total number of bit-wires is unchanged.

3.3 Basic Constructs and Notation

The basic constructs (atoms) of the language are the previously described reversible gates, the identity gate, elements for wire permutation, and wire reordering. The gates are only included in their non-generalised form and named as in Sec. 2 (Not, Feyn, Toff, Fred). A notation for using gates with permuted inputs is introduced below. The identity gate is named Id.

Wire permutations are written using one-line notation in curly brackets. For example, $\{3, 2, 1\}$ is the 3-wire permutation that swaps the first and third wire but keeps the second in place. Some frequently used arbitrary-sized wire permutations have been specified with a name. These are the flip[1] permutation (Flip), which reverses all the wires ($\{n, ..., 2, 1\}$), the roll down (Rdn), which barrel rolls all wires towards the lower positions ($\{n, 1, ..., n - 1\}$) and the roll up (Rup), which does the same in the opposite direction ($\{2, ..., n, 1\}$).

Wire reordering (mainly used to ensure the correct type for compositions) consists of the transposing function Zip, which takes N by M wire-types and returns them ordered as M by N, a function (Concat) for grouping an n-tuple containing similar types to a list of length n, and ungrouping wires (Split), which does the inverse of Concat.

Notation. To avoid writing too many permutations and parallel identity gates we adopt the following notation: writing a permutation as a subscript to a gate is shorthand for applying the permutation, followed by the standard version of the gate, followed by the inverse permutation, *e.g.*,

$$\mathsf{Toff}_{\{2,3,1\}} \equiv \{2, 3, 1\} \, ; \mathsf{Toff} \, ; \{2, 3, 1\}^{-1} \, .$$

Similarly, if the permutation is wider than the gate itself, then a number of identity gates are added to make the composition of the correctly typed, *e.g.*

$$\mathsf{Feyn}_{\{1,3,2\}} \equiv \{1, 3, 2\} \, ; [\mathsf{Id}, \mathsf{Feyn}] \, ; \{1, 3, 2\}^{-1} \, ,$$

because Feyn is a two input/output gate.

3.4   Basic Compositions

The language has two ways of composing circuits: serial and parallel. The *serial composition* of two circuits f and g is written as

$$f \, ; g \, . \hspace{4cm} \text{(serial composition)}$$

To ensure a simple correspondence between the standard diagrams and the language, we use *left-to-right* notation (see Fig. 7). This is contrary to the *right-to-left* notation of function composition used in FP.

The *parallel composition* of two circuits is written as

$$[f, g] \, , \hspace{4cm} \text{(parallel composition)}$$

---

[1] The name Flip has been chosen over the more common *reverse* to avoid any confusion with the term *reversibility* and the inversion combinator (f^{-1}).

Fig. 7. Serial composition: $f;g$ **Fig. 8.** Parallel composition: $[f,g]$

where the first group of wires are inputs to f and a second group inputs to g as shown in Fig. 8. This construct differs from FP in that f and g do not get the same input. We write $[f,g,h,...]$ as a short-hand for $[f,[g,[h,[...]]]]$.

Some basic laws for composing circuits are as follows: (1) Id is the identity element for serial composition (there is none for parallel composition), (2, 3) both serial and parallel compositions are associative, and (4) serial composition is distributive over parallel composition.

$$f;\mathsf{Id} = \mathsf{Id};f = f \quad (1) \qquad\qquad [[f,g],h] = [f,[g,h]] \quad (3)$$
$$(f;g);h = f;(g;h) \quad (2) \qquad\qquad [f,g];[h,k] = [f;h,g;k] \quad (4)$$

Both the Toffoli and the Fredkin gate are universal gates, so either of these gates together with these two compositions is enough to describe the functionality of all circuits (including permutations).

3.5   Conditionals

The language has one conditional construct and two special cases of this conditional. The two special-case conditionals are included because they are well-suited for optimisation. All conditionals are implemented as reversible updates with the restriction that the updating function must be reversible. The conditional (if f then g else h) is written as

$$f ? (g,h) \qquad\qquad \text{(conditional)}$$

and to implement it as a reversible update, the conditional has two inputs. The first input is used as input for f and is unchanged over the conditional, while the second input is used as input to g and h as shown in Fig. 9. This results in different laws for lifting a function out of the conditional compared to FP. In (5) and (6) we must use the identity gate in parallel with g.

$$f ? (g;h, g;k) = [\mathsf{Id}, g];(f ? (h,k)) \qquad\qquad (5)$$
$$f ? (h;g, k;g) = f ? (h,k);[\mathsf{Id}, g] \qquad\qquad (6)$$

The first of the special-case conditionals,

$$f ? g = f ? (g, \mathsf{Id}), \qquad\qquad \text{(true-conditional)}$$

has only the then-case while the second,

$$f ! g = f ? (g, g^{-1}), \qquad\qquad \text{(inversion-condition)}$$

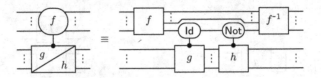

Fig. 9. General conditional: f ? (g,h). The Boolean value of the lowest wire after computing f is used as the control.

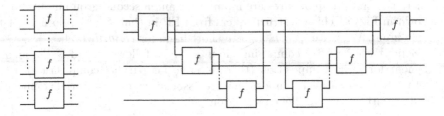

Fig. 10. Apply to all: αf **Fig. 11.** Ripple down: $\backslash f$ and ripple up: $/f$

applies g if f is true and otherwise applies g^{-1}. These specialised combinators are included because they are closer to actual logic implementation than the general conditional. The first has the control structure of the basic logical gates. The second, in some cases, can be beneficial to use, because the physical realisation can be made with only one circuit implementation of g: using the control-function f to choose *execution direction*, the single implementation of g can be used for both g and g^{-1}. This requires a small overhead in the implementation of f, but if g is large enough then the overhead is easily saved by removing the implicit duplication of g in the circuit for g^{-1}.

3.6   Apply-to-All and Rippling

The reversible version of *apply-to-all* (or map) is very conventional. It is written

$$\alpha f , \qquad \text{(apply-to-all)}$$

and takes a number of inputs, applies f to each of these and yields the same number of outputs (see Fig. 10).

More interesting are the ripple-circuits as they are both non-standard and important for giving structure to the descriptions. They are written as

$$\backslash f \quad \text{and} \quad /f , \qquad \text{(down and up ripple)}$$

where f must be a two-input function (see Fig. 11). The behaviour of the reversible ripple-circuits is very similar to the scan-left and right list operators in Haskell.

Of algebraic laws relating to these operations we have that (9) apply-all is distributive over serial composition, (7, 8) ripple-up is related to ripple-down via the flip permutation and *vice versa*, and finally that (10) ripples with the identity gate at some of the inputs can be rewritten to apply-all.

$$\backslash f = \text{Flip}; /(\text{Flip}; f; \text{Flip}); \text{Flip} \quad (7) \qquad \alpha(f; g) = \alpha f; \alpha g \quad (9)$$

$$/f = \text{Flip}; \backslash(\text{Flip}; f; \text{Flip}); \text{Flip} \quad (8) \qquad \backslash[\text{Id}, f] = /[\text{Id}, f] = [\text{Id}, \alpha f] \quad (10)$$

Again, the language does not have general recursion, but uses other regular constructs, such as ripples, that are better suited for optimisation. The ripple structure, of course, is not the only existing regular construct and the language can be extended with others, such as parallel prefix networks [9].

3.7 Inversion

The inversion combinator is unique to this language, and we write the inversion of f using the standard notation

$$f^{-1}. \qquad \text{(inversion)}$$

Inversion upholds the expected laws, in that (11) the inverse of an inverse function is the function itself and (12) a function in sequence with its inverse is the identity.

$$(f^{-1})^{-1} = f \quad (11)$$

$$f^{-1}; f = f; f^{-1} = \text{Id} \quad (12)$$

The following gives the algebraic rules for inverting basic constructs. In general, they show that the gates are self-inverse and that permutations and wire reordering are either self-inverse or pairwise inverse:

$$\text{Id}^{-1} = \text{Id} \quad (13) \qquad \qquad \text{Toff}^{-1} = \text{Toff} \quad (16)$$

$$\text{Not}^{-1} = \text{Not} \quad (14) \qquad \qquad \text{Fred}^{-1} = \text{Fred} \quad (17)$$

$$\text{Feyn}^{-1} = \text{Feyn} \quad (15)$$

$$\text{Flip}^{-1} = \text{Flip} \quad (18) \qquad \qquad \text{Zip}^{-1} = \text{Zip} \quad (21)$$

$$\text{Rup}^{-1} = \text{Rdn} \quad (19) \qquad \qquad \text{Concat}^{-1} = \text{Split} \quad (22)$$

$$\text{Rdn}^{-1} = \text{Rup} \quad (20) \qquad \qquad \text{Split}^{-1} = \text{Concat} \quad (23)$$

Rewriting the inverse of compositions is also very simple: (24) the inverse of sequential composition is analogous to function inversion, (25) inversion is distributive over parallel composition, (26) the inverse of a conditional propagates the inversion only to the updating functions (not the controlling function), (27) – (29) inversion of map and ripples are propagated to the inner function, and as an example of a more intricate law (30) part of a conditional with forward/backward execution, in some cases, can be lifted out.

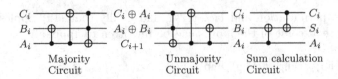

Fig. 12. Bit-slice of a reversible binary adder. Figure from [30].

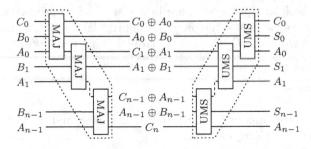

Fig. 13. n-bit ripple-carry CDKM-adder. MAJ is the majority circuit and UMS is the combined unmajority and sum calculation circuit. Figure from [30].

$$(f;g)^{-1} = g^{-1}; f^{-1} \quad (24) \qquad\qquad (\alpha f)^{-1} = \alpha f^{-1} \quad (27)$$

$$[f,g]^{-1} = [f^{-1}, g^{-1}] \quad (25) \qquad\qquad (\diagdown f)^{-1} = \diagup f^{-1} \quad (28)$$

$$(f \mathbin{?} (g,h))^{-1} = f \mathbin{?} (g^{-1}, h^{-1}) \quad (26) \qquad\qquad (\diagup f)^{-1} = \diagdown f^{-1} \quad (29)$$

$$f \mathbin{!} (g; h; g^{-1}) = [\mathsf{Id}, g]; (f \mathbin{!} h); [\mathsf{Id}, g^{-1}] \quad (30)$$

4   Example: Binary Adder

The following example is based on an existing binary adder design and is intended to show both how the language can be used to describe reversible circuits and also how rewriting can improve the circuit design. All the optimisations are known from the literature, but are here derived using the algebraic laws above.

The conventional approach of using full-adders is not suitable for reversible binary adders, because calculating both the sum and carry-out in parallel in a full-adder with exactly 3 inputs cannot be done reversibly.[2] This problem is resolved by a novel adder design [11, 33] that uses the fact that the carry-out (C_{i+1}) is *not* needed to calculate the sum bit (S_i) and *vice versa* (see [30] for a more detailed description.) The reversible binary adder (Fig. 12) first calculates the carry-out in a *majority* circuit, then uses the carry-out in the next bit-slice, and finally uncomputes using the *unmajority* circuit followed by the *sum* circuit. Implementing an n-bit adder (Fig. 13) is done with a *downward* ripple of majority circuits followed by an *upward* ripple of unmajority-and-sum circuits.

---

[2] Embedding a 3-to-2 full-adder in reversible logic requires a 4-bit circuit which leaves non-trivial garbage.

We can define this binary adder in the language by first describing the majority (maj) and the sum circuit (sum), both of type $\tau \to \tau$, where $\tau = \mathtt{w} * \mathtt{w} * \mathtt{w}$. Using these two descriptions, the adder $(adder)$ is described using the forward and backward ripple structure and will have the type $\tau' \to \tau'$, where $\tau' = \mathtt{w} * (\mathsf{N} \times \mathtt{w}) * (\mathsf{N} \times \mathtt{w})$.

$$ord1 = [\mathsf{Id}, \mathsf{Split}]$$
$$ord2 = [\mathsf{Id}, \mathsf{Concat}; \mathsf{Zip}]$$
$$maj = \mathsf{Feyn}_{\{1,3,2\}}; \mathsf{Feyn}_{\{2,3,1\}}; \mathsf{Toff}_{\{1,2,3\}}; \mathsf{Flip}$$
$$sum = \mathsf{Feyn}_{\{1,3,2\}}; \mathsf{Feyn}_{\{3,1,2\}}$$
$$adder = ord2; \backslash(ord1; maj; ord1^{-1}); /(ord1; maj^{-1}; sum; ord1^{-1}); ord2^{-1}$$

4.1 Optimisation / Rewriting

We have a ripple-up of the serial composition $maj^{-1}; sum$. We can rewrite this as follows.

$$\begin{aligned}
maj^{-1}; sum &= (\mathsf{Feyn}_{\{1,3,2\}}; \mathsf{Feyn}_{\{2,3,1\}}; \mathsf{Toff}_{\{1,2,3\}}; \mathsf{Flip})^{-1}; sum \\
&\stackrel{a}{=} \mathsf{Flip}^{-1}; \mathsf{Toff}_{\{1,2,3\}}^{-1}; \mathsf{Feyn}_{\{2,3,1\}}^{-1}; \mathsf{Feyn}_{\{1,3,2\}}^{-1}; sum \\
&\stackrel{b}{=} \mathsf{Flip}^{-1}; \mathsf{Toff}_{\{1,2,3\}}^{-1}; \mathsf{Feyn}_{\{2,3,1\}}^{-1}; \mathsf{Feyn}_{\{1,3,2\}}^{-1}; \mathsf{Feyn}_{\{1,3,2\}}; \mathsf{Feyn}_{\{3,1,2\}} \\
&\stackrel{c}{=} \mathsf{Flip}^{-1}; \mathsf{Toff}_{\{1,2,3\}}^{-1}; \mathsf{Feyn}_{\{2,3,1\}}^{-1}; \mathsf{Feyn}_{\{3,1,2\}} \\
&\stackrel{d}{=} \mathsf{Flip}; \mathsf{Toff}_{\{1,2,3\}}; \mathsf{Feyn}_{\{2,3,1\}}; \mathsf{Feyn}_{\{3,1,2\}}
\end{aligned}$$

First (a) we can rewrite the inversion of the serial compositions (24) in maj. Next (b) we substitute the definition of sum. For (c) we notice that an inverse Feynman gate is serially composed with the same Feynman gate. Feynman gates are self-inverse (15), so this is equal to the identity gate (12), which is removed in the same step (2). Then (d) we rewrite the inverse flip (18) to get the final combined circuit. The unmajority and sum circuits is then merged into one *unmajority-and-sum* circuit, reducing the depth by two gates.

5 Example: Linear Cosine Transform

In the introduction, we mentioned loss-less multimedia transforms as an application of reversible logic, due to the fact that these transforms are injective. We will here show the implementation of the cosine transform used in the H.264/AVC encoding [23]. The implementation draws heavily on the binary adder design from the above example (Sec. 4).

To make the design reversible we must first redesign the (irreversible) butterfly structure of the transform to the (reversible) *lifting scheme* [13] shown in Fig. 14. This redesign is fairly straightforward and information about this can be found

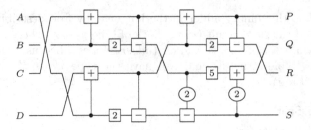

Fig. 14. Lifting scheme for the H.264 linear cosine transform. The letters denotes integer values. Figure from [15].

in [15]. Second, we need to extend the design with two ancilla lines in positions 1 and 2 to be used with the adders. This results in the following design for the transform (of the type $\tau \to \tau$ where $\tau = \mathtt{w} * \mathtt{w} * \tau' * \tau' * \tau' * \tau'$ and $\tau' = \mathsf{N} \times \mathtt{w}$). Circuits for constant multplication ($mul2$ and $mul5$) have been omitted.

$$subtr = \{1, 3, 2\}; adder^{-1}; \{1, 3, 2\}$$

$$lift2 = adder; [\mathsf{Id}, \mathsf{Id}, mul2]; subtr$$

$$lift5 = [\mathsf{Id}, mul2, \mathsf{Id}]; subtr; [\mathsf{Id}, (mul2^{-1}; mul5), mul2]; adder; [\mathsf{Id}, \mathsf{Id}, mul2^{-1}]$$

$$H264 = \{1, 5, 4, 2, 6, 3\}; [lift2, lift2]; \{1, 2, 5, 4, 3, 6\}; [lift2, lift5]; \{1, 4, 2, 5, 3, 6\}$$

6   Implementation and Future Work

The language is currently implemented (in standard ML) by means of the simple type system, shown in Fig. 6, that can ensure reversibility of the circuit descriptions. The type system will be extended further to support the following concepts: ancillae and reversible updates.

6.1   Ancillae

Ancillae are an important concept in reversible (and quantum) computing. Adding more ancillae can reduce both the logic depth and the number of used gates. Therefore, the core language should allow the user to both introduce and remove such temporary wires. The problem is that, in general, it is hard to ensure that the removed ancillae are indeed reset to zero, as they must be to guarantee reversibility. For a high-level language this would be done at run-time, but that is not a viable option here.

  If we can identify the ancillae wires in the circuits it is possible to improve optimisation by adding more specialised rewriting rules. We can reuse the ancillae wires between functions and use existing ancillae wires that are unused to optimise sub-circuits.

6.2   Reversible Updates

Identifying reversible updates is also important and equally hard. In the conditional, computing a function, using the result and then uncomputing it again is an obvious example of wires that are unchanged over some number of computations. Another example that is much harder to identify mechanically is the above example of the binary adder circuit (Sec. 4). In this case we note that the forward-ripple computes the majority function and the backwards-ripple computes the unmajority-and-sum function. We therefore know that it is only the sum function that actually changes the values of wires over the circuit, so only the sum-wire is changed.

If we can identify such reversible updates, then we will have a much better chance to do optimisations, as it would yield more possibilities for rearranging (and removing) gates.

6.3 Term Rewriting

One of the aims of this work is to enable circuit designs that are better than the circuits produced by existing synthesis methods: for this we will use term rewriting that encapsulates the algebraic laws of the language. However, for more and better rewriting opportunities we must support reversible updates, and be able to recognise these in larger circuits.

7 Conclusion

The design of reversible logic circuits is currently either done by hand (slow, and difficult to verify) or by using synthesis approaches (which means high gate counts and many ancillae/garbage lines). We have here presented a functional language, based on a few simple combinators, that is suitable for describing reversible logic circuits. Using only static analysis (type checking), we can ensure that the described circuits are indeed reversible. For this language we have identified a number of algebraic laws that are useful for circuit optimisation by a rewriting approach.

We applied the language to an example of binary reversible adders and found that the circuits were fairly easy to describe in the language and the algebraic laws could be used to optimise the adder design. We also applied the language to the cosine transform of the lossless H.264 encoding, which was easy using the adder description.

Further work is still needed on the type system of the language in relation to a good formalisation of ancillae and reversible updates. These concepts are important to add more specialised algebraic laws and, thereby, to improve the automatic optimisation in the rewriting system.

Acknowledgments. The author thanks Robert Glück and Holger Bock Axelsen for discussions about this work. Special thanks to Mary Sheeran and John Hughes for their interest in, and comments on the work. This work was supported by the Danish Strategic Research Council under the MicroPower research project.

References

1. Altenkirch, T., Grattage, J.: A functional quantum programming language. In: Proceedings of 20th Annual IEEE Symposium on Logic in Computer Science, LICS 2005, pp. 249–258. IEEE (2005)
2. Athas, W.C., Svensson, L.: Reversible logic issues in adiabatic CMOS. In: Workshop on Physics and Computation (1994)
3. Axelsen, H.B., Glück, R.: What Do Reversible Programs Compute? In: Hofmann, M. (ed.) FOSSACS 2011. LNCS, vol. 6604, pp. 42–56. Springer, Heidelberg (2011)
4. Axelsen, H.B., Glück, R., Yokoyama, T.: Reversible Machine Code and Its Abstract Processor Architecture. In: Diekert, V., Volkov, M.V., Voronkov, A. (eds.) CSR 2007. LNCS, vol. 4649, pp. 56–69. Springer, Heidelberg (2007)
5. Backus, J.: Can programming be liberated from the von Neumann style? A functional style and its algebra of programs. Communications of the ACM 21, 613–641 (1978)
6. Barenco, A., Bennett, C.H., Cleve, R., DiVincenzo, D.P., Margolus, N., Shor, P., Sleator, T., Smolin, J.A., Weinfurter, H.: Elementary gates for quantum computation. Physical Review A 52(5), 3457–3467 (1995)
7. Bennett, C.H.: Logical reversibility of computation. IBM Journal of Research and Development 17, 525–532 (1973)
8. Berut, A., Arakelyan, A., Petrosyan, A., Ciliberto, S., Dillenschneider, R., Lutz, E.: Experimental verification of landauer/'s principle linking information and thermodynamics. Nature 483(7388), 187–189 (2012)
9. Brent, R., Kung, H.: A Regular Layout for Parallel Adders. IEEE Transactions on Computers C-31(3), 260–264 (1982)
10. Burignat, S., Thomsen, M.K., Klimczak, M., Olczak, M., De Vos, A.: Interfacing Reversible Pass-Transistor CMOS Chips with Conventional Restoring CMOS Circuits. In: De Vos, A., Wille, R. (eds.) RC 2011. LNCS, vol. 7165, pp. 112–122. Springer, Heidelberg (2012)
11. Cuccaro, S.A., Draper, T.G., Kutin, S.A., Moulton, D.P.: A new quantum ripple-carry addition circuit. arXiv:quant-ph/0410184v1 (2005)
12. Cuykendall, R., Andersen, D.R.: Reversible optical computing circuits. Optics Letters 12(7), 542–544 (1987)
13. Daubechies, I., Sweldens, W.: Factoring wavelet transforms into lifting steps. Journal of Fourier Analysis and Applications 4(3), 247–269 (1998)
14. De Vos, A.: Reversible computing. Progress in Quantum Electronics 23(1), 1–49 (1999)
15. De Vos, A., Burignat, S., Thomsen, M.K.: Reversible implementation of a descrete integer linear transform. Journal of Multiple-Valued Logic and Soft Computing, Special Issue: Reversible Computation 18(1), 25–35 (2012)
16. De Vos, A., Van Rentergem, Y.: Reversible computing: from mathematical group theory to electronical circuit experiment. In: Computing Frontiers Proceeding, pp. 35–44. ACM Press (2005)
17. Feynman, R.P.: Quantum mechanical computers. Optical News 11, 11–20 (1985)
18. Fredkin, E., Toffoli, T.: Conservative logic. International Journal of Theoretical Physics 21(3-4), 219–253 (1982)
19. Gershenfeld, N.: Signal entropy and the thermodynamics of computation. IBM Systems Journal 35(3-4), 577–586 (1996)
20. Koller, J.G., Athas, W.C.: Adiabatic switching, low energy computing, and the physics of storing and erasing information. In: Workshop on Physics and Computation, pp. 267–270 (1992)

21. Landauer, R.: Irreversibility and heat generation in the computing process. IBM Journal of Research and Development 5(3), 183–191 (1961)
22. Lutz, C.: Janus: A time-reversible language. A letter to R. Landauer (1986), http://tetsuo.jp/ref/janus.pdf
23. Malvar, H.S., Hallapuro, A., Karczewicz, M., Kerofsky, L.: Low-complexity transform and quantization in H. 264/AVC. IEEE Transactions on Circuits and Systems for Video Technology 13(7), 598–603 (2003)
24. Merkle, R.C.: Reversible electronic logic using switches. Nanotechnology 4(1), 21–40 (1993)
25. Morita, K.: A Simple Universal Logic Element and Cellular Automata for Reversible Computing. In: Margenstern, M., Rogozhin, Y. (eds.) MCU 2001. LNCS, vol. 2055, pp. 102–113. Springer, Heidelberg (2001)
26. Nielsen, M., Chuang, I.L.: Quantum Computation and Quantum Information. Cambridge University Press (2000)
27. Patra, P., Fussell, D.: On efficient adiabatic design of MOS circuits. In: Workshop on Physics and Computation, pp. 260–269 (1996)
28. Sheeran, M.: muFP, A language for VLSI design. In: Proceedings of the 1984 ACM Symposium on LISP and Functional Programming, LFP 1984, pp. 104–112. ACM (1984)
29. Sheeran, M.: Hardware design and functional programming: a perfect match. Journal of Universal Computer Science 11(7), 1135–1158 (2005)
30. Thomsen, M.K., Axelsen, H.B.: Parallelization of reversible ripple-carry adders. Parallel Processing Letters 19(1), 205–222 (2009)
31. Thomsen, M.K., Glück, R., Axelsen, H.B.: Reversible arithmetic logic unit for quantum arithmetic. Journal of Physics A: Mathematical and Theoretical 43(38), 382002 (2010)
32. Toffoli, T.: Reversible Computing. In: de Bakker, J.W., van Leeuwen, J. (eds.) ICALP 1980. LNCS, vol. 85, pp. 632–644. Springer, Heidelberg (1980)
33. Vedral, V., Barenco, A., Ekert, A.: Quantum networks for elementary arithmetic operations. Physical Review A 54(1), 147–153 (1996)
34. Wille, R., Drechsler, R.: Towards a Design Flow for Reversible Logic. Springer Science (2010)
35. Wille, R., Offermann, S., Drechsler, R.: SyReC: A programming language for synthesis of reversible circuits. In: Proceedings of the Forum on Specification & Design Languages, pp. 1–6. IET, Southhampton (2010)
36. Yokoyama, T., Axelsen, H.B., Glück, R.: Towards a Reversible Functional Language. In: De Vos, A., Wille, R. (eds.) RC 2011. LNCS, vol. 7165, pp. 14–29. Springer, Heidelberg (2012)
37. Yokoyama, T., Glück, R.: A reversible programming language and its invertible self-interpreter. In: Proceedings of Partial Evaluation and Program Manipulation, pp. 144–153. ACM Press (2007)

Hardware Design with Generalized Arrows

Adam Megacz

Computer Science Division, UC Berkeley
megacz@cs.berkeley.edu

Abstract. Ordinarily, a compiler for a multi-level language will contain some knowledge of the object language; for example, in a multi-stage programming language with runtime code generation, the compiler will know how to produce code which emits machine code for object language expressions. This means that adding, extending, or replacing the object language requires knowledge of compiler internals.

Generalized arrows act as an intermediate language, separating the meta language compiler from the object language implementation. Two-level expressions are *flattened* [11] into ordinary one-level expressions polymorphic in an instance of the GArrow class, which is used to represent object language expressions. Operations on object language expressions are then packaged in an instance of the GArrow class, which is a library rather than part of the compiler.

This paper presents an example application of this approach: a bit-serial circuit which searches for SHA-256 hash collisions. A two-level circuit-building program is passed through the GHC flattening pass (which is not specific to hardware design in any way) and the resulting one-level program is combined with a GArrow instance that emits Verilog code; this instance is an ordinary Haskell library which can be written without knowledge of compiler internals.

1 Introduction

Hardware design in functional languges has a long history, starting with Backus' 1978 lecture [1] introducing the combinator language FP, which served as the basis for Sheeran's μFP [18]. Since then, many researchers have investigated the use of functional programming languages to describe hardware circuits. There are several challenges in this area; this paper will focus on four in particular:

1. Enforcing a phase distinction
2. Disallowing higher-order functions in circuits
3. The need for application-specific compiler modifications
4. Distinguishing recursive structure from feedback

Not all of these challenges are necessarily regarded as major problems, but the solutions chosen are helpful in distinguishing different approaches.

A. Gill and J. Hage (Eds.): IFL 2011, LNCS 7257, pp. 164–180, 2012.

Enforcing a Phase Distinction. Hardware design in functional languages is an example of heterogeneous metaprogramming: a software program generates a hardware program, and the resulting hardware program must be free of any dependencies on further software computation. This is independence is called a *phase distinction*. Monadic systems such as Chalmers Lava (Bjesse, Claessen, Sheeran, and Singh Bjesse et al. [2]) make a phase distinction in expressions by limiting the primitives which may be used to construct circuits. However, there is no phase distinction in the type system; for example, `CircuitMonad m => m Bit -> m Bit` is both the type of one-input/one-output circuits as well as the type of circuit-transformers that turn a one-output circuit into another one-output circuit. A few systems – notably reFL^{ect} [7] and Sheard's Ωmega [17] – are based on multi-level languages [13] in which the type $\langle \tau_1 \to \tau_2 \rangle$ of object language functions is different from the type $\langle \tau_1 \rangle \to \langle \tau_2 \rangle$ of meta language functions that transform object language expressions. In homogeneous multi-level languages these types are related by the "isomorphism for code types" [19, Section 8].

Disallowing Higher-Order Functions in Circuits. Functional languages allow higher-order functions: functions which take other functions as arguments. Unfortunately this does not correspond to anything meaningful in the world of circuits: one cannot have a circuit which takes another circuit as its input. Any approach to hardware design in a functional language must address this issue: higher-order functions must not be allowed *in circuits themselves*, but are desirable in the software programs which *generate the circuits*. Most existing work addresses this issue via a sort of implied well-foundedness lemma, whereby circuits with a type suitable for top-level operations (synthesis, execution, etc) can be proved to be free of irreducible higher-order subcircuits. For example, Chalmers Lava represents a circuit with input of type A and output of type B as a Haskell value of type `CircuitMonad m => A -> m B`. Since `Circuit` is a subclass of `Monad`, it is possible to create values of type `CircuitMonad m => (Bit -> m Bit) -> m B`. Values of such a type would appear to correspond to "higher-order circuits." Fortunately, since the primitives of the `CircuitMonad` class (such as `xor`, `nand`, etc) do not include higher-order operations, it can be shown that any paradoxical "higher-order circuits" occur within ordinary circuits only as part of a reducible subexpression.

The Need for Application-Specific Compiler Modifications. Converting a functional program to Verilog or VHDL requires an understanding of the application domain (hardware). Ideally the compiler writer should not have to understand the application domains in which the compiler might be used. This is usually a disadvantage of systems based on multi-level languages; as Sheard and Linger [17] write "there is usually only a single object-language, and it must be built into the meta-language." Chalmers Lava avoids application-specific compiler modifications by using a *monadic embedding* of the circuit object language into unmodified Haskell. Producing Verilog is then a matter of selecting the symbolic interpretation [2, Section 3.2] by supplying the appropriate `instance CircuitMonad T` for some type `T` that represents Verilog program text. Kansas Lava [6] avoids hardware-specific compiler modifications by requiring only that compiler's `IO` monad implementation support the `StableName` extension [5].

Distinguishing Recursive Structure from Feedback. One of the most difficult problems with representing circuits in functional languages is dealing with sharing. In Chalmers Lava's monadic embedding this distinction is made by using different language constructs for recursion and feedback: Haskell's `let` is used for recursive structure and a special `mfix` operator (of the `MonadFix` class [4]) is used for feedback. In Hawk [10] both repetitive structure and feedback are represented using Haskell's recursive `let` construct; in order to produce HDL it must be possible to distinguish these. Later versions of Hawk extracted this additional information from the program text using a mechanism called *observable sharing* [3, 5]. Early versions of Kansas Lava took a similar approach, but replaced observable sharing with IO-based reification [5]; later versions carry both a shallow embedding and a deep embedding at the same time [6].

1.1   Contribution

This paper serves as a small yet nontrivial example of a metaprogramming task carried out using a two-level language and generalized arrows. The task in question is one of hardware design: create a bit-serial circuit that implements the SHA-256 hash function. This example demonstrates how an approach based on a two-level language and generalized arrows provides a unique combination of soloutions to the challenges above:

1. The phase distinction is enforced using a two-level source language with environment classifiers [20]. The phase distinction extends to the types: the type of circuits with input A and output B is different from the type of circuit-transformers whose arguments have output type A and whose results have output type B.
2. Higher-order functions are kept out of circuits by restricting the object language to κ-calculus.
3. Application-specific compiler modifications are not required. The *flattening transformation* [11] – which converts two-level programs into one-level programs polymorphic in a `GArrow` instance – is the only compiler modification involved and it is not specific to hardware design in any way.
4. Recursive structure is distinguished from feedback: recursive `let` bindings in the object language produce feedback while recursive `let` bindings in the meta language produce repetitive structure.

1.2   Overview of the Paper

The methodology used here is introduced in four steps, each motivated by the need to solve one of the above challenges. Section 2 addresses the challenge of enforcing a phase distinction: programs are written and typechecked in a two-level language. Section 3 explains how higher-order functions are kept out of the object language: the object language based on κ-calculus. Section 4 explains how the need for application-specific compiler modifications is avoided: the compiler produces expressions of type (`forall g. GArrow g => g x y`); these `GArrow`-polymorphic expressions are then instantiated with a Verilog-specific instance of the `GArrow` class. Section 5 highlights the distinction between recursive structure and feedback. Section 6 covers a simple example circuit: a bit-serial SHA-256 hashing core.

2   Enforcing a Phase Distinction via Two-Level Languages

This paper will focus on the following fragment of Haskell:

$x ::= \ldots$	*(variables)*
$\alpha ::= \ldots$	*(type variables)*
$e ::= x \mid \backslash x \rightarrow e \mid e\ e \mid \ldots$	*(expressions)*
$\tau ::= \tau \rightarrow \tau \mid \alpha \mid \ldots$	*(types)*

Extending the fragment above to a two-level language involves adding expression forms `<{e}>` for bracketing and `~~e` for escape, as well as code types `<{τ}>@α`. The code types are indexed by an environment classifier [20], which is a type variable.

$e ::= \ldots \mid$ `<{e}>` $\mid$ `~~e` $\mid \ldots$	*(expressions)*
$\tau ::= \ldots \mid$ `<{τ}>@α` $\mid \ldots$	*(types)*

Expression brackets delimit object language expressions. The escape operator appears within an object language expression and is applied to a meta language expression; the type of the meta language expression must be a code type, and the resulting code value is spliced into the surrounding object language expression. For example, the venerable pow example is shown in Figure 1.

```
pow :: Int -> <{ Int -> Int }>@a
pow 0 = <{ \x -> 1 }>
pow 1 = <{ \x -> x }>
pow n = <{ \x -> x * ~~(pow (n - 1)) x }>
```

Fig. 1. The two-level pow function; pow n produces an object-language expression specialized to the task of raising integers to the nth power

In this paper, object language expressions will be used to represent circuits; here is a very simple example: a synchronous circuit whose output oscillates whenever its input is true and holds its previous value when the input is false:

```
class Hardware a where
   -- ...
   xor :: <{ Bit -> Bit }>@a
   reg :: <{ Bit -> Bit }>@a

oscillator :: Hardware a =>
                <{ Bit -> Bit }>@a
oscillator =
   <{ \input ->
           let output  = ~~xor input delayed
               delayed = ~~reg output
           in output }>
```

3   Disallowing Higher-Order Functions in Circuits

Unfortunately, the <{e}> construct introduced in the previous section is too powerful: it allows arbitrary λ-calculus expressions in the object language. This means that it is possible to write two-level expressions corresponding to "higher-order circuits":

```
applyCircuit :: <{ (Bit -> Bit) -> Bit }>@a ->
                <{  Bit -> Bit         }>@a ->
                <{  Bit -> Bit         }>@a
applyCircuit =
   <{ \higherOrderCircuit -> \arg -> higherOrderCircuit arg }>
```

The expression above is syntactically correct and well-typed, yet cannot be translated into meaningful hardware. The problem is that λ-calculus allows functions of *higher type*; i.e., expressions of type $(\tau \rightarrow \tau) \rightarrow \tau$. When the need arises to restrict the use of such functions, the most straightforward approach is a "syntactic separation" in the grammar for types:

$$\sigma ::= \text{Bool} \mid \text{Int} \mid \ldots \qquad \qquad \textit{(ground types)}$$
$$\tau ::= \sigma \mid \sigma \rightarrow \tau \qquad \qquad \textit{(first-order types)}$$

This approach is effective, but does not scale well. Consider adding polymorphism: two syntactical categories of type variables are required: one for ground types and one for first-order types. This in turn requires two syntactic quantifier forms, and subsequently two different kinds for polymorphic expressions; the duplication of effort grows rapidly: most language constructs must occur in two different "flavors."

3.1 κ-Calculus

Hasegawa's κ-calculus [8] provides a more manageable approach, motivated as a *syntax for morphisms in a contextually-closed category*. κ-calculus can also be seen[1] as a type theory for Milner's algebraic theory of action calculi [12]. The following grammar is taken from Hasgawa's paper [8, Section 3], substituting[2] symbols which are more familiar to Haskell users.

$$\tau ::= \text{()} \mid \tau * \tau \mid \ldots \qquad\qquad\qquad\qquad \textit{(types)}$$
$$k ::= x \mid \texttt{id} \mid \texttt{first } k \mid \kappa x{:}\tau \texttt{ -> } k \mid k \texttt{ >>> } k \qquad\qquad \textit{(expressions)}$$

A typing judgment $\Gamma \vdash k : \tau_1 \rightsquigarrow \tau_2$ assigns an expression k a *pair* of types: τ_1 is the *source type* and τ_2 is the *target type*. Similarly, contexts Γ associate a pair of types to each variable. The source type of an expression can be thought of as a list of arguments, represented as a "right imbalanced" *-tree terminated by (). For example, a function taking exactly three arguments of types A, B, and C and returning a result of type D would have the types A*(B*(C*())) ~~> D.[3]

The most significant difference between κ-calculus and λ-calculus is the typing rule for abstractions:

$$\frac{\Gamma, x{:}\text{()} \rightsquigarrow \tau_1 \vdash e{:}\tau_2 \rightsquigarrow \tau_3}{\Gamma \vdash \kappa x{:}\tau_1 \texttt{ -> } e \; : \; \tau_1 * \tau_2 \rightsquigarrow \tau_3} \quad [\kappa\text{-Abs}]$$

As with λ-abstraction, the typing rule for κ-abstraction is applicable when the body of the abstraction is typeable under an additional assumption about the type of the abstracted variable. However, in the case of κ-calculus, that assumption must have the unit type () as the source type of the free variable. This is how the "first order" nature of κ-calculus is enforced. If polymorphism is added there is no need for two "flavors" of each language construct since the first order restriction is enforced at the site of *use* rather than at the site of *binding*.

In the syntactically-separated first-order λ-calculus of the previous subsection, a function taking two arguments of types A and B and yielding a result of type C has the type A -> (B -> C). In κ-calculus such a function has the pair of types (A*(B*()))~~>C. The () is necessary as an indication that B is the *second and*

---

[1] Specifically, κ-abstraction corresponds to the "non-functorial" version of the abstraction operator ab_x described in [12, Section 4.9]. The κ-calculus expression **first f** is similar to the action structure $\texttt{f} \otimes \texttt{id}$, although the algebraic laws of action calculi [12, Section 2.2] require that for all **f** and **g** the equalities $(\texttt{f} \otimes \texttt{id})\texttt{>>>}(\texttt{id} \otimes \texttt{g}) = (\texttt{f>>>id}) \otimes (\texttt{id>>>g}) = (\texttt{id>>>f}) \otimes (\texttt{g>>>id}) = (\texttt{id} \otimes \texttt{g})\texttt{>>>}(\texttt{f} \otimes \texttt{id})$ hold. Since these equalities do not necessarily hold for all **Arrows**, the theory of action calculi is not quite general enough for use as syntax for arrows or generalized arrows.

[2] We write () for 1, **first** for lift, * for $\otimes$, **f>>>g** for $\texttt{g} \circ \texttt{f}$, and $\kappa x{:}\tau\texttt{->}k$ for $\kappa x.k$.

[3] In both Hasegawa's and Milner's presentations the underlying category's monoidal structure is assumed to be strict; as a consequence, the type *equalities* $()*\tau = \tau = \tau*()$ and $\tau_1*(\tau_2*\tau_3) = (\tau_1*\tau_2)*\tau_3$ hold. In this paper these are assumed only to be *isomorphisms*; they will be invoked explicitly via a family of typing rules [$\cong$].

final argument rather than *a list of all but the first argument*; this is similar to how the principal typings of the Haskell expressions a:b:[] and a:b differ in the type of b.

Juxtaposition $k_1 k_2$ is an abbreviation for first k_2 >>> k_1; its typing rule [κ-App] is derivable:

$$
\begin{array}{c}
\text{[First]} \dfrac{\Gamma \vdash k_2 : ()\,{\sim\!\sim\!\!>}\,\tau_1}{\Gamma \vdash \text{first } k_2 : ()*\tau_2\,{\sim\!\sim\!\!>}\,\tau_1*\tau_2} \\[2ex]
[\cong] \\
\text{[Comp]} \dfrac{\Gamma \vdash \text{first } k_2 : \tau_2\,{\sim\!\sim\!\!>}\,\tau_1*\tau_2 \qquad \Gamma \vdash k_1 : \tau_1*\tau_2\,{\sim\!\sim\!\!>}\,\tau_3}{\Gamma \vdash \text{first } k_2 \text{ >>> } k_1 : \tau_2\,{\sim\!\sim\!\!>}\,\tau_3}
\end{array}
$$

Unlike "uncurried" function types (A,B,C)->D, κ-calculus functions can be partially applied without knowledge of their arity – just as with curried functions in λ-calculus *but without the use of higher types*. For example, the following judgment is derivable for any α, and therefore for functions f of any arity:

$$f : A*\alpha\,{\sim\!\sim\!\!>}\,B \ , \ e:()\,{\sim\!\sim\!\!>}\,A \ \vdash \ f\,e : \alpha\,{\sim\!\sim\!\!>}\,B$$

The ability to type a partial application without knowing the function's arity ensures that standard Damas/Hindley/Milner type inference algorithms can be used.

To improve readability, the parser and pretty-printer treat * as right-associative and omit parentheses where possible. Also, a source type enclosed in an outermost layer of parentheses is another way of writing a trailing (). This means that the type A*(B*(C*())) ~~>D can be written as (A*B*C) ~~>D; however, this is different from A*B*C~~>D, which abbreviates A*(B*C) ~~>D.

3.2 A Two-Level λ-κ-Calculus

The next step is to include κ-calculus expressions as an object language; these will be enclosed in square <[..]> brackets rather than curly ones <{..}>:

```
k ::= x | \x -> k | kk | ~~e | ...          (κ expressions)
e ::= ... | <[k]> | ...                     (λ expressions)
τ ::= ... | () | τ*τ | <[τ ~~> τ]>@α | ...  (types)
```

Here is a simple example program showing κ-application inside brackets:

```
applyBrak :: <[    a*b ~~> c ]>@d ->
             <[    () ~~> a ]>@d ->
             <[     b ~~> c ]>@d
applyBrak x y = <[ ~~x ~~y ]>
```

The following functional illustrates κ-abstraction; it reverses the order of the first two arguments of a function.

```
swap :: <[ a*b*c ~~> d ]>@e ->
          <[ b*a*c ~~> d ]>@e
swap f = <[ \x y -> ~~f y x ]>
```

Notice that swap works for functions f of any arity greater than one. The following attempt to write the applyCircuit example from the previous section using <[..]> brackets will fail:

```
applyCircuit =
  <[ \higherOrderCircuit -> \arg -> higherOrderCircuit arg ]>
```

The program above is rejected by the GHC typechecker, which gives the following error message:

```
Fail.hs:2:37:
    Couldn't match expected type 't0*t1' with actual type '()'
    Expected type: t0*t1~~>t3
      Actual type: ()~~>t2
    In the expression: higherOrderCircuit arg
    In the expression: \ arg -> higherOrderCircuit arg
```

Since higherOrderCircuit is brought into scope by a κ-abstraction, the type inference algorithm uses rule [κ-Abs] and proceeds under the assumption that higherOrderCircuit has type ()~~>t2 for some type t2. When it encounters the application higherOrderCircuit arg it uses the (derived) rule [κ-App], attempting to unify ()~~>t2 with t0*t1~~>t3; this unification fails since () and t0*t1 cannot be unified.

With the extended grammar and type system, it is now possible to express the oscillator example as a two-level program:

```
class Hardware a where
  -- ...
  xor :: <[ Bit ~~> Bit ]>@a
  reg :: <[ Bit ~~> Bit ]>@a

oscillator :: Hardware a => <[ Bit ~~> Bit ]>@a
oscillator =
  <[ \input ->
        let output  = ~~xor input delayed
            delayed = ~~reg output
        in output ]>
```

The full definition of the Hardware type class can be found in Figure 4.

4   Avoiding Application-Specific Compiler Modifications

The changes described in the previous section require altering the compiler's
parser and typechecker so that it is aware of two-level expressions, code types,
and κ-calculus expressions. This leaves the question of what the rest of the
compiler ought to do with these two-level expressions once they have been parsed
and typechecked.

4.1   Generalized Arrows

The two-level expressions introduced in the previous section are not executed
directly; the back end of the compiler has not been extended to produce code for
them. Instead, these expressions are *flattened* into ordinary Haskell expressions
parameterized by an instance of the GArrow class. The definition of the GArrow
class is shown in the appendix. The appendix also includes an instance which
turns any Control.Arrow intance (including (->)) into a canonical GArrow instance; this is partial justification for the name *generalized* arrows. After the
translation, the type of the oscillator example becomes:

```
oscillator :: (GArrow a, Hardware a) => a Bit Bit
```

Any one-level modules which import this code will see the type above, rather
than the two-level type Hardware a => <[Bit ~~> Bit]>@a. A number of
things can be done with the flattened version of oscillator above, depending on what instance of GArrow is provided. This section will show three examples: an instance GArrowPretty which pretty-prints the flattened expression,
an instance GArrowTikZ which renders the flattened expression visually using
the TikZ graphics library, and an instance GArrowVerilog which emits Verilog
code suitable for hardware synthesis. All of these instances are ordinary libraries
rather than compiler backends.

4.2   A GArrow Instance for Pretty-Printing

One of the simplest GArrow instances is GArrowPretty, which uses
pretty-printing combinators [9] to turn a GArrow expression into equivalent
Haskell source code; it is analogous to the Show class. Here is a partial
definition:

```
import Text.PrettyPrint.HughesPJ
type Precedence = Int
data SourceCode a b = SC Precedence Doc

instance GArrow SourceCode (,) () where
  ga_first (SC 0 f) = SC 1 $ text "ga_first" f
  ga_first (SC _ f) = SC 1 $ text "ga_first" $ parens f
  -- ...
  ga_cancell        = SC 0 $ text "ga_cancell"
  -- ..
```

It is also possible to give a `Hardware` instance for `SourceCode`:

```
instance Hardware SourceCode where
  high       = SC 0 $ text "high"
  -- ...
  fifo   len = SC 0 $ text "fifo"   <+> (text . show) len
  probe  id  = SC 0 $ text "probe"  <+> (text . show) id
  loop   vals = SC 0 $ text "loop"  <+> brackets $ hcat $ vals'
      where
        vals' = punctuate comma $ map (text . show) vals
```

Using these instances, it is possible to write:

```
showHardware ::
   (forall g . (Hardware g, GArrow g) => g x y) .
   -> String
```

Notice the rank-2 type; the `showHardware` operation must be able to supply its own type g and `GArrow` instance to its argument; on the other hand, the type of the input x and output y are chosen by the caller. The `GArrow` representation of object language expressions is an example of *induction principle representation* of datatypes in System F_ω. This representation was as described by Pfenning and Paulin-Mohring [15, Definitions 13 and 14]; it was first used by Pfenning and Lee [14] in LEAP to represent polymorphic λ-calculus.

Instantiating `oscillator` with this instance declaration and rendering the resulting Doc gives:

```
ga_loopl (ga_first reg >>>
          xor >>>
          ga_copy)
```

The `SourceCode` instance demonstrates one reason for using `GArrows` instead of `Arrows`. The `Arrow` type class allows `arr :: (x -> y) -> a x y` to be applied to any Haskell function `f :: x -> y`. Unfortunately, arbitrary Haskell functions cannot be inspected – there is no `Show` instance for function types.

4.3 A `GArrow` Instance for Drawing Penrose Diagrams

Reading `GArrow` expressions in the text form above can be quite difficult for larger examples; it is often more convenient to visualize `GArrow` terms as Penrose diagrams [16]. The instance `GArrowTikZ` renders these diagrams as TikZ code, using the `lp_solve` linear solver to produce a pleasing visual layout. Figure 3 shows the result of using the `GArrowPretty` instance on the `oscillator` example; Figure 2 contains two larger examples.

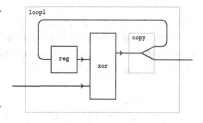

Fig. 2. Penrose diagram for the `oscillator` example

```
tikzExample1 =
  ga_copy             >>>
  ga_swap             >>>
  ga_first ga_drop >>>
  ga_cancell
```

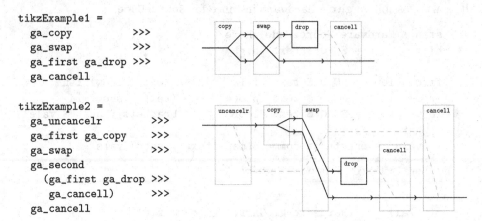

```
tikzExample2 =
  ga_uncancelr        >>>
  ga_first ga_copy    >>>
  ga_swap             >>>
  ga_second
    (ga_first ga_drop >>>
     ga_cancell)      >>>
  ga_cancell
```

Fig. 3. Two sample `GArrow` expressions and their visualization as a Penrose diagrams

4.4 A `GArrow` Instance for Emitting Verilog

The instances given so far are useful for debugging; this section will describe the `GArrowVerilog` instance for generating HDL output. The Verilog output is produced in two passes. The first pass allocates `wire` declarations to components using a bidirectional propagation algorithm similar to unification. Once `wire` declarations have been allocated, producing the HDL text is straightforward. Here is the result of instantiating `oscillator` with `GArrowVerilog`:

```
module demo(inputWire)
  wire wire0;
  wire wire1;
  wire wire2;
  reg (wire1, wire0);
  xor (wire2, wire1, inputWire);
endmodule
```

5 Distinguishing Recursive Structure from Feedback

Recursion *outside the code brackets* represents repetitive structures, whereas recursion *inside the brackets* represents feedback loops. This is illustrated by the following two examples; the first shows recursion *inside the brackets*, which produces feedback:

```
feedbackDemo =
  <[ \x -> let out   = (3 * out) * x
             in   out ]>
```

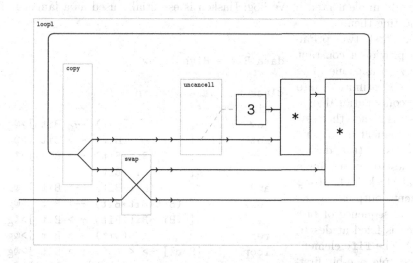

The following example demonstrates recursion *outside the brackets*, which produces repetitive structures, using the pow function from Figure 1:

`repetitiveStructureDemo = pow 6`

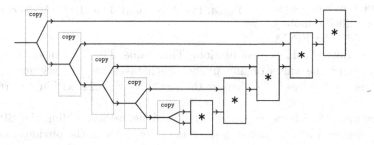

This distinction between recursion inside the brackets and recursion outside the brackets is closely related to monadic *value recursion* [4]. In fact, an expression which uses recursive `let` inside the brackets will be flattened to a `GArrow` expression which relies on `ga_loopl`. This expression may then be instantiated for any `MonadFix`, since `Control.Arrow.Kleisli` provides a `ArrowLoop` instance for any `MonadFix`, and the appendix provides a `GArrowLoop` instance for any `ArrowLoop`. When instantiated in this manner, `ga_loopl` will be realized as `mfix`. By contrast, recursion outside the brackets is not altered by the flattener.

6   Example: Bit-Serial SHA-256

The SHA-256 engine is defined in terms of the primitives shown in Figure 4, which appear as opaque elements in Haskell. Each of the primitives was manually implemented in Verilog; Haskell is essentially used as a language for connecting them.

The first two primitives provide a constant logic zero and one. The next six primitives are basic combinational logic elements, and the seventh element is a simple register (the design assumes only a single global clock). The loop element outputs a repeating sequence of bits (which is fixed at design time). The fifo element is a simple one-bit first-in-first-out queue.

The oracle is much like loop, except that the value being repeated can be modified remotely from outside the FPGA

```
data Bit = High | Low

class Hardware g where
  high   :: <[                 () ~~> Bit ]>@g
  low    :: <[                 () ~~> Bit ]>@g
  not    :: <[           (Bit) ~~> Bit ]>@g
  xor    :: <[       (Bit*Bit) ~~> Bit ]>@g
  or     :: <[       (Bit*Bit) ~~> Bit ]>@g
  and    :: <[       (Bit*Bit) ~~> Bit ]>@g
  mux2   :: <[ (Bit*Bit*Bit) ~~> Bit ]>@g
  maj3   :: <[ (Bit*Bit*Bit) ~~> Bit ]>@g
  reg    :: <[           (Bit) ~~> Bit ]>@g
  loop   :: [Bool] -> <[   () ~~> Bit ]>@g
  fifo   :: Int    -> <[(Bit) ~~> Bit ]>@g
  probe  :: Int    -> <[(Bit) ~~> Bit ]>@g
  oracle :: Int    -> <[   () ~~> Bit ]>@g
```

Fig. 4. Primitives needed for the SHA-256 circuit

using the device's JTAG connection. This same JTAG connection can be used to query the value of any probe. Each takes an Int argument which is used as an "address" to identify the probe or oracle within the running design.

There are a few basic subcircuits to build before assembling the SHA-256 hashing engine. First, we define a three-input xor gate in the obvious manner:

```
xor3 = <[ \x y z -> xor (xor x y) z ]>
```

The xor3 can be used to code a bit-serial adder, shown below. The firstBit produces a repeating pattern of 32 bits, the first of which is a one; this signal is used to clear the internal carry-bit state (carry_out).

```
adder =
  <[ \in1 in2 ->
     let firstBit  = ~~(loop [ i/=0 | i<-[0..31] ])
         carry_out = reg (mux2 firstBit zero carry_in)
         carry_in  = maj3 carry_out in1 in2
     in  xor3 carry_out in1 in2 ]>
```

Finally, the circuit below performs a bitwise right-rotation. Since the circuit is bit-serial, it has a latency of 32 bits.

```
rotRight n =
  <[ \input ->
     let sel   = ~~(loop [ i >= 32-n | i<-[0..31] ])
         fifo1 = ~~(fifo (32-n)) input
         fifo2 = ~~(fifo  32   ) fifo1
     in  mux2 sel fifo1 fifo2
  ]>
```

Using these subcircuits, it is now possible to express the SHA-256 algorithm, which can be found in Figure 5.

Below is the implementation of the core of the SHA-256 algorithm. The circuit is initialized by holding load high for 8 × 32 cycles while shifting in the initial hash state on the input wire. The 64 rounds of the SHA-256 algorithm are then performed by holding load low and waiting for 64 × 32 clocks. Finally the result is read out by holding load high and monitoring the circuit's output for the following 8 × 32 clocks.

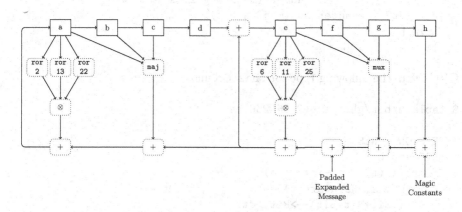

Fig. 5. The SHA-256 Algorithm. Each solid rectangle is a 32-bit state variable; the path into each rectangle computes its value in the next round based on the values of the state variables in the previous round. The standard specifies initialization values for the state variables prior to the first message block. The ⊗ symbol is bitwise xor, the + symbol is addition modulo 2^{32}, ror is bitwise right rotation, maj is bitwise majority, and mux is bitwise mux (e[i]?f[i]:g[i]). For each block of the message the algorithm above is iterated for 64 rounds; the values in the eight state registers afterwards are added to the values they held before the block before starting the next block. The hash of a message consists of the concatenation of the values in the eight state variables after the last block has been processed.

```
sha256round =
  <[ \load input k_plus_w ->
     let a   = ~~(fifo 32) (mux2 load a_in input)
         b   = ~~(fifo 32) a
         c   = ~~(fifo 32) b
         d   = ~~(fifo 32) c*
         e   = ~~(fifo 32) (mux2 load e_in d)
         f   = ~~(fifo 32) e
         g   = ~~(fifo 32) f
         h   = ~~(fifo 32) g
         s0  = xor3 (~~(rotRight  2) a_in)
                    (~~(rotRight 13) a_in)
                    (~~(rotRight 22) a_in)
         s1  = xor3 (~~(rotRight  6) e_in)
                    (~~(rotRight 11) e_in)
                    (~~(rotRight 25) e_in)
        a_in = adder t1 t2
        e_in = adder t1 d
        t1   = adder (adder h s1)
                     (adder (mux2 e g f) k_plus_w)
        t2   = adder s0 (maj3 a b c)
     in h
  ]>
```

GHC infers the following type for `sha256round`:

```
$ inplace/bin/ghc-stage2 SHA256.hs

TYPE SIGNATURES
  sha256round ::
    forall (t :: * -> * -> *) a.
      (Num a, Hardware t) =>
      <[(Bit*Bit*Bit)~~>Bit]>@t
```

References

1. Backus, J.: Can programming be liberated from the von neumann style? a functional style and its algebra of programs. Communications of the ACM 21(8), 613–641 (1978), http://doi.acm.org/10.1145/359576.359579
2. Bjesse, P., Claessen, K., Sheeran, M., Singh, S.: Lava: hardware design in haskell. In: ICFP 1998 (January 1998), http://portal.acm.org/citation.cfm?id=289440
3. Claessen, K., Sands, D.: Observable Sharing for Functional Circuit Description. In: Thiagarajan, P.S., Yap, R.H.C. (eds.) ASIAN 1999. LNCS, vol. 1742, pp. 62–73. Springer, Heidelberg (1999)
4. Erkök, L., Launchbury, J.: Recursive monadic bindings. In: Proceedings of ICFP 2000, pp. 174–185. ACM (2000), http://doi.acm.org/10.1145/351240.351257

5. Gill, A.: Type-safe observable sharing in haskell. In: Haskell Symposium, pp. 117–128. ACM (2009), http://doi.acm.org/10.1145/1596638.1596653
6. Gill, A., Bull, T., Kimmell, G., Perrins, E., Komp, E., Werling, B.: Introducing Kansas Lava. In: Morazán, M.T., Scholz, S.-B. (eds.) IFL 2009. LNCS, vol. 6041, pp. 18–35. Springer, Heidelberg (2010), http://www.ittc.ku.edu/csdl/fpg/sites/
7. Grundy, J., Melham, T., O'leary, J.: A reflective functional language for hardware design and theorem proving. Journal of Functional Programming 16(2), 157–196 (2005), http://journals.cambridge.org/abstract_S0956796805005757
8. Hasegawa, M.: Decomposing Typed Lambda Calculus into a Couple of Categorical Programming Languages. In: Johnstone, P.T., Rydeheard, D.E., Pitt, D.H. (eds.) CTCS 1995. LNCS, vol. 953, pp. 200–219. Springer, Heidelberg (1995), http://dx.doi.org/10.1007/3-540-60164-3_28
9. Hughes, J.: The Design of a Pretty-Printing Library. In: Jeuring, J., Meijer, E. (eds.) AFP 1995. LNCS, vol. 925, pp. 53–96. Springer, Heidelberg (1995), http://dx.doi.org/10.1007/3-540-59451-5%5f3
10. Matthews, J., Cook, B., Launchbury, J.: Microprocessor specification in hawk. In: Proceedings of 1998 International Conference on Computer Languages, pp. 90–101 (May 1998)
11. Megacz, A.: Multi-Level Languages are Generalized Arrows. CoRR, abs/1007.2885 (2010), http://arxiv.org/abs/1007.2885, DBLP, http://dblp.uni-trier.de
12. Milner, R.: Calculi for interaction. Acta Inf. 33(8), 707–737 (1996), http://dx.doi.org/10.1007/BF03036472
13. Nielson, F., Neilson, H.R.: Two-Level Functional Languages. Cambridge University Press, Cambridge (1992)
14. Pfenning, F., Lee, P.: Metacircularity in the polymorphic λ-calculus. Theoretical Computer Science 89(1), 137–159 (1991), http://www.sciencedirect.com/science/article/pii/030439759090109U
15. Pfenning, F., Paulin-Mohring, C.: Inductively Defined Types in the Calculus of Constructions. In: Schmidt, D.A., Main, M.G., Melton, A.C., Mislove, M.W. (eds.) MFPS 1989. LNCS, vol. 442, pp. 209–228. Springer, Heidelberg (1990), http://www.sciencedirect.com/science/article/pii/030439759090109U
16. Selinger, P.: A survey of graphical languages for monoidal categories (August 23, 2009), http://arxiv.org/abs/0908.3347
17. Sheard, T., Linger, N.: Programming in omega. Tech. rep., 2nd Central European Functional Programming School (2007)
18. Sheeran, M.: muFP, A language for VLSI design. In: LISP and Functional Programming, pp. 104–112 (1984)
19. Taha, W., Sheard, T.: Multi-stage programming with explicit annotations. SIGPLAN Not. 32(12), 203–207 (1997) ISSN: 0362-1340, doi: 10.1145/258994.259019, http://doi.acm.org/10.1145/258994.259019
20. Taha, W., Nielsen, M.F.: Environment classifiers, pp. 26–37 (2003), http://doi.acm.org/10.1145/640128.604134

A GArrow Type Class and Arrow Instance

```
class Category g => GArrow g (**) u where
--id           :: g x x
--(>>>)        :: g x y -> g y z -> g x z
  ga_first     :: g x y -> g (x ** z) (y ** z)
  ga_second    :: g x y -> g (z ** x) (z ** y)
  ga_cancell   :: g (u**x)           x
  ga_cancelr   :: g     (x**u)       x
  ga_uncancell :: g     x        (u**x)
  ga_uncancelr :: g     x           (x**u)
  ga_assoc     :: g ((x** y)**z ) ( x**(y **z))
  ga_unassoc   :: g ( x**(y **z)) ((x** y)**z )

class GArrow g (**) u => GArrowCopy g (**) u where
  ga_copy      :: g x (x**x)

class GArrow g (**) u => GArrowDrop g (**) u where
  ga_drop      :: g x u

class GArrow g (**) u => GArrowSwap g (**) u where
  ga_swap      :: g (x**y) (y**x)

class GArrow g (**) u => GArrowLoop g (**) u where
  ga_loopr     :: g (x**z) (y**z) -> g x y
  ga_loopl     :: g (z**x) (z**y) -> g x y

instance Arrow a => GArrow a (,) () where
  ga_first     = first
  ga_second    = second
  ga_cancell   = arr (\((),x) -> x)
  ga_cancelr   = arr (\(x,()) -> x)
  ga_uncancell = arr (\x -> ((),x))
  ga_uncancelr = arr (\x -> (x,()))
  ga_assoc     = arr (\((x,y),z) -> (x,(y,z)))
  ga_unassoc   = arr (\(x,(y,z)) -> ((x,y),z))

instance Arrow a => GArrowDrop a (,) () where
  ga_drop      = arr (\x -> ())

instance Arrow a => GArrowCopy a (,) () where
  ga_copy      = arr (\x -> (x,x))

instance Arrow a => GArrowSwap a (,) () where
  ga_swap      = arr (\(x,y) -> (y,x))

instance ArrowLoop a => GArrowLoop a (,) () where
  ga_loopr     = loop
  ga_loopl f   = loop (ga_swap >>> f >>> ga_swap)
```

Author Index

Achten, Peter   116
Amsden, Edward   17
Axelsson, Emil   85

Barzilay, Eli   100

Chang, Stephen   100
Clements, John   100

Elyasov, Alexander B.   1

Felleisen, Matthias   100
Fluet, Matthew   17

Koopman, Pieter   116

Maier, Patrick   35
Megacz, Adam   164
Middelkoop, Arie   1

Naylor, Matthew   69

Page, Rex   134
Persson, Anders   85
Plasmeijer, Rinus   116
Prasetya, Wishnu   1

Reich, Jason S.   69
Runciman, Colin   69

Schilling, Thomas   51
Svenningsson, Josef   85

Thomsen, Michael Kirkedal   148
Trinder, Phil   35